Feminist Views on the English Stage

This is an exciting and insightful study of contemporary drama from a
feminist perspective, one that challenges an idea of the 1990s as a
'post-feminist' decade and pays attention to women's playwriting
marginalized by a 'renaissance' of angry young men. Working through a
generational mix of writers, from Sarah Kane, the iconoclastic 'bad girl'
of the stage, to the 'canonical' Caryl Churchill, Elaine Aston charts the
significant political and aesthetic changes in women's playwriting at
the century's end. Aston also explores new writing for the 1990s in
theatre by Sarah Daniels, Bryony Lavery, Phyllis Nagy, Winsome
Pinnock, Rebecca Prichard, Judy Upton and Timberlake Wertenbaker.

ELAINE ASTON is Professor of Contemporary Performance at Lancaster
University. She is internationally known for her research into
contemporary women's theatre and playwriting. Her publications
include *Introduction to Feminism and Theatre* (1995), *Caryl Churchill*
(1997; 2001), *Feminist Theatre Practice* (1999) and (as co-editor) the
Cambridge Companion to Modern British Women Playwrights (2000).

CAMBRIDGE STUDIES IN MODERN THEATRE

Volumes for Cambridge Studies in Modern Theatre explore the political, social and cultural functions of theatre while also paying careful attention to detailed performance analysis. The focus of the series is on political approaches to the modern theatre with attention also being paid to theatres of earlier periods and their influence on contemporary drama. Topics in the series are chosen to investigate this relationship and include both playwrights (their aims and intentions set against the effects of their work) and process (with emphasis on rehearsal and production methods, the political structure within theatre companies, and their choice of audiences or performance venues). Further topics will include devised theatre, agitprop, community theatre, para-theatre and performance art. In all cases the series will be alive to the special cultural and political factors operating in the theatres examined.

Books published
Brian Crow with Chris Banfield, *An introduction to post-colonial theatre*
Mario DiCenzo, *The politics of alternative theatre in Britain, 1968–1990: 7:84 (Scotland)*
Jo Riley, *Chinese theatre and the actor in performance*
Jonathan Kalb, *The theatre of Heiner Müller*
Richard Boon and Jane Plastow, eds., *Theatre matters: performance and culture on the world stage*
Claude Schumacher, ed., *Staging the Holocaust: the Shoah in drama and performance*
Philip Roberts, *The Royal Court Theatre and the modern stage*
Nicholas Grene, *The politics of Irish drama: plays in context from Boucicault to Friel*
Anatoly Smeliansky, *The Russian theatre after Stalin*
Clive Barker and Maggie B. Gale, eds., *British theatre between the Wars, 1918–1939*
Michael Patterson, *Strategies of political theatre: post-war British playwrights*

Feminist views on the English stage

Women playwrights, 1990–2000

Elaine Aston

CAMBRIDGE
UNIVERSITY PRESS

PUBLISHED BY THE PRESS SYNDICATE OF THE UNIVERSITY OF CAMBRIDGE
The Pitt Building, Trumpington Street, Cambridge, United Kingdom

CAMBRIDGE UNIVERSITY PRESS
The Edinburgh Building, Cambridge, CB2 2RU, UK
40 West 20th Street, New York, NY 10011–4211, USA
477 Williamstown Road, Port Melbourne, VIC 3207, Australia
Ruiz de Alarcón 13, 28014 Madrid, Spain
Dock House, The Waterfront, Cape Town 8001, South Africa

http://www.cambridge.org

First published 2003

Printed in the United Kingdom at the University Press, Cambridge

Typeface Trump Mediaeval 9.25/14 pt. and Schadow BT   *System* LATEX 2_ε [TB]

A catalogue record for this book is available from the British Library

Library of Congress Cataloguing in Publication data
Aston, Elaine.
Feminist views on the English stage : women playwrights, 1990–2000 / Elaine
Aston.
   (Cambridge studies in modern theatre)
Includes bibliographical references and index.
1. Feminist drama, English – History and criticism.   2. Feminism and
literature – Great Britain – History – 20th century.   3. Women and
literature – Great Britain – History – 20th century.   4. English drama – Women
authors – History and criticism.   5. English drama – 20th century – History
and criticism.   I. Title.   II. Series.
PR739.F45A77   2003
822′.914099287 – dc21   2003051551

ISBN 0 521 80003 x hardback

For Magdalene and Daniel

My children

Our future

Contents

vii

Contents

viii

Contents

Acknowledgements

The completion of this volume was only made possible through research leave funded by the Arts and Humanities Research Board and Lancaster University.

My special thanks go to commissioning editor Vicki Cooper and to series editor David Bradby, both of whom took the time to read and to comment on draft chapters and offered invaluable support at critical moments during the project.

Several of the writers whose work appears in this volume offered helpful comments and criticisms, and were willing to share scripts. In particular I should like to thank Sarah Daniels, Bryony Lavery, Phyllis Nagy, SuAndi, Rebecca Prichard, Anna Reynolds and Timberlake Wertenbaker. I am extremely grateful to Mel Kenyon for putting me in touch with playwrights and for her assistance with the theatre of the late Sarah Kane (Chapter 5). I am also indebted to Sue Parrish of The Sphinx Theatre Company for tracking down materials and checking information.

So many friends and theatre colleagues have given their support to this project. In particular, I should like to thank new friends and colleagues at Lancaster, and members of the Feminist Theatre Group of the International Federation for Theatre Research whose insightful comments over the years have always proved invaluable. I also wish to thank Graham Saunders and John Stokes who created opportunities for sharing and discussing portions of this work in progress.

I would not have got through this project without the support of my family: my mother, June; my children, Magdalene and Daniel, all of whom have been especially patient throughout. And a final thank you to Clare Scobling who sorted out the practicalities of our lives by finding us somewhere to live during the final stages of producing the manuscript!

1 A feminist view on the 1990s

A dominant view of the British stage as it entered the final decade of the twentieth century was that it was in a critical state; was on a downward spiral as it struggled to survive the draconian effects of the Thatcher years. In particular, paralleling the millennial moment of 100 years earlier, the 1990s, like the 1890s, were apparently suffering from a lack of 'new drama'.[1] The 'most telling indicator of diminishing theatrical vitality', writes Christopher Innes in conclusion to his epic study *Modern British Drama 1890–1990*, 'is the comparative absence of new playwrights'.[2] When Innes arrives at 1990, the final moment in a century of theatre that he traces back to Shaw in 1890, he presents a bleak picture of playwrights withdrawing from theatre (Harold Pinter), not developing (Howard Barker and Howard Brenton), retreating into commercialism (Peter Schaffer), or becoming part of an 'old guard' (David Hare, Tom Stoppard, Alan Ayckbourn).

However, in contrast to the downward trend in British drama as viewed through his list of male playwrights, Innes cites the emergence of women dramatists as a potentially energising force, given their political drive and desire to experiment. 'Present tense – feminist theatre' is how Innes titles his final chapter, set apart and signalling a new departure from the patterns and categories of playwriting through which he maps his century of drama.[3] Innes was not alone in noting the energies of feminist theatre. Playwright David Edgar signals 'the explosion of new women's theatre' in the 1980s, and theatre critic Benedict Nightingale, endorsing Edgar's view, cites women's drama as the 'most positive aspect' of the 1980s, an otherwise 'barren decade for new drama'.[4] From the vantage point of a new century it might be reasonable, therefore, to expect to be looking back on a decade when women dramatists, capitalizing on their advancement in the 1980s, finally moved centre stage.

This is not, however, what happened. Although the British stage claimed its renaissance in the mid-1990s, it was not represented as feminist, but was, in a majority view, associated with a wave of writers, that, like the Osborne generation before them, were (mostly) angry young men.[5] Theatre history of the 1990s is, as Alex Sierz's, *In-Yer-Face Theatre: British Drama Today* testifies, written as a 'shock-fest' of violent drama by mostly angry young men, joined by a few angry young women.[6]

There is a danger, however, that 'in-yer-face' theatre history may write out all playwriting that is not considered central to a drama of 'new laddism'.[7] Feminist theatre scholarship has demonstrated how women's contribution to drama, theatre and performance always has been susceptible to loss; has been frequently 'written out', culturally marginalised and 'lost' to view. In consequence, theatrical recovery has been a mainstay of feminist activity. Despite the close proximity of the period studied to the moment of writing, this project was originally conceived as an act of feminist recovery; of making those dramatic energies of women in the 1990s a matter of public record, rather than allowing them to disappear.

'Boys in trouble': a backlash 1990s

Susan Faludi's *Backlash: The Undeclared War Against Women*, published in Britain in 1992,[8] offers extensive documentation of the media-created myth of a 'post-feminist' 1980s; the promotion of anti-feminist views at the very moment that feminist women generally, like theatre women specifically, had made a few, albeit limited, advances. The backlash, Faludi argues, was galvanised by men realising what they stood to lose, and women lost out because they did not 'capitalise' on their 'historic advantage'.[9] However, on a similar note to Innes, although in a broader cultural, rather than a specifically theatrical context, Faludi concludes *Backlash* with the observation: 'there really is no good reason why the 1990s can't be their [women's] decade. Because the demographics and the opinion polls are on women's side. Because women's hour on the stage is long, long overdue'.[10] Optimism for the 1990s as a women's decade, was, however, short-lived. As testimony to the 'war' against women, undeclared or otherwise, that Faludi and others claimed,[11] the battle between the sexes began to appear in print and performance. Neil Lyndon's *No More Sex War* (1992) and David Thomas's *Not Guilty* (1993) are key examples of men claiming victim status and blaming feminism for the oh-so-much-harder-lives men have compared to women.[12] On the London stage in 1993, David Mamet's highly controversial *Oleanna* staged the gender war in a dramatic two-hander in which a male professor, accused by a female student of political incorrectness, harassment and rape, turns angry and violent.[13]

Understanding the unabated hostility of men towards women informs Faludi's subsequent study, *Stiffed*, published at the close of the decade in 1999. The 'betrayal of modern man', the book's subtitle, signals Faludi's interest in ways in which men have been betrayed by capitalist and patriarchal systems effecting their displacement from their traditional roles in employment and family. One of Faludi's key findings is that in response to these 'betrayals', 'men prefer to see themselves as 'battered by feminism than shaped by the larger culture'.[14] As masculinity in crisis, the boys in trouble, comes to dominate the decade, the unwillingness to lay the blame anywhere other than at feminism's door, accounts for the anti- (sometimes virulently anti-) feminist feel to the decade. A culture of feminist blame, however, does not resolve, rather deepens masculinity in crisis, and as the playwriting examined in Chapter 3, 'Saying no to Daddy: child sexual abuse, the "big hysteria"' illustrates, places women and children at greater risk.

'Boys' on television, film and stage

Faludi's *Stiffed* primarily relates to American culture. America in the 1990s was a scene of 'men behaving badly', from celebrity boxers (Mike Tyson, convicted for the rape of Desiree Washington) to American presidents (Bill Clinton, impeached for his alleged affair with Monica Lewinsky). Britain in the 1990s was arguably not dissimilar. 'New lad' misogyny, media created by magazines such as *Loaded* (1994), displaced the earlier, 1980s image of the 'new man' and provided testimony to a masculinist culture that derided women in attempts to bolster a vulnerable male ego. The television review, *Goodbye to the '90s*, broadcast on BBC2 at the close of 1999, for example, images Britain as a nation dominated by designer drugs and football. Significant in the documentary are the gender lines created through the choice and juxtaposition of clips. Popular entertainment, culture and sport, emerge as overwhelmingly male-dominated, as exemplified in programmes such as *Fantasy Football League*, which offers men the best of both worlds: football in a comedy format. When women occasionally take part, they are aiming to prove they can be as good as the boys (Miss Great Britain appeared on *Fantasy Football* drinking a pint of beer), or they are thoroughly degraded (as in Brigitte Nielson's drunken appearance on *Fantasy World Cup Live* in 1998). In brief, what the review makes clear is the way in which the 'new lad' culture that emerged in the 1990s was effective in silencing (degrading, even) women's representation.

British film in the 1990s also offers an at-a-glance view of an emergent masculinist culture.[15] Like theatre, British film had suffered a crisis of funding in the 1980s and was struggling to support new work. Significant among the films that helped to revive the fortunes of the cinema industry in the 1990s were those that variously represented masculinity in crisis. The adaptation of Irvine Welsh's *Trainspotting* (1996) gave expression to a 1990s generation of Thatcher's children: disaffected young men who, in the absence of any purpose – political, social or otherwise – locate directionless lives in an urban world of designer drug-taking. The success of the film was in part dependent on a style of innovative film-making that aesthetically captured the mood of disaffection and its attendant sub-cultural, drug-taking lifestyle. Financially, however, the film was only modestly successful compared to the next major 'boys in trouble' movie: *The Full Monty* (1997).[16] *The Full Monty* locates masculine disaffection in a community of ex-steel workers from Sheffield. Displaced from marriages, families, homes and jobs, the men take up stripping: their only means of survival is in the objectified ornamental role, traditionally reserved for women. The internecine struggles of male communities – communities that were felt to be under threat in real life – were generally popular in the 1990s,

4

though varied in representation from the openly misogynist *Brassed Off* (1996) ('girl' tries to join the boys' brass band at a local colliery), to Jez Butterworth's Quentin Tarentino-influenced 1950s gangland *Mojo* (1997), or Kevin Elyot's circle of gay friends in *My Night with Reg* (1997).

Both *Mojo* and *My Night with Reg* were plays before they were movies, and both were staged in seasons at the Royal Court that remained heavily engaged with boys' drama throughout the decade. Mark Ravenhill's consumerist take on sexual relations, *Shopping and F***ing* (1996), with ex-Royal Court director Max Stafford-Clark and his new company Out of Joint, was greeted by many as theatre's answer to *Trainspotting*. Masculinity was represented with a harsh and violent edge in the plays of Antony Nielson, but given a more gentle (although arguably more forceful, persuasive) treatment in Jonathan Harvey's gay play, *Beautiful Thing* (1993, also given cinematic treatment). Women were 'peaches' in Nick Grosso's debut play (*Peaches*, 1994), absent in Patrick Marber's all-male gambling community in *Dealer's Choice* (1995) and 'offstage' (at the end of a telephone) in Simon Block's *Not a Game for the Boys* (1995). It is not that these plays group together in terms of style or register, but that, as David Edgar argues, they share an 'over-arching theme': 'these plays address masculinity and its discontents'.[17] So if 'masculinity and its discontents' culturally and theatrically moved centre stage in the 1990s, what happened to women and to feminism?

Feminist directions in the 1990s
To extend, for a moment, the at-a-glance view of British cinema in the 1990s to representations of women, it is much harder to find positive (progressive) imaging. 'Viewing' is hindered by the numerous costume dramas and the continued success of (heterosexual) romance narratives (*Four Weddings and a Funeral* 1994; *Notting Hill* 1999). Influenced by Hollywood 'killer women' films, such as *Thelma and Louise* and *Terminator II* (both 1991),[18] the 'bad girl' began to make an appearance. Tank Girl, a British comic strip creation of the late 1980s, for example, was turned into a movie in 1995. The collision of power, femininity and personal happiness was given a more political

treatment in *Elizabeth* (1999), although was arguably more forcefully imaged through the real life events surrounding the death of Princess Diana in 1997.

One particular image of young women, however, came to dominate Britain in the 1990s: the confident, aggressive, girls-together image promoted by the The Spice Girls (1996) and packaged in their 'Cool Britannia' styled *Spice World: The Movie* (1997). The band promoted 'girl power' as a 'new' feminism for the 1990s, and member Geri Halliwell cited Margaret Thatcher as 'the original Spice Girl'.[19] 'Girl power' was this contradictory mix of feminist and anti-feminist discourses that promoted an image of aggressive 'sisterhood' and feminine glamour through a creed of selfish individualism designed to 'get what you want out of life'. It was precisely the damaging consequences of this kind of 'right-wing' feminism on the lives of young women that so concerned Caryl Churchill in *Top Girls* (1982) revived some ten years later as a 'bookend to the Thatcher period' (see Chapter 2).[20] Later in the decade, playwrights like Rebecca Prichard and Judy Upton would dramatise the gap between social reality and the 'girl power' myth for communities of disadvantaged young women in the 1990s (see Chapter 4).

'Girl power' also signals a generational gap in feminism in the 1990s. The binarism of 'old' and 'new', or 'victim' and 'power' models of feminism crudely separated an older style of second-wave feminism from a third generation of feminism. Among American feminists, 'power' feminism is exemplified by Naomi Wolf's *Fire with Fire: The New Female Power and How it will Change the 21st Century* (1993) or Katie Roiphe's *The Morning After: Sex, Fear and Feminism* (1993). *Fire with Fire* sees an older style of 'victim' feminism as a hindrance to women advancing their increased access to power in the wake of what Wolf argues as the 'genderquake' of the 1990s.[21] Roiphe takes a narrower focus and concentrates on the idea of 'victim feminism' in the context of rape, particularly date rape, a phenomenon of the 1990s in both America and Britain,[22] accusing feminism of promoting a culture of fear and excessive political correctness.

In British feminism, an example of 'new' styled feminism can be found in Natasha Walter's *The New Feminism*, where Walter accuses second-wave feminists of taking 'feminism to a dead end'.[23] Briefly, her argument is that second-wave feminism paid too much attention to bodies; that the 'new feminism' is more political and less personal in approach. There are, however, very serious problems with Walter's account of feminism, not least of which is the idea that second-wave feminism was somehow not interested in the 'material basis of economic and social and political inequality'.[24] Moreover, despite claims to a materialist feminist base to her 'new feminism', Walter's feminism has most in common with an old style of bourgeois feminism, the least radical of the established feminisms that proposed modest changes in the interests of increasing power to a minority of a few (already privileged) women. This, as Imelda Whelehan observes, turns out to be a prevalent problem with strands of 'new feminism': 'the implication is that they have something original to say about feminism, but on closer inspection it is clear that the main thrust of their arguments are very old indeed – an improbable mixture of early second-wave positions, coupled with classic anti-feminist sentiments'.[25] In brief, if the 'new' style of feminism represented women waking up to what Faludi argued as their missed opportunity of the 1980s, it was, nevertheless, problematic on account of its failure to bridge the 'gap' between advantaged and disadvantaged communities of women.

Feminism in the 1990s was also experiencing a difference of views over the issue of identity politics. The editorial to the 1989 spring issue of *Feminist Review: The Past Before Us, Twenty Years of Feminism*, marks feminism as having reached the point of recognising differences and inequalities between women (of race, sexuality, class). 'The danger now lies', cautions the editorial, 'in the reification of differences rooted in experiential identities'.[26] For identity to reside wholly through the personal, the individual, runs the risk of inherent essentialism and, in terms of a feminist movement, fragmentation and divisiveness between groups of women (as happened in the 1980s).

The 1990s challenge to identity politics came from feminist philosophy associated principally with Judith Butler and Eve Sedgwick. In the wake of Butler's *Gender Trouble* (1991) especially, ideas of gender and performativity came into wide critical and theoretical circulation. *Gender Trouble* and its sequel *Bodies that Matter* (1993)

7

proposed that there is no subject to decide on its gender; no subject who gets to choose. Rather, gender is a matter of reiteration: the regulated, forcible citation of gender 'norms' established and maintained by dominant cultural and social systems that invest heavily, if not exclusively, in the heteronormative.

Closer to home, in the field of performance studies, Peggy Phelan also proposed a critique of identity politics and the visible in her influential *Unmarked* (1993), arguing that 'there are serious limitations to visual representation as a political goal', and 'real power in remaining unmarked'.[27] On the other hand, leading international feminist theatre scholars, Sue-Ellen Case and Janelle Reinelt among them, have challenged the way that critical projects like Phelan's or Butler's involve the possible evacuation of a political agenda. As Case argues in *The Domain-Matrix: Performing Lesbian at the End of Print Culture* (1996), while such projects claim a 'less essentialist base', they risk abandoning the 'materialist discourses that signalled to activist, grassroots coalitions'.[28] Chapter 6 looks at aspects of this debate through two different responses to identity politics: Bryony Lavery's staging of lesbian love stories and Phyllis Nagy's dramatisation of gender trouble and identity displacement.

In desiring beyond a reductive model of 1980s identity politics, feminism in the 1990s also began to think transnationally. The influence of cultural and literary theorists such as Gayatri Spivak encouraged engagement with the colonising binary of first and third world feminisms. An emergent transnational feminism in the 1990s looked to ways of acknowledging the global and the local, of making cross-border connections, resistant to the colonial 'othering' of gender, race and nation. Chapter 7 looks at crossing cultural and theatrical borders in black and Asian writing as feminism connects to a multicultural 'scene'. Transnational thinking also informs Chapter 8: an examination of Timberlake Wertenbaker's cross-border politics that links contemporary feminism to issues of European citizenship as a major issue for the twenty-first century.

There is another feminist view circulating throughout this study: my own. As a title, 'Feminist Views on the English Stage' is designed to signal feminism as double, meaning both a feminist approach to the playwrights and playwriting considered in this volume, and the idea that some (though not necessarily all) of the writers and plays directly engage with feminism. Again, it is possible to see a generational gap in attitudes towards feminism, from, for example, Caryl Churchill's enduring and evolving commitment to socialist-feminism, to Sarah Kane's 'I have no responsibility as a woman writer because I don't believe there's such a thing'.[29] My own view is one that carries with it a history of teaching and researching feminist plays and performances over the past twenty years or more, a feminist history that I hope is useful to the study in being able to make sense of the 'present' within the context of an immediate, contemporary, past. Unlike Walter, I would not argue for a 'new' feminism, but for a continuum: an understanding of feminism as a political field that responds intrinsically and extrinsically to social and cultural change, but always with a view to understanding and, if not radically transforming, then at the very least ameliorating the social and cultural conditions under which a majority, and not a privileged minority, of women, variously and heterogeneously, live their lives.

Feminist structures of feeling

The explosion of explicitly feminist theatre-making in the 1970s was an artistic response to the lived experience of social and cultural exclusion. That, as Innes explained, women dramatists departed from the categories of theatre that had been in place for a century, reflects their need for different 'patterns', styles and aesthetics to give expression to experiences of social and cultural marginalisation. To mark a break, a rupture, with cultural tradition is indicative, as cultural materialist critic Raymond Williams explains, of a response to dominant culture's 'selective tradition', in this instance, one that had effectively written women out/off.[30] Quite what form feminist drama took, what radical break it made with the theatrical 'past', was dependent upon what kind of feminism coloured the stage picture,[31] but, overall, the break was indicative of what Williams describes as a 'a radical kind of *contemporary* change' giving rise to 'new structures of feeling'.[32]

When Williams explains the break with the past as reflecting '*contemporary* change' his use of the word '*contemporary*' is

9

significant. What was contemporary for the 1970s is no longer contemporary in the 1990s, and what needs to be acknowledged is that
structures of *feminist* feeling are a matter of evolution; a response
to differently lived lives and experiences of women in the 1990s that
were not those of an earlier generation of 1970s feminist women.[33]
Williams explains: 'One [feminist] generation may train its successor,
with reasonable success, in the social character or the general cultural pattern, but *the new generation will have its own structure of
feeling*'.[34]

In presenting a selection of women's playwriting from the
1990s, I have aimed to mix playwriting generations and feminism to
illustrate a 1970s feminist legacy circulating among different feminist
structures of feeling that reflect a world that seems a whole lot darker
and more violent. Women are still represented as victims of male violence and abuse, as in the theatre of Sarah Daniels and other abuse
plays examined in Chapter 3, but women are also perpetrators of violence. In Phyllis Nagy's *Butterfly Kiss* a daughter kills her mother.
In Caryl Churchill's *The Skriker* a young woman has killed her baby
and in Daniels's *Esme and Shaz* a young girl has killed her half-sister.
Young women seeking 'girl power' in reality are shown to live damaged (street) lives, as in the girl gang communities of Judy Upton and
Rebecca Prichard, or in the women who smuggle drugs for a living in
Winsome Pinnock's *Mules*. Situating the 1990s canon of Sarah Kane
at a mid-point in the study was also designed to ask what it means for
a feminist landscape to be ruptured by a playwright whose rejection
of the idea of a woman writer, as Graham Saunders argues, 'seem[ed]
to both simultaneously reject issues of gender and sexuality operating
in the work itself and abruptly cut Kane off from any "tradition" or
pattern for British women writing in the medium of theatre since the
1950s'.[35] Yet as much as I was drawn, on the one hand, to the insights
that such discontinuities and ruptures offered, I was, on the other,
excited by feminist continuities and connections. Most significant in
this respect was an emergent urgency and concern for the child (literally and metaphorically) at risk in a world where feminist agency
is lost to the individualist, materialist principles of late twentieth-
century capitalism – a world which, as the title of Caryl Churchill's

first play of the twenty-first century suggests, is not so very 'far away'.

While so many of the masculinity-in-crisis plays are inward-looking, nihilistic and lacking in political direction, much of the theatre I consider here engages with the dangers of a contemporary world, its inequalities and injustices, in a way that strives to be forward-looking, political and hopeful. Even in the darkest of pictures – such as Kane's *Blasted* or Lavery's *Frozen* – there is a glimmer of hope. As Kane argued, 'sometimes we have to descend into hell imaginatively in order to avoid going there in reality. If we can experience something through art, then we might be able to change our future'.[36]

Theatre contexts

I am aware that my own study is also, out of necessity, 'selective'. In seeking to balance a breadth of feminist argument with detailed play analysis, I could not be inclusive of all writers and all plays.[37] Nor, in view of these constraints, was it possible to widen my scope from the English to the British stage (a limitation that I hope future feminist theatre research will address).[38]

My view of the English stage is determined or shaped by a focus on those venues and companies dedicated to new writing. Key among them are the London based venues: the Royal Court, the Bush, the Hampstead and the Red Room. What these venues had in common in the 1990s were directors prepared to give their support to new writing: Stafford-Clark at the Court until 1993, succeeded by Stephen Daldry and Ian Rickson;[39] Dominic Dromgoole at the Bush until 1996, followed by Mike Bradwell; Jenny Topper, artistic director throughout the decade at the Hampstead; and Lisa Goldman at the Red Room, from its inauguration in 1995. Also important is the Soho Theatre Company, dating back to 1972 which, at the end of the 1990s, after a chequered history, secured a permanent home, courtesy of Lottery funding.[40] The National Studio (surviving the threat of closure in 1997 when the Old Vic and its annexe, where the Studio is housed, went up for sale) operates as an important resource for writers, offering them the opportunity to workshop and to develop scripts. Touring company Paines Plough commissioned new work in the early 1990s under the direction of Anna Furse (1990–4). Latterly the company was re-invigorated under Vicky Featherstone (director of Kane's *Crave*, 1998). Although woefully underfunded, Max Stafford-Clark's Out of Joint found a way of making new writing 'pay' by pairing a revival of a classic or popular play with a piece of new writing, and finding co-producers or partners for productions.[41] As co-producers and hosting venues, regional theatres have been vital to sustaining new drama. Out of Joint's production of Wertenbaker's *The Break of Day*, for example, was co-produced with Leicester Haymarket and paired with Chekhov's *Three Sisters*, while the Birmingham Repertory Theatre, under Bill Alexander's direction, has staged a variety of new writing in its studio venue (including, for example, plays by Bryony Lavery and Judy Upton), at the same time as building and sustaining a relationship with Asian women-led company, Tamasha.

While this describes the new writing scene generally it does not, or rather cannot, account for the complex web of relationships between writers and the people who manage, direct and produce their work, and the contexts of these relations – personal, social, cultural, material and theatrical – in any one given moment, that affect whether or not a play gets put on. Clearly, finding and sustaining relations between writers and their directors, practitioners and agents is vital to having plays performed. While it is possible to cite several examples of where women writers have benefited from specific relations – Caryl Churchill and Timberlake Wertenbaker with director Max Stafford-Clark, Judy Upton with director Lisa Goldman, Sarah Daniels with director Jules Wright, or Sarah Kane and Phyllis Nagy with agent Mel Kenyon – it is also the case that women playwrights generally perceive themselves as relatively disadvantaged when compared to male writers. This emerges as a constant complaint in the interviews in *Rage and Reason: Women Playwrights on Playwriting*: 'men get opportunities. They get staged. They get coverage' (Phyllis Nagy, *Rage*, p.28); 'statistically more women go to the theatre than men and yet women seem to have so little power over what they see and over what is chosen on their behalf' (Pam Gems, *Rage*, p.97), or 'all writers are dependent on the vagaries of whoever runs theatres, except it's often the vagaries of men because men still really do run theatres' (April de Angelis, *Rage*, p.59). Complaints of inequality are borne out by statistics, such as those produced by the Women's Playhouse Trust, a producing company set up in 1981 to create opportunities for women in British theatre and to give support to new writing by women.[42] Such figures show that women still have less share of the theatrical cake, and that complaints about the high profile given to the boys' plays in the 1990s are legitimate. Of writer Judith Johnson, Bush director Dominic Dromgoole comments, for example, 'an assured, still and sane voice, Judith Johnson was swamped by the explosion of boys' plays that appeared at the same time as her'.[43] Even established playwrights like Timberlake Wertenbaker felt squeezed out by the demand for a 'different kind of play; male violence, homoerotica' (*Rage*, p.137). In brief, doing battle with the vogue for boys' plays in the 1990s has made it all the harder for women on the new writing circuit, making successful relations with managements, directors and agents, all the more critical.

Although new writing generally has the support of companies and venues as cited, women's playwriting also finds a small outlet in the few surviving companies, mostly formed in the more liberal climate of the 1970s, who are dedicated to producing theatre committed to a programme of social change, sexual politics or feminism (or possible combinations of these). The few companies of this kind that have kept going are nothing compared to the number of groups that folded as a result of losing funding. Casualties of funding cuts at the end of the 1980s and beginning of the 1990s include, for example, the lesbian theatre company, Siren, and Monstrous Regiment, which had regularly commissioned plays by British and European women writers.[44] Gay Sweatshop, financially vulnerable at the start of the decade, found a brief new lease of life as a touring company of queer theatre and performance, but ceased in 1996 after further funding cuts. A company that has endured is Clean Break, formed in 1979 as a group of predominantly female ex-offenders, playing to prisons, touring nationally, and commissioning some of the women writers who appear in this volume (Sarah Daniels, Winsome Pinnock, Rebecca Prichard and Anna Reynolds). Exceptionally, in 1998 Clean Break secured a building base in Kentish Town, North London. Two long-standing companies currently provide opportunities for women to devise: Scarlet Theatre (formerly Scarlet Harlets) and Foursight Theatre. Only one of the 1970s women's new playwriting companies remains: The Sphinx Theatre Company, formerly The Women's Theatre Group.[45]

The Sphinx Theatre Company: (re)-presenting women writers

The Women's Theatre Group dates from 1973 and has been instrumental in creating opportunities for women writers to develop their craft. While an early phase of the company's work was committed to collaborative devising, in the late 1970s the company began to commission writers and nurtured the emergent careers of a number of playwrights, among them Bryony Lavery, Claire McIntyre, Timberlake Wertenbaker and Winsome Pinnock. At the end of the 1980s, as a response to financial pressures, the company abandoned its original collective style of management and pared down to a management team of five. Shortly afterwards, the group was re-named as The Sphinx Theatre Company and, under the artistic direction of Sue Parrish, continued throughout the 1990s to pursue a policy of commissioning new work or adaptations by women.[46] The company also hosted annual 'Glass Ceiling' conferences to provide a public platform for the discussion of the role and place of women in the arts.

The change of company name was a response to a desire to challenge an outmoded perception of the group as producing an 'agit-prop, political, seventies-style' of theatre.[47] 'The Sphinx Theatre Company' is a more 'enigmatic' and less descriptive name than The Women's Theatre Group, formerly radical in its indexing of a women's-only space for feminist theatre-making, but subsequently (especially given the demise of other women's companies) problematic in its implied homogeneity: one group as representative of all women.

The same problem obtains for the label 'woman playwright', which on the one hand claims a (political) identity, and on the other risks the reductive, essentialist 'fixing' of identity. The problem, as Butler observes, is how 'provisionally to institute an identity and at the same time to open the category as a site of permanent political contest'.[48] Three plays in the 1990s repertoire of The Sphinx

14

Theatre Company 'open up' the category of 'woman writer' and as a final, introductory point, help to reflect on the work by women playwrights that is detailed in this volume. The plays are Hélène Cixous's *Black Sail/White Sail* (1994), Pam Gems's *The Snow Palace* (1998) and Eileen Atkins's *Vita and Virginia* (1999). Respectively, these represent the lives of the Russian poet Anna Akhmatova, the Polish dramatist Stanislawa Przybyszewska, and Virginia Woolf and Vita Sackville-West. Each of the three plays points towards moments of crisis in the history of Europe: the prospect of Hitler in *Vita and Virginia*, the French Revolution in Stanislawa's writing, and Stalinist Russia in *Black Sail/White Sail*.

Of the writers given a dramatic treatment, Virginia Woolf arguably and easily is the best known – a reminder that 'canonical' writing is not an entirely male preserve. More importantly, however, is the way that Atkins's two-hander, drawing on the love-letters between Virginia and Vita, represents not one, but two writing lives where fictionalities and sexualities are not distinct but are constantly crossing over. Orlando, in Woolf's 'biography' *Orlando*, 'turns out to be Vita',[49] and 'writing', Vita observes '. . . is really the most intimate part of one'.[50] *Vita and Virginia* connects (sexualised) bodies to writing in a way that echoes Cixous's manifesto for an *écriture féminine*.

'Writing women' can take many different forms and there is no one style to characterise the work of women playwrights in the 1990s. Stylistically, they defy categorisation. What they do share, however, is, as Innes observed of post-1970s women's playwriting, a refusal of 'standard dramatic forms',[51] whether this is a revisioning of (white) realism by black and Asian women writers, Kane's more explosive treatment of realism in *Blasted*, Nagy's jazz-style compositions, Churchill's experiments with words and bodies, or Upton's techniques of mimetic distortion.

In Gems's *The Snow Palace*, the money and 'room of one's own' that Woolf argued as necessary to women's writing is reduced to a poor wooden hut. The writer Stanislawa lives and dies in abject poverty. Her work was not produced in her lifetime.[52] There is nothing romantic about her starving, penniless existence as a writer, and no way of surviving without the support of either state or family, all of which

15

is a salutary reminder for contemporary funding bodies and theatrical managements.

The snow bound, solitary woman writer offers a stark contrast to the subject of her writing: the French Revolution. Hers is an epic drama of revolutionary politics that conjures up the figures of Robespierre, Danton and St Just in public debates about issues of citizenship and democracy. In a contemporary world, Timberlake Wertenbaker observes that the opportunities for public debate are diminishing, making theatre as a public forum all the more important.[53] Like Stanislawa, it is the 'big issues' that attract contemporary women playwrights. As Rebecca Prichard argues 'plays where a writer has refused to limit the scope of her work to women's issues, but instead has simply written about the world' are those that she finds most exciting.[54] Critic Michael Billington also made this gendered observation: 'there is a new school of male playwrights fascinated by hermetic worlds. But there is an equally powerful corps of women playwrights capable of tackling anything under the sun: domestic and public violence, the problem of childless fortysomethings, late 20th-century despair'.[55] I would argue both of these slightly differently: that it is not so much a question of women playwrights turning to the 'world' as a subject, but of them *re-presenting women's issues as major issues of our time*. Violence towards the maternal reproductive body; the abuse of children and the increasing numbers of 'missing' children; the dispossessed communities of women, or the continued 'othering' of race, gender and sexuality, are not issues that concern a 'minority' of women, but are matters of local, national and international importance.

Theatre has the political power to stage the world that is and to invite us to see the other worlds that might be. Consequently, 'power', Cixous argues, 'is afraid of poetry [theatre]'.[56] In Cixous's *Black Sail/White Sail* Anna Akhmatova is punished on account of the subversive power of her poetry: her son, Liova, has been exiled to Siberia for seventeen years. Whether her son will come home and whether her poems will get published are the two issues that concern Anna. Both herald the possibility of a better future. Like the 'sisters' in Timberlake Wertenbaker's *The Break of Day*, Anna and her circle of female friends have lived in hope of a better future: 'for forty years we've been here craning our necks in an effort to leap up to Heaven'.[57] Perhaps, one of her friends suggests in the closing moments of the play, they might 'receive a telegram' in an afterlife telling them how things turned out: 'Poems arrived safely. Signed: on the banks of the 21st century' (*Black Sail/White Sail*, p.81).

Looking back from 'the banks of the 21st century', women's playwriting of the 1990s is shown to be concerned with the kind of future the world will inherit; which flag, the black or the white, it will 'sail' under is of major concern. The new century cannot, as the final image of Stanislawa frozen in the act of writing, her gaze directed towards the chair so recently vacated by the revolutionary Robespierre suggests (*Snow Palace*, p.71), be one where women are marginal to a politics of 'democratic' citizenship debated only by men. They must have parts to play; voices to be heard. In brief, as Faludi argued, 'women's hour on the stage is long, long overdue'.[58]

2 Telling feminist tales: Caryl Churchill

Caryl Churchill has the longest playwriting career of any of the writers profiled in this volume. For many years, she was one of only two contemporary women playwrights in the English theatre to receive critical and scholarly attention (the other was Pam Gems). In consequence, Churchill's theatre has been enormously important to subsequent generations of playwrights (women and men) and to the evolution of a contemporary feminist theatre practice and scholarship on the English stage and in the theatre academy.

Where several of the playwrights covered in this volume do not necessarily see themselves as feminist writers especially, Churchill is someone whose playwriting career and political outlook have consciously been shaped by a continuing commitment to feminism and to socialism. Socialism and feminism are not 'synonymous' in Churchill's view, but as she explained in an interview in the late 1980s, 'I feel strongly about both and wouldn't be interested in a form of one that didn't include the other'.[1] Her stage plays from the 1970s and 1980s are centrally concerned, therefore, with theatricalising a socialist and feminist critique of the injustices and inequalities produced by late twentieth-century western capitalism and patriarchy. Historicising the past in the interests of the present, she sought to make visible the politics of power and of social control: the regulation of sexuality (*Cloud Nine*, 1979), land (*Light Shining*, 1976), property (*Owners*, 1982) and punishment (*Soft Cops*, 1984). She demonstrated the risk to 'future histories' in her dramatisations of transnational capitalism (*Fen*, 1983; *Serious Money*, 1987) and cultural values (*Ice Cream*, 1989). Philosophical, socialist and feminist writings that influenced her thinking and theatre-making variously include works

18

by Michel Foucault, Franz Fanon, Hannah Arendt and Kate Millett. Foucault especially has been important to her desire to make sense of contemporary culture and social systems through historical perspectives. Moreover, what makes her playwriting so distinctive is the way in which her socialist and feminist politics are not just a matter of content, but also of theatrical form: the political is as much a 'subject' of her theatrical apparatus as it is of her dramatic content.

In contradistinction to her earlier work, where socialist and feminist politics were clearly (although by no means exclusively) staged through a Brechtian–feminist dramaturgy, Churchill's theatre since has experimented more with stylistic registers and has cross-fertilised drama with dance and music. Most significant here are her dance–theatre collaborations with the choreographer Ian Spink and the company Second Stride. Churchill first worked with Spink on *A Mouthful of Birds* (co-written with David Lan, 1986), and subsequently with Second Stride on *Lives of the Great Poisoners* (1991), *The Skriker* (1994) and *Hotel* (1997). Such collaborations reflect Churchill's desire to keep experimenting with form, a desire that has influenced a younger generation of writers, and has been appreciated, admired even, by those more experienced in stagecraft. Martin Crimp asserts that Churchill 'never loses sight of the playfulness of form',[2] while Sarah Daniels refers to her as the 'Picasso' of theatre.[3]

Churchill's formal experimentation is also inextricably bound up with the political. While the possibility of revolution and social transformation has remained a constant and consistent theme of her theatre (see, for example, *The Hospital* (1972) *Light Shining* (1976) or *Mad Forest* (1990)), the recognition that socialism and feminism have been losing rather than gaining ground has strongly influenced the shape of her 1990s canon. Explicit about the world she would like to see, a world that in 1982 she described as 'decentralised, nonauthoritarian, communist, non-sexist',[4] Churchill has since had to find ways of writing about, or giving theatrical expression to, a world in which her vision of greater democratisation and equality has become less and less attainable.

Characteristic of her playwriting in the 1990s, therefore, is a concern to make audiences see the potentially catastrophic consequences of late twentieth-century capitalism (to which events of 9.11 bear witness). Within this theatrical landscape women's lives continue to emerge as the most at risk; the most damaged. More specifically it is the organisation of mother–child relations in a social and cultural economy that continues to privilege production over reproduction, that remains a focus of her feminist critique. In support of this, I will examine Churchill's resistant representations of the maternal in the revival of *Top Girls* (1991) and in *The Skriker* (1994). I look at the fiction of the familial in *Blue Heart* (1997), and close with a brief reference to *Far Away* (2000), to show Churchill's concern with the 'gap' between personal 'happiness', and social and political responsibility.

Top Girls: from 1982 to 1991

Top Girls figures as a major work, not just in terms of Churchill's canon, but also in the context of contemporary feminist theatre and in the broader context of the contemporary English stage. 'I read *Top Girls* at least once a year and I weep', writes Mark Ravenhill, 'One day, I think to myself, one day I'll write something as good.'[5] Ravenhill also describes *Top Girls* as 'the best play of the past 20 years', while *Guardian* critic Michael Billington lists it in his ten best British plays of the twentieth century.[6] Specific to women dramatists, Shelagh Stephenson argues that with *Top Girls* 'Caryl Churchill hacked out a path for a whole generation of female playwrights.'[7]

The Royal Court staged a major revival of *Top Girls* in 1991, with several members of the 1982 cast and the play's original director, Max Stafford-Clark. A televised version of the production was also made for BBC broadcast. At the time of seeing the revival and broadcast in 1991, I was working on a student production of *Top Girls*. It struck me then – and possibly even more so now in the wake of the late 1990s style of 'new feminism' – how important, relevant and necessary the play's critique of top girl 'feminism' remains.

If earlier drama had signalled the difficulty of socialism without feminism,[8] *Top Girls* shows the dangers of feminism without socialism. For Churchill, a commitment to socialist-feminism meant that the women-as-achievers principle of bourgeois feminism was not adequate to the task of improving the lives of a majority of women. When *Top Girls* was first performed it was some three years after Thatcher came to power (1979) and a year before her re-election for a second term of office. Already, the idea of the materially driven 'Superwoman', Churchill's kind of 'top girl' Marlene figure, was taking hold. But career and economic advancement consequent upon inter- and intra-sexual oppression, a kind of 'right-wing feminism' (as Churchill also termed it),[9] does not necessarily provide a progressive way forward; can hardly, as the play shows, be equated with feminism in any positive sense at all.

Back in 1982, critical attention focused on the play's opening dinner scene and its innovatory technique of overlapping dialogue that has since influenced a number of British playwrights (Ravenhill included), and attracted feminist interest for the way in which it fostered ideas about breaking up language in the interests of finding a 'voice' in which women's concerns might be heard, or heard differently. 'Legendary and much imitated', as Clare Bayley described it on the play's revival in 1991,[10] the restaurant scene, in which women come together to celebrate Marlene's 'top job' promotion in an employment agency, defied all conventions of stage realism with its dinner guests: Isabella Bird (Victorian traveller); Lady Nijo (Japanese courtesan, turned Buddhist nun); Dull Gret (figure from a Brueghel painting); Pope Joan (woman disguised as a man and thought to have been Pope between 854 and 856), and Patient Griselda (the obedient wife from Chaucer's 'The Clerk's Tale' in *The Canterbury Tales*).

In 1982, moreover, it was exceptional to have an all-female stage picture and a play with roles exclusively for women. As reviewer Robert Cushman observed, 'a chap has to take notice' when the two best plays of the year (*Top Girls* and Louise Page's *Salonika*) are written by women.[11] Though more all-female casts have followed in the wake of *Top Girls* (Charlotte Keatley's *My Mother Said I Never Should* significant among them), in the longer term, the change was neither as dramatic nor as extensive as the 'chaps' expected. In the late 1990s, for example, Ravenhill compared Mamet's *Glengarry Glen Ross* with *Top Girls*, observing that both plays were performed within a year of each other, and both had opening scenes in restaurants followed

by office scenes designed to question capitalist forces and human relations. 'Why then', asks Ravenhill, 'has Mamet's been followed by
scores of all-male plays and Churchill's by only a handful of all-girl?'[12]

Top Girls itself points towards an answer: unless women, in the
interests of economic and professional advancement are prepared to
make sacrifices, particularly of the domestic and maternal kind, and
espouse masculinist values then they do not 'get on' (or, in the case of
theatre, get 'put on'). The politics of a selfish versus selfless creed is
staged in *Top Girls* in the relationship between two sisters, Marlene
and Joyce. As Marlene enjoys her high-flying career, her working-class
sister Joyce has a less 'successful' (in economic terms) life caring for
Marlene's daughter, Angie (a low achiever and unlikely to become a
'top girl'). The difficulty of combining work and family life is posed
as an unresolved problem in *Top Girls*, while the dangers of espousing
Marlene's masculinist, capitalist values, oppressive to other women
(and men), are signalled in the final line of the play, delivered by Angie:
'Frightening'.

That Churchill chose the kitchen as the site for the play's political debate between the Thatcherite Marlene and her working-class
sister Joyce is highly significant in feminist terms. As a visual echo
of the 1970s feminist creed, 'the personal is political', it signalled the
on-going need for feminism to examine and to include the politics of
the kitchen, of the domestic, as part of the broader, epic struggle of the
'us and them' divide that would become a feature of British politics
and class-warfare in the 1980s. Kit and Angie's scene also works in a
similar way. Hiding out in their junk shelter in Joyce's backyard, the
two girls talk of a different kind of warfare:

> KIT. When there's a war, where's the safest place?
> ANGIE. Nowhere.
> KIT. New Zealand is, my mum said. Your skin's burned right
> off. Shall we go to New Zealand?[13]

The girls hiding out in the makeshift 'shelter', keeping out of sight of
the mother-figure who, though she tries, can no longer fulfil her role as
maternal protector, stages one of Churchill's most enduring political

concerns: the child, the girl-child in particular – trying to keep safe in an unsafe world.[14]

By the time of the play's revival in 1991, a feeling that the world was an unsafe place resonated throughout due to the civil wars and revolutions breaking out in former East European countries. Churchill's first play of the 1990s, *Mad Forest*, for example, depicted the revolution in Romania: the fall of Ceauşescu and the election of Illiescu and the National Salvation Front. The moment of post-revolutionary chaos was so vividly captured in the play's surreal image of a vampire and dog: Romania, the poor, starving, ownerless, stray dog, missing the hated master and looking to the vampire as a new blood-sucking owner.[15] Closer to home, Thatcher had, finally, by the November of 1990, been forced out of office and replaced by John Major and a Cabinet from which women were conspicuous by their absence. In a worsening British economy, the country headed into a deepening recession. By 1992 the unemployment figure stood at 2.6 million. The 1980s years of earning 'ridiculous money', being 'pissed and promiscuous', as Ian Dury's lyrics in *Serious Money* (1987) described, were well and truly over.

This being the case, reviewers of the *Top Girls* revival warmed to the heightened irony in Marlene's prediction for the 1980s of a 'stupendous' time ahead and an economy that would get Britain back on its feet. 'Caryl Churchill's prescient ode to Thatcherism rings brilliantly with bitter, retrospective ironies, not least because the recession is screwing the coke-and-shampoo set as ruthlessly as they screwed up the '80s', observed James Christopher in *Time Out*.[16] Or, 'Caryl Churchill's observations about the Thatcherite Top Girls of the '80s seem even sharper as the recession bites' wrote Ros Asquith in *City Limits*.[17] It was, as Ravenhill later summarised, 'a masterstroke to revive it [*Top Girls*] as a bookend to the Thatcher period. Nobody else got it quite so right, that epic struggle between two different value systems'.[18] In brief, received in 1982 as a socialist-feminist critique of bourgeois feminism, *Top Girls* in 1991 was 'read' as an 'epic', state-of-the-nation debate about the Thatcher legacy of a materially divided, 'us and them' Britain.

For feminists in particular, the early 1990s was a moment for looking back at the impact that the materialist 1980s had had on their lives. Clare McIntyre's *My Heart's a Suitcase*, staged at the Royal Court in 1990, for example, presented three women each with different attitudes towards money: Chris who moans about not having any, Hannah who enjoys making do without and Tunis who has lots of money and no interest in life other than spending it. Are women allowed to like money, or not? Should they have careers, or not? Children, or not? What gets debated through all of this is the issue of social responsibility: how are women to find 'value' in their lives, to be responsible, for themselves and for others, in the debris left behind by the Thatcherite 1980s? The play poses some challenging (and inevitably unanswered, or rather, irresolvable) questions for women at the start of the 1990s.

The consequences of a Thatcherite style of 1980s 'free market' feminism have been widely debated in feminist studies, although as Joni Lovenduski and Vicky Randall write, 'few would argue that they have been good'.[19] While feminists mostly have been critical of the kind of 'successful' woman Thatcher stood for and encouraged other women to be like, there are a 'few' who argue in Thatcher's favour. Natasha Walter, for example, reclaims Thatcher as 'the great unsung heroine of British feminism'.[20] Walter argues her case for Thatcher on the grounds that she 'normalised female success':

> She allowed British women to celebrate their ability not just to be nurturing or caring or life affirming, but also to be deeply unpleasant, to be cruel, to be death-dealing, to be egotistic. It was cathartic for us to acknowledge those possibilities in the female character writ so large.
>
> (Walter, *The New Feminism*, p.174)

However, as *Top Girls* shows, to accept as cathartic the possibility of 'female success' based on egotism, cruelty, 'death-dealing', would mean somehow taking pleasure in Angie's 'Frightening' moment. What this highlights is the 'gap' between Churchill's socialist-feminist commitment and the 'new' feminism, gaining ground in the 1990s, that espouses 'female success' and continues to ignore the economic and class factors that militate against the idea that all women are able to 'compete' on an equal basis. Two key issues that emerge from the socialist-feminist politics of *Top Girls* set against the material and cultural backdrop of the early 1990s are the difficulty of combining work and motherhood, and the social reality for young, disadvantaged girls, like Angie.

If, in the early 1980s, in the wake of 1970s legislation that encouraged women's greater equality in the workforce, the emphasis was on women and work, by the early 1990s the focus was on the idea of the working mother. Researching for the 1991 revival, for example, and looking back at the 1982 *Top Girls*, cast members and Stafford-Clark noted the change in emphasis, from childless career woman to mother with career.[21] Researching and working on the 1991 student production of *Top Girls* I cited earlier, I noted a similar change. By then, images of glamorous, shoulder-padded executive businesswomen felt like museum or media (*Dallas* and *Dynasty*) pieces. These had been replaced by glamorous images of professional working mothers. I particularly remember the car advertisements from the early 1990s because I had just had my own first child, and could not (in spite of myself) resist the fantasy of the executive-looking-mother-in-suit strapping a placid, smiling baby into car seat. My own stressful reality was of early morning drives (6a.m. starts) to child-minders (the most affordable form of child care) with a not always smiling baby, and on to work, with the minimal amount of attention to my own personal appearance. The glamorous image bore little relation to a stressful reality. My own experience is one to be found in the countless stories of other working mothers from this time; the post-1980s stress of having to combine parenting with paid work. As one reviewer wrote of the *Top Girls* revival, 'progress means that now, financially unassisted by the state women are expected to embrace both [work and motherhood]'.[22] Hard as this was for women in professional jobs, like myself, it was significantly harder for those women with low-income jobs for whom child care was simply not affordable.

Moreover, 'buying' into a 1980s vision of female 'success' had not addressed the relative impoverishment of the lives of young working-class women and Angie's nightmare vision had, by the 1990s, become a social reality. It is Angie's 'frightening' story that, over time, has arguably shifted to become the focus of the play. Having taught *Top Girls* now for many years, my own primary focus, like that of the reviewers of the first production, began with the dinner scene, moved to the kitchen scene, and, then, to Angie's story.[23]

Angie's story of gender and class oppression is the 'underside' of Marlene's 'top girl' success; for there to be a 'top' there must be a 'bottom'. The dismissal of Angie by Marlene as a girl who is 'not going to make it' reinforces her own position as a woman who has made it, and by virtue of her 'success' is empowered to decide which other women get to the top or are forced to stay at the bottom of the career ladder (as illustrated in the interview scenes set in the employment agency). Although not yet a mother, the adult–child playing of Angie, doubled with the role of the monosyllabic working-class, peasant mother of ten, Dull Gret, foretells that her life will map out in some way like Joyce's: as domestic–maternal drudge.

Not that Angie is entirely accepting of her 'position' as 'docile body' (as Foucault terms it). She tries everything in her limited 'power' to change her life (travelling to London to see Marlene, or telephoning Marlene in order to get her to visit herself and Joyce in East Anglia).[24] Disadvantaged in social and economic terms, she fantasises a different life for herself – one in which she experiences limited agency, not waiting for a prince to rescue her, but trying to rescue herself. Fairy tales, as Marina Warner explains, 'play to the child's hankering after nobler, richer, altogether better origins, the fantasy of being a prince or a princess in disguise, the Freudian "family romance"'.[25] Angie's desire for 'altogether better origins' centres on Marlene. Of course the twist in Churchill's tale is that Marlene, Angie's 'fantasy' and real mother, does not come to claim her long lost daughter; there is no restoration of the 'Freudian "family romance"', a point that Churchill has repeatedly insisted on, in earlier plays such as *Cloud Nine* (1976) and later theatre like *Blue Heart* (1997). If Churchill is telling tales then she does it not to conceal a psychic-social reality, but to make it the subject of her tale. In contrast to the revival of interest in tales in which a child learns about *him*self and successfully saves the world, current at the time of writing this chapter,[26] Churchill connects the damage of the child-mother to an unsafe, damaged world that it is becoming increasingly harder to save, as exemplified in her 1994 production of *The Skriker*.

The Skriker

Concern for future generations – particularly future generations of women – links *Top Girls* to Churchill's mid-1990s production of *The Skriker*.[27] The Skriker is a figure that Churchill's directions describe as '*a shapeshifter and death portent, ancient and damaged*'; a figure drawn from Lancashire folklore.[28] The Skriker emerges from her underworld to attach herself to two young teenage girls. One girl, Josie, is in a mental institution for having killed her baby; the other, Lily, is pregnant and running away from home. As the Skriker haunts the two girls, shapeshifting through a number of disguises, she tries to entice them both into her underworld. Josie is the first to be taken there, and, after what seems to her to be like years, is returned to the 'real' world, seemingly just a few seconds after she left it. Lily, however, has a very different and much darker experience. At the close of the play, she leaves her baby behind and agrees to accompany the Skriker to the underworld, believing that, like Josie, she too will be returned in a matter of seconds to her own world and to her baby. Instead, she is 'tricked, tracked, wracked' into 'another cemetery, a black whole hundred yearns' – the future world of her granddaughter and great-great-granddaughter (*The Skriker*, p.290).

However, while thematically there are links between *Top Girls* and *The Skriker* and a parallel to be found in the paired friendships between girls (Kit and Angie, Lily and Josie), stylistically the two plays are radically different. The Brechtian–feminist dramaturgy of the former is now replaced by a corporeal and textual composition with movement 'written' by Ian Spink and words 'choreographed' by Churchill. It is important to note this dramaturgical and stylistic shift and its possible significance. As previously noted, *Top Girls* belongs to an earlier phase of theatre-making, when playwrights and practitioners with feminist concerns and interests paid attention to the inequalities of dominant social, sexual, cultural and political systems. Drawing largely on a Brechtian dramaturgy, their widely shared aim was to make visible the invisible gender (class/race) apparatus: to denaturalise or destabilise gender in order that it might be 'seen' differently. In order to demonstrate the effects of dominant gender ideology, this might, theatrically, involve showing the 'other', the abject. In her illuminating commentary on Churchill's *Fen* (1983), for example, Elin Diamond notes the shifts from the play's 'episodic but coherent text concerned with mimetic accuracy' to what she terms the 'death-space': a space in which the dead figure of Val releases the misery and pain of the other Fen women (past and present). 'To tamper with this space – and with the fictional dramatic world in which the dead stay dead – is', Diamond explains, 'to insist on a different way of seeing, a different order'.[29] With Churchill's dramaturgical, stylistic shift in *The Skriker*, however, the hold on 'mimetic accuracy' has lessened. The dramatic fiction of *The Skriker* is accessed not through the mimetic, but through the Skriker's underworld. It is the spirit world that frames our 'own' (or the closest we can find to it in the world of Josie and Lily).[30] The mimetic is disturbed and 'taken in' by the 'other' world, spilling out of the margins to which it was previously confined. It is the underworld, a world whose rules 'disobey' the logic of time, space and (im)mortality, that distorts the 'real', makes it barely recognisable. Moreover, accessed through the Skriker's underworld, the 'real', the mimetic, as we conventionally know it, is only a small, tiny part – visually suggested in the production by the boxed-in effect of Annie Smart's set design. Cubic and clinical, this setting, in which several of the encounters between the girls and the Skriker were staged, was haunted constantly by figures from the spirit world: a physical counterpointing to the logos of the 'real'.

Unlike *Top Girls*, *The Skriker* did not enjoy a warm critical reception, because reviewers apparently found it a hard piece to make any sense of at all – let alone political sense. At home with the Brechtian–feminist dramaturgy of *Top Girls*, they could not find a way into the physical style of *The Skriker*. Reviews are replete with critics expressing their anxieties about having to give an account of a performance they felt they had not understood, or, like Benedict Nightingale, asking 'what's the point and purpose of it all?'[31] Like Nagy's *The Strip*, Wertenbaker's *The Break of Day* or Kane's *Blasted* (see relevant chapters for discussion of each of these), *The Skriker* stands in the Churchill canon as arguably the play the critics least understood and were most hostile to.[32] Significantly, there has been no major revival of *The Skriker* on the English stage since its 1994 production in the Cottesloe studio theatre at the Royal National Theatre.

Reviewers were particularly hostile to the physical register that Spink used to create the spirit world, made up of fairy tale figures that 'ghost' through the 'real' world of the teenage girls. 'The dancing spirits . . . never seem at home', wrote one critic.[33] 'The choreography is dull when it isn't risible', wrote another.[34] Irrespective of whether one might want to argue the effectiveness of Spink's arrangement, failure to 'read' the physical register meant an elision of the political significance of the underworld. One critic referred back to Churchill's earlier play *Vinegar Tom* to claim that she was contradicting herself by creating a spirit world that she had previously argued did not exist.[35] Skriker may be 'part witch' as Janelle Reinelt argues,[36] but she and the other spirits do not reinstate or reinscript the demonisation of women forcefully critiqued in *Vinegar Tom*. Rather, they come, figuratively, to stand for the damaged semiotic (in the Kristevan sense): the marginalised 'other' that haunts the symbolic order – an invisible, repressed world, made visible. A better, more appropriate, understanding of the politics of *The Skriker's* underworld, and the spirits who represent it, emerges by going back not to *Vinegar Tom* as a point of reference, but to *Cloud Nine*.

Cloud Nine has mainly attracted critical interest on account of its gender role reversal and cross-race casting. Exceptionally, Alice Rayner's excellent and illuminating essay, 'Caryl Churchill's Furious Ghosts', examines the play from the point of view of mother–child relations, arguing that in *Cloud Nine* Churchill attempts to work out such relations in excess of or more complex than the 'idea of compulsory motherhood'.[37] Her argument includes analysis of the park scene (Act Two, Scene Three), in which brother and sister, Edward and Victoria, along with Lin (lesbian friend to and would-be lover of Victoria) try to conjure up the goddess Isis. As a setting, the park is a site of contradictions: where characters desire to be socially and sexually different to the heteronormative, but where children and an outmoded, traditional view of the family lay claim to their lives and time. Isis, archaic goddess 'who walked in chaos and created life' does not appear.[38] Previously, like the characters in the play, I found this ritual hard to take seriously and had concerns about the possible essentialist overtones of an archaic maternal.[39] Now (with hindsight) I would argue that the park ritual marks a crucial and critical moment: the archaic goddess, sign of an alternative order to the idea of Mother, does not (cannot) appear. Instead, 'war' (a dead soldier from the combat in Northern Ireland) comes in her place. In this militaristic displacement of an alternative maternal, one can see the political logic of Churchill's later work, through to the spirits of *The Skriker* and on to the chilling evocation of transnational war in *Far Away*. Looked at in this way, the Skriker and her underworld serve as a haunting reminder of the goddess figure that did not, could not, appear in the park: the lost possibility of mother–child relations figured differently to that determined and defined by the law of the father. With the further warnings of Angie's 'frightening' future unheeded, it is this lost opportunity which, in the damaged form of the Skriker and the other spirits, comes back to haunt the symbolic.

Skriker comes from an ancient, pagan, pre-Christian time. The damage marked on and through the spider-like body of the spirit is, I would argue, of a double kind: one consequential upon both pre- and post-Christian lives. As an androgynous, archaic spirit, the Skriker offers the possibility of a point of origin outside of the gender binary, but one that s/he is not allowed to take up; is not allowed to 'be'. It is significant, for example, that the Skriker cannot actually remember living in a time when s/he was made welcome, when s/he and the other spirits 'mattered', rather s/he has to 'think it was so' that that was how 'it should have been' (*The Skriker*, p.257). Instead, s/he is forced to live through centuries of man-made 'history'.

The spirit body of the Skriker, as played by Kathryn Hunter in the production, was evocative of the twisted, distorted body of the hysteric, as was the semiotic babble of the Skriker's jumbled-up tale-telling.[40] In human guise, the Skriker acts out the roles of the Freudian 'family romance': appearing as child (needy for a mother), the 'prince' or would-be lover and father, or fairy (god)mother (who grants dangerous wishes). But the disguises slip and the spirit body is never far out of sight. Similarly, other human figures in the play are haunted or doubled by spirit bodies: businessmen have Thrumpins riding on their backs, without knowing they are there. The damaged semiotic makes itself felt, will not go away. Rather it is taking its revenge on a world that has created and yet denied its existence.

Making visible the repressed, marginalised, 'monstrous' world of the Skriker, however, does not bring with it the possibility of *jouissance*. If there is a moment of *jouissance* to be found in *The Skriker* it occurs in the 'mutual gazing' relations between Lily and the baby: 'I know everyone's born. I can't help it. Everything's shifted round so she's in the middle' (*The Skriker*, p.277). As E. Ann Kaplan discusses, in the 'mutual gaze' of mother–child relations, lies an alternative possibility of mutual recognition.[41] However, this exchange between Lily and her baby is no match for the Skriker's gaze: one that 'sees' through centuries of pain, hurt and damage. In demanding the various attentions of Lily and of Josie, the Skriker plays low status (a needy child, an old woman) and high status roles (business woman, would-be lover) – but always in relations that are hierarchical, vampiric and never mutual. And Lily's baby is always in the 'middle' of the power games; is the 'object' or objective. Ultimately, I am inclined to argue the Skriker as a nemesis figure: an ancient, avenging figure unleashed on a world that continues to neglect its mothers, its children, its future. The other spirits, too, are mostly those that prey on children, and are, therefore, evocative of a nightmarish world in which children cannot be kept safe.[42] Mother and child are constantly separated, torn apart. This is not done to express some kind of failure on the part of the biological mother, nor to reinstate a biologically determinist view of the maternal. Rather it aims to show the economic, social and familial relations that stand in the way of an alternative, arguably more hopeful, set of mother–child relations.[43]

As a nightmare world, the spirit underworld is a time out of time. Yet time is also running out. The fairy tale telling which underpins Skriker is crumbling, corrupted. 'Shape-shifting is', Marina Warner explains, 'one of fairy tale's dominant and characteristic wonders: hands are cut off, found and reattached, babies' throats are slit, but they are later restored to life'.[44] But in *The Skriker*, restorative powers are running out. The idea of a tale as somehow universal, endlessly repeated, a constant, a known, a given, is collapsing; is damaged. More specifically, Skriker's tale telling spins together a number of pieces which point not to the conventional 'happy' ending but always to disaster.

The 'happy ever after' ending to the conventional fairy tale implies an idea of monumental, eternal time in the moment of narrative closure. In the ending is the beginning of a time in which the rescued heroine will be eternally 'happy'. The Skriker's tale not only demolishes this gendered (matrimonial) myth of the 'happy ever after', but it further demonstrates that the comfort of a world that goes on without us – through nature, through children – is also at risk: 'It was always possible to think whatever your personal problem, there's always nature. Spring will return even if it's without me. . . . This has been a comfort to people, as long as they've existed. But it's not available any more' (*The Skriker*, p.282). The idea of time running out, through a spirit world that grows ever bleaker, is a way of signalling imminent global catastrophe; the millennial pressures of 'a cemetery, a black whole hundred yearns' (p.290), in which nature is ruined, damaged to the point of extinction: 'wide open wide world hurled hurtling hurting hurt very badly' (p.271).

There is a connection or doubling between the ancient oppression of the Skriker and the young girls in the present: a way of reading *The Skriker* as a kind of tale for a contemporary moment. It is important to note that at the time of the production, the then Conservative government were mounting an increasingly hostile campaign against young single mothers. In a moral panic about the rising numbers of young women either choosing to or being forced to raise children on their own, initiatives were proposed to reduce welfare benefits. However, as the dramatisation of the child-mother Lily and killing-mother Josie warns, without systems of support – such as family, friends, money – mother-child and child are both at risk.

Traditional tales in which young women get rescued from danger, poverty and loneliness may have their uses as fantasy, but bear no relation to the social reality of the Angies, Lilies and Josies in the modern, urban world of the 1990s. For these young girls there is no 'magical' way in which their lives are suddenly transformed, made better. If there is a metanarrative or archetypal tale to be identified in *The Skriker*, it is that Lily's act of individual kindness to the Skriker is no (political) solution for her child, or her child's children and all of their futures.

'The Mother of Invention': *Blue Heart*[45]

If the Skriker is some kind of nemesis figure, then s/he is also feminism's nemesis: feminism's failure fully to address the issue of mothering. The problem that in the 1960s Betty Friedan called 'the problem that has no name',[46] can now be named, but is still a problem. Women may have got themselves out of the kitchen and into paid work, and out of dual and into single models of parenting in greater numbers, but without the radical transformation of society and family, so much desired and expected in the 1970s, actually taking place. With the family ideologically intact (even if somewhat ragged at the edges and periodically in need of being re-mythologised by the various, successive Conservative governments), women's changing social realities have had to co-exist with an outmoded, yet prevalent sense of the familial. It is a myth that continues to be 'naturalised', and one, therefore, that Churchill took apart in her 1997 production of *Blue Heart*.

Blue Heart consists of two plays: *Heart's Desire* and *Blue Kettle*. 1997, the year that finally saw the election of a New Labour government after eighteen years of Conservative rule, was also a major year for Churchill. In addition to *Blue Heart*, revivals of *Cloud Nine* and *Light Shining* were staged at the Old Vic and the National theatres respectively, and Churchill produced two more new works: *Hotel* (an exploration of urban isolation, again in collaboration with Spink and Second Stride) and *This is a Chair* (a short, Brechtian styled critique of personal lives divorced from major political and social issues, staged at the Royal Court). This body of work was all the more significant, given that Churchill had spent three years away from the stage after the production of *The Skriker* and her translation of *Thyestes* for the Royal Court, both in 1994.[47]

Blue Heart brought Churchill back together with director Max Stafford-Clark – although not at the Royal Court from which Stafford-Clark had relinquished his post in 1993, but with his newly formed touring company, Out of Joint. In 1979, Stafford-Clark's Joint Stock production of *Cloud Nine* played out dangerous family fictions and hidden sexualities across an impossible (in realistic terms) nineteenth- and twentieth-century time span, as lives encompassed a colonial past and a contemporary present. In *Heart's Desire*, Out of Joint staged a family caught up not in some kind of 'impossible' chronology, but a time loop, as a father, mother, aunt and brother wait for the daughter of the family to come home. Except that the homecoming is constantly delayed and deferred as the play is made to start several times over, and is picked up and left off at various different points. Set in a realistically staged kitchen in the Out of Joint production, it was nevertheless a kitchen variously invaded by gunmen (who burst in and shoot everybody dead); a man who comes demanding the family's papers, a ten-foot tall bird, and hoards of children who rush out of the kitchen cupboards. This parallels the nightmarish stories that begin to emerge during the monotony of waiting: stories of a dead body in the garden, of the father's urge to eat himself, or the aunt's fear of dying. It is a style of magic realism that turns the family inside out: from the ordinary, domestic, into a possible site of high, violent drama. In particular, it is important to note that the daughter, though she makes a very brief appearance, does not, in effect, return home. The father, who most desires her return, does not get to reclaim his daughter, rather, as he states and repeatedly states as the opening line to the play, 'She's taking her time'.[48] In taking *her* time, the daughter is the one not to come home.

Less playful in composition than *Heart's Desire*, *Blue Kettle* dramatises a young man, Derek, conning several elderly women into making them believe he is their long lost son. As a child, Derek's favourite tale was the Enid Blyton story of *The Magic Faraway Tree*: each time you climbed it, it took you to a different, magical country (*Blue Heart*, p.60). With each 'mother' he sets out to trick, he invents a different 'country' in which landscape figures the story of a lost son returned. The maternal need to believe in the filial fiction is treated stylistically, not realistically, and primarily through a play with language in which the words 'blue' and 'kettle' (and eventually just syllables and sounds from these two words), come to replace all others. The surface play with language at one level, like the ordinary, the domestic in *Heart's Desire*, allows for the possibility of another, 'deeper', 'narrative' to emerge, in this instance the emotional lives of the mothers, all separated from their sons who were given up for adoption.

A few critics were annoyed or irritated by the playfulness of *Blue Heart*, but most gave it a warm reception. While *The Skriker* had confused and bewildered, *Blue Heart*, particularly after Churchill's three-year absence, afforded the critics the opportunity to applaud her capacity for reinventing herself. Benedict Nightingale claimed Churchill as 'the most inventive, unpredictable British dramatist now at work',[49] while Paul Taylor described her as 'the most playfully and profoundly innovative dramatist',[50] and John Peter wrote of her as 'the most radical and stylistically innovative dramatist writing today other than Pinter'.[51] 'Inventive', 'unpredictable', 'innovative', or 'radical' highlight Churchill's desire to experiment, rather than signalling the broadly political or more particularly feminist edge to her work. More appropriately, however, I would wish to argue Churchill as a writer who remains concerned with all of these elements: innovative, political and feminist. The playfulness of *Blue Heart* may not have the feminist impact of *The Skriker* (as is argued in this chapter), but its inventiveness relates directly to one of feminism's on-going concerns: the family.

Far Away

To endorse my claim for Churchill's constant and consistent feminist political concerns linked to her inventiveness, I conclude with a brief mention of *Far Away*, Churchill's first play of the twenty-first century. From the perspective of a new century, *Far Away* provides a kind of 'bookend' to *Top Girls*: shows how the failure to care differently, less oppressively, for future generations of children, leads to global destruction. In *Far Away*, it is, finally, the child's turn to tell the tale. Like Angie in *Top Girls*, Joan in *Far Away* is staying with her aunt, Harper.

Also like Angie, Joan has trouble sleeping. The play opens with Joan downstairs, explaining to her aunt that she cannot sleep. Harper offers her comfort and the conviction that her house in the country where they are staying is a 'safe' place. The child's logic gradually unravels the fiction of the adult. Seen through the eyes of the child, Harper's house is re-presented as a place of violence, in which those seeking help (asylum) are being brutalised, killed even.[52]

However, the child Joan who asks many questions grows up into a young woman who asks fewer questions of the capitalist hat-making industry she comes to work for. As in *This is a Chair*, personal lives take priority over and become divorced from social and political realities. Joan and her boyfriend Todd are more interested in each other than the world around them – most forcibly imaged in *Far Away* as prisoners on their way to death: men, women and children, parade (holocaust style) in the hats made by Joan and Todd. In C.S. Lewis's children's fiction *The Lion, the Witch and the Wardrobe*, inhabitants of the other world, Narnia, have to look out for these creatures and even trees which are on the side of the wicked White Witch. Unlike Lewis's Narnia, the world in *Far Away* is so mixed up and so much at war, that it is not even possible to know 'whose side the river [is] on'.[53] In Churchill's tales, the victory of good over evil is no longer told. Children can no longer save the world, but are forced to live its dangerous realities.

Far Away is a cautionary tale, not least for feminism. The cross-generational betrayal of women, of Harper and Joan, who choose complicity in the (male-authored) crimes against humanity committed in their 'home', contributes to catastrophe. Education and labour systems that teach and train young women (and men) to make beautiful objects, but fail to instruct in the politics of their learning or their labour are dangerous. Where a 1970s style of feminism argued the need for an understanding of the personal as political, Churchill's late twentieth-century feminism is arguing, in brief, for the need to close the gap between the personal and the political.

3 Saying no to Daddy: child sexual abuse, the ' big hysteria'

In Churchill's *Far Away*, introduced briefly to conclude the last chapter, Joan probes the violent 'secrets' of her uncle's house. The tale the child tells in the opening scene is of people and children hidden in a lorry and attacked, hit by her uncle. The child has discovered 'something secret' and the aunt asks her to keep the secret. 'Sometimes', she explains, 'you get bad children who even betray their parents.'[1] Yet, as *Far Away* Illustrates, coercing the child into keeping violence within the home a secret has long term damaging consequences, not least for the child herself.

One particular form of damage to the child concerns me in this chapter: child sexual abuse. Where, as the previous chapter showed, Churchill figuratively expresses the damage done to young women and children, especially in *The Skriker*, others have elected to focus more concretely on abuse as an issue for the 1990s, albeit in a range of theatrical forms and with different, but related, concerns. With this in mind, I begin this chapter with an account of plays by Sarah Daniels from the early 1990s that concentrated on child abuse as a key issue. The chapter then progresses through a range of work that offers a dramatic treatment of abuse that insists on exposing rather than keeping secrets: *Augustine (Big Hysteria)*, Anna Furse; *Easy Access (for the Boys)*, Claire Dowie; and *Frozen*, Bryony Lavery. I conclude with Eve Ensler's *The Vagina Monologues* to connect abuse to the continuum of violence against women's bodies.

From silence to silence: child sexual abuse 1970s–1990s

I was listening to Radio Four . . . It was an item about clichés of all things . . . Apparently the cliché which summed up the Seventies was 'corridors of power'. I've forgotten what the Eighties was supposed to be but the one for the Nineties, according to this programme is 'denial'.[2]

Like domestic violence and rape, child sexual abuse was brought to public attention via the women's consciousness-raising groups in the 1970s. Encouraged and supported by the feminist group environment, abused women found the courage to speak out, which in turn led to self-help initiatives[3] and to women writing about their experiences. Among those women first to speak out and to write about child sexual abuse was Louise Armstrong, American writer and author of *Kiss Daddy Goodnight* (1978), that merges her own experiences collectively with those of other women in a painful, but arguably cathartic, process of sharing.

However, since the 1970s the issue of child sexual abuse has itself been a specific victim of the general backlash against feminism. Looking back over the years since her feminist 'speak out' volume, Armstrong's *Kiss Daddy Goodnight: Ten Years Later* (1987) and *Rocking the Cradle of Sexual Politics* (1994) document the 'post-feminist' climate in the US, favouring the professional and corporate 'top girl' success (that so concerned Churchill). Such a climate did not, however, favour women protesting the idea of male violence and abuse, more frequently dismissed as a 'radical man-hating ploy'.[4] The exoneration of fathers involved blaming mothers, and in some cases, instead of receiving help, mothers seeking to protect their children from suspected abuse were punished (lost custody of the very children they were trying to protect).[5]

A similar backlash can be traced in Britain,[6] but one particular event, the Cleveland affair (as it became known) is significant. In 1986 a BBC broadcast on child abuse, *Childwatch*, put abuse firmly in the public eye and launched the national children's help-line.[7] The following year in the county of Cleveland a growing number of children were diagnosed as having been sexually abused and were removed from family homes and taken in to care. Highly emotive media reporting of events in Cleveland in 1987 tended to exonerate parents and blame the professionals – two (women) in particular: paediatrician, Dr Marietta Higgs, and social worker, Sue Richardson. Opposition to the efforts of Higgs and Richardson to remove allegedly abused children from the possibility of further abuse came largely from men in positions of authority (police, politicians, clergy). As Jean la Fontaine summarises: 'the media presented the Cleveland crisis not merely as one of Parents versus the State but as Men against Women.'[8] Missing from the representation of the Cleveland case was, as Beatrix Campbell's analysis demonstrates, any discussion of 'masculinity as a political problem',[9] and no attempts to empower the mothers. Thatcherism had served to sanctify, to protect the family in a way that failed to protect the children.[10] Media and school campaigns that, in the interests of protecting children, have repeatedly urged them to 'Say No to Strangers', could not possibly conceive of running a campaign with the slogan 'Say No to Daddy'.

Sarah Daniels

One playwright who has not been afraid of saying no to 'Daddy' is Sarah Daniels. Like Churchill, Daniels is a well-established figure on the contemporary English stage, is one of the feminist 'canonicals'. She describes herself as a feminist, though states that she did not set out 'thinking, I'm going to be a feminist dramatist'.[11] Where Churchill's theatre has engaged with a socialist-feminist politics, Daniels's drama frequently examines what (her) critics have viewed as a radical-feminist politics of male domination. In plays such as *Ripen Our Darkness* (Royal Court Theatre Upstairs, 1981) and *The Devil's Gateway* (Royal Court Theatre Upstairs, 1983), Daniels focused on the male domination of women in the home, from drudgery to domestic violence. The darkly comic register that characterises her work is exemplified in the suicide note that Mary, oppressed and longsuffering housewife and mother of three boys in *Ripen Our Darkness*, leaves for her husband: 'Dear David, your dinner and my head are in the oven.'[12] In *The Devil's Gateway* women abandon their boring and unhappy domestic lives (and their husbands) for the women's peace camp at

Greenham Common. Ill at ease with Daniels's representation of men in domestic settings, her male (and some female) critics were positively outraged and incensed by her feminist attack on pornography in *Masterpieces* (Royal Exchange Theatre, Manchester and Royal Court Theatre Upstairs, 1983). *Masterpieces* remains the most controversial play in the Daniels canon, that has since included the abuse plays discussed here, an adaptation of Pat Barker's novel, *Blow Your House Down* (1995), that treats women prostitutes in fear of a Yorkshire Ripper styled figure, and, more recently, a dramatisation of elderly women resisting teenage violence in *Morning Glory* (2001).[13]

The hysterical, sometimes violent criticism of Daniels's plays in the 1980s is indicative of the growing backlash against feminism. Responding to a question about her views on feminism in the 1990s, Daniels stated 'that in its origin feminism had a very radical agenda to do with rights and justice and of course neither of those things have been too popular recently'.[14] Undeterred by this, Daniels entered the 1990s with three plays that involve a feminist treatment of child abuse: *Beside Herself* (1990), *Head-Rot Holiday* (1992) and *The Madness of Esme and Shaz* (1994).[15]

Beside Herself

Daniels's staging of *Beside Herself* in 1990 joins with those publications, such as Campbell's *Unofficial Secrets* (1988), Judith Herman's *Trauma and Recovery* (1992) or Armstrong's *Rocking the Cradle* (1994), that were seeking to make a feminist case for the testimony of women and children. As Herman comments, when bearing witness to abuse, the 'bystander is forced to take sides', must choose between 'victim and perpetrator'.[16] In *Beside Herself* the side that Daniels takes, and invites her audience to take, is that which by the 1990s was increasingly being silenced by the media reporting of abuse: that of the abused child/woman. Directed by Jules Wright of the Women's Playhouse Trust, also a trained psychotherapist, *Beside Herself* shows remarkable insight into the issue of child sexual abuse.

The figure of the abused child/woman is represented through Daniels's construction of a split subject, Evelyn/Eve, where Evelyn is the adult woman accompanied by Eve, her abused, childhood self.

Visually this represents the phenomenon that Herman describes as the adult being 'prisoner of her [abused] childhood'.[17] In the production, though played by an adult, Eve was represented as a child, as a kind of Alice-lost-in-wonderland figure, in her girl's dress and Alice hair band. Eve can speak that which her adult self represses; cannot bring herself to put into words. As a theatrical device, the split subject is also a means of representing the dissociative state that abuse victims create to defend themselves; to cut themselves off from the reality they cannot face.[18] Except that this repressed, abused 'other', is one that remains a haunting absent presence until the truth, the father, is confronted. At the point where Evelyn achieves this in the close of the play, Eve slips away.[19]

The play opens with a surreal scene that sets female biblical figures – Mrs Lot, Jezebel, Delilah, Eve and Martha – in a blood red supermarket, before switching to a naturalistic scene in which Evelyn (accompanied as always by Eve) is seen unpacking the shopping she has done for her father (abuser). Some critics suggested a parallel between the opening scene and the dinner scene in *Top Girls* that is an appropriate analogy in so far as both scenes reflect concerns subsequently touched on and developed in the respective plays. In *Beside Herself*, the biblical shopping motif captures the idea that from times ancient to modern, women bear the burden of nurturing the family, whilst also carrying the guilt for everything that goes wrong in it. The scene includes the image of a mother in the supermarket, harassed to the point of threatening to mow down one of her children with a supermarket trolley, an incident that is referred to again in the play (*Beside Herself*, pp.159–60), reinforcing the idea that women carry primary responsibility for the 'health' of the family. If the mother has 'lost her trolley' (as Jezebel suggests, p.103), then this is only a way of signalling maternal madness as a social 'norm'; of barely being able to conceal maternal rage. *Beside Herself* is replete with stories of women who, though abused, carry on nurturing, providing. Evelyn shopping for her father typifies the behaviour of abused women who, as Herman explains, with an inadequate sense of self-protection are unable to 'imagine themselves in a position of agency or choice', carry on administering to the needs of the abuser.[20]

When not shopping for her father, Evelyn fulfils her wifely duties (she is married to an MP) by attending to a number of charitable causes. Her involvement on the committee of St Dymphna's, a community group home, brings her into contact with a number of 'caring' professionals, hierarchically arranged along gender lines: psychiatric social worker, doctor and reverend who embody male 'authority'; a house manager, home help and nurse in positions of auxiliary domestic and medical care. In their management of the community home, the men show themselves to be the least caring and the most bigoted, exemplified in the figure of the homophobic vicar.[21] Failure to care is dramatised through the death of a newly admitted patient to the home: Dave, a gay schizophrenic. Everyone tries to blame everyone else for his dying unattended and unnoticed, and as Evelyn feels that somehow the others are blaming her for the death, so the event becomes the catalyst for her finally to confront her father.[22]

To confront the father as abuser contests the masculine order that keeps the Father in 'his' (dominant) place. As Campbell writes: 'sexual abuse of children now presents society with the ultimate crisis of patriarchy, when children refuse to protect their fathers by keeping their secrets'.[23] The 'ultimate crisis of patriarchy' may be understood as the undoing of the heterosexual masculine, as Daniels's dramatisation of Evelyn's paternal confrontation and recovery in *Beside Herself* illustrates. To clarify: Daniels uses the death of the homosexual patient, Dave, to bring Evelyn to the point of confrontation. The homosexual body stands in for, is an historicisation of, the child's abused body.[24] What connects the two is the anal orifice, acknowledged as a site of homosexual activity and of child abuse.[25] As Lynda Hart describes, the anus is 'the opening to the body that historically has been most associated with "unnatural sexuality"'.[26] Acceptance of abusing fathers means accepting that 'unnatural sexuality' is not exclusive to homosexual activity but is a 'normal' practice for heterosexual males. In consequence, the binarism of hetero/homo is undone. As Beatrix Campbell argues, 'the presence of anal dilatation as a sign of buggery in child sexual abuse has blurred that distinction, that enforcement of sexual difference *between men*'.[27]

Staging child abuse, therefore, invites an audience to think the 'unthinkable', mirroring the way that mothers of abused children are forced to believe the 'unbelievable'. The unwillingness to believe is heightened in *Beside Herself* in a second abuse narrative: the mother and estranged (abused) daughter dramatised in the relationship be-tween Lil and Nicola. As an abused child of her mother's second hus-band, Nicola deserted her mother when she refused to believe that her second husband was abusing her daughter. While Daniels ends the play with the possibility of Nicola and Lil reuniting (as Lil closes the door behind her on her husband), the mother–daughter relation-ship primarily highlights the powerlessness of mothers to cope with abuse. If they bring themselves to believe, how are they to cope? Who is there to help? Most significantly, who will believe them? As Daniels dramatises, those (men) in positions of authority, like those in real life cases, are more likely to disbelieve them.

In staging the 'unspeakable', Daniels uses theatre as a forum for a feminist 'speak out'. This explains why dramaturgically she con-centrates on the dramatisation of abuse as a political rather than a personal issue. The medium of theatre provides a feminist forum to make public women's testimonies of abuse beyond the private con-fessional sphere of the therapist, to which, in the absence of a femi-nist movement, they became increasingly confined and de-politicised in the 1990s. Theatre becomes a means of publicly bearing witness. That is not to say that the play does not offer a therapeutic or cathar-tic possibility for an audience, but the realisation of that possibility necessarily resides in a willingness to believe in the suffering and to take pleasure in the recovery.

In staging a feminist view on child sexual abuse Daniels nec-essarily attracts criticism from critics and spectators who are more persuaded by the mainstream (male-dominated) view. Significantly, there were those who thought the play should not be appearing on a mainstream stage. 'Seen on the small studio stage upstairs by a special-ist audience of sexual social workers,' wrote Sheridan Morley, '*Beside Herself* might have some purpose that on the main stage it seems to lack.'[28] The idea of the 'specialist audience', however, sidesteps the issue of the prevalence of abuse in the ordinary family.[29] To force the play off the 'main stage' is to counter Daniels's aim to bring the abuse of women and children out of silence.

Head-Rot Holiday and The Madness of Esme and Shaz

Laying claim to performance space for women's theatre remains, as my introductory chapter argues, difficult in the 'boys' club'. *Beside Herself* was made possible through the joint funding of the Women's Playhouse Trust and the Royal Court.[30] *Head-Rot Holiday*, the second of Daniels's 'women and madness' plays, also had women's support: *Head-Rot* was a commission for Clean Break theatre company. The play, researched with the help of WISH (Women in Special Hospitals), opened at the BAC (Battersea Arts Centre). Exceptionally, Daniels was again able to work with an all-women's production team that she argues is important to her theatre.[31] Paulette Randall directed, and the lighting and set designers from *Beside Herself*, respectively Jenny Crane and Jenny Tiramani, worked on *Head-Rot*. Tiramani's design for *Head-Rot* was particularly effective: a larger than life-size committal document, dominating the lives of the women played out in front of it.

In *Head-Rot* it is possible to feel the exigencies of small-scale touring. *Head-Rot* was cast with three women each taking three roles: a patient, a nurse and an outsider figure. Due to the casting constraints, there are times when scenes feel hampered by the logistics of who is available to be on or off stage. Despite such limitations, however, *Head-Rot* is a hard-hitting play that focuses on the abusive juridical and medical systems that fail adequately to care for women who have been abused and/or are suffering from mental health problems. The figure of the mother 'off her trolley' in *Beside Herself* haunts *Head-Rot*. What happens to women who do lose control is dramatised in the figure of Claudia, a mother who loses her children because of her depression,[32] and loses her freedom after attacking her social worker with a potato peeler. The attack with a domestic utensil rather than a knife is significant. The 'offence' committed by the mother, Daniels suggests, is nothing compared to the 'crime' committed against her.

While Daniels brings humour to her dramatisation of the special hospital, it is of the blackest, bleakest kind, summed up, for example, in the hospital disco, where the women patients are encouraged to dress themselves up to dance with male inmates, many of whom are convicted rapists. As patient Dee argues: 'if I was on the outside and I made a relationship with a serial killer or rapist or both you'd consider me mad but that's what you have to do in here to prove you're sane. Now what's more loony, me or that?' (*Head-Rot*, p.239). The women survive but all are severely damaged by the end of the play: Dee has cut herself, Ruth has attempted suicide by hanging (provoked by seeing her step-mother who failed to stop her being abused), and Claudia has got into trouble for reporting a nurse who hit a patient. There is no sign of the women ever managing to leave the hospital.

By contrast, *The Madness of Esme and Shaz* (1994), though painful and black in its treatment of abuse and women's damaged lives, offers a more hopeful note. Esme, an elderly, retired civil servant, single and a Christian, is invited by hospital authorities to take care of her thirty-three-year-old niece, Shaz, whom she has never seen. Shaz has been detained in a Regional Secure Unit attached to a Psychiatric Hospital. Much later in the play it is made known that her incarceration was due to her killing her step-sister, the baby daughter of her abusing father. What sets out in a mostly realistic frame becomes more and more surreal as, to save her niece, Esme holds a (female) hospital doctor at (replica) gunpoint, hires a (stolen) car she is not qualified to drive and 'escapes' with her niece to the Greek island of Limnos.

The reviewers were mostly critical, arguing that the play 'starts hot and goes cold', is 'well-meaning but obscurely patronising' or dismissing it as a 'maddening experience'.[33] Several deplored what they described as the play's Shirley Valentine motif, and some responded with their customary male panic. 'I feel ill at ease in her [Daniels's] universe', wrote Benedict Nightingale, 'and so, I suspect', he conspiratorially reassured his readers, 'will most of you.'[34] 'In Daniels's earlier play *Masterpieces* the only place for a man was under the wheels of a tube train, and judging from their portrayal here it doesn't look as if the author's position has changed much', wrote another.[35]

While hysterically insisting on the problems of Daniels's all-female dramatic universe, in which they claimed that men are represented as uniformly 'bad' and women 'good', reviewers were over-looking the complexities of her argument and the shift in feminist focus. In the 1980s Daniels's theatre was characterised by a feminist anger; a kind of polemical anger that cried out at the injustices of a man-made world; a scream of outrage that was also screaming that the world simply had to change. In the 1990s she concentrates less on re-vealing the (man-made) enormity of what women are up against, and more on women striving to help each other despite the odds stacked against them. Some feminist criticism of her 1980s work that either lamented the lack of a positive 'solution' (for example, to Mary's do-mestic crisis), or what in *Masterpieces* was perceived by some as a lack of 'space for radical feminist solidarity',[36] is answered by her 1990s evolution of a feminism that seeks collaboration between women, whatever their 'crimes' and whatever their differences.

Daniels also works to complicate or to problematise the ex-pectation that feminism provides an automatic guarantee of mutual support among women. When, for example, Shaz confesses her crime to her girlfriend Pat, explaining that she murdered a girl and not a boy child, Pat abandons her (*Esme and Shaz*, p.297). It is not a coincidence that Pat's feminism is a kind of textbook, academic feminism: one inadequate for dealing with the complexities and absurdities of life (of which her own life is empty to the point that she invents stories about herself). Feminism, so Daniels suggests, must challenge its own orthodoxy and aim to be more rather than less inclusive. As her the-atre also shows, when women fail each other, the consequences can be disastrous, fatal even.[37]

The Madness of Esme and Shaz is particularly concerned with the need for women to be supportive of each other. Daniels herself ar-gued that the play 'celebrated female solidarity and resourcefulness'.[38] Whether one 'reads' the abuse literally or figuratively (as standing for the ways in which women's lives are damaged), recovery, the play ar-gues, is only possible if women are able to find commonality while working through and learning to accept difference. The 'and' of the play's title which joins Esme and Shaz together is important. Working across class, cultural, spiritual, sexual and generational differences,

Esme and Shaz find ways of helping each other. In particular, Daniels's style of cross-collaborative feminism offers an alternative 'faith' to the Christian church (so heavily critiqued throughout her theatre). Where Mary opts for a feminist heaven in *Ripen Our Darkness*, Esme and Shaz find a more earthly 'heaven' out in the Mediterranean. The biblical motif of *The Madness of Esme and Shaz*, encoded not just in Esme's outlook, but also made visually present in the production in Kate Owen's triptych set design, is heightened in the closure as, bathed in sunlight, Shaz, with Esme's help, bears her (self) wounds. Christ-like (no coincidence perhaps that Shaz is aged thirty-three), Shaz makes visible the signs of her damaged and damaging body; invites an audience to bear witness and to believe in her suffering and the possibility of her healing. Kane's theatre arguably would make a more provocative case for loving the 'monster' (see Chapter 5), yet Daniels movingly signals finding purpose, direction and love in the most unlikely and unexpected of relations between women in her mid-1990s feminist landscape.

The production of *The Madness of Esme and Shaz* also brings me back to the issue of space, or rather lack of it, for women's theatre. It was seeing the production squeezed into the Theatre Upstairs at the Court in 1994, while Downstairs, Stephen Daldry, the then newly appointed director, worked with a cast of twenty-eight in a revival of Arnold Wesker's *The Kitchen*, in a lavishly rearranged auditorium (with stall seats taken out to accommodate the set), that so outraged and left me 'beside myself'.[39] I was not alone in my reaction. In a feature article for the *Guardian*, Claire Armistead contrasted the relative success of both Caryl Churchill and Sarah Daniels on the British stage in the 1980s, but went on to ask why, given their 1980s success, they were not, therefore, well-established on the main stages. In looking at some of the reasons put forward explaining why women are not more significantly represented on main stages, Armistead observes that neither *The Skriker* nor *The Madness of Esme and Shaz* would be considered main-house productions: *The Skriker* in terms of its experimental style; *The Madness of Esme and Shaz* in respect of its separatist, feminist politics.[40]

47

To this I would also add that both plays treat a feminist politics of damage that is out of tune with the 'power' feminism of the 1990s. In concentrating on feminist 'success', the issue of what happens to women who do not make it (like Angie in *Top Girls*), remains hidden. Both Josie and Shaz are child killers; damaged and damaging young women. This raises an important and neglected issue: the need to consider what happens to abused or damaged women (exactly what happened in Josie's past is never made clear). Sylvia Fraser, in her account of coming to terms with being abused by her father, acknowledges the 'resources' (social and educational) that enabled her to survive and to recover.[41] For those less advantaged or fortunate, like Josie, or Shaz without Esme, there is every possibility that unresolved self-hatred and self-loathing will turn in on themselves and outwards to others; cause selfharm and possibly harm to others (children).[42] Not to acknowledge this risks the kind of world seen at the close of *Far Away* where Joan thinks nothing at all of talking about killing a child under five.

Refiguring Freud

While the 1970s Women's Liberation Movement had revealed that abuse was much more likely to occur inside rather than outside of the home, and with the father rather than a stranger, it was precisely this revelation that was at the heart of subsequent, so-called 'post-feminist' denial. However, denial of abuse was not exclusive to the 1990s. Freud himself had acknowledged and then subsequently denied women's complaints of child abuse as fantasy rather than reality, preferring to attribute them to the 'normal' development of the feminine Oedipal complex, by which girls come to attach to the father rather than the mother. 'Stories' of abuse, could, therefore, be argued in the Freudian frame as fantasies of paternal seduction. Elaine Showalter explains Freud's reversal as threefold: the lack of therapeutic success in his treatment of hysteria as seduction; the inability to distinguish truth from reality in the seduction narratives; and, most significantly, the implication that *'the incidence of fathers abusing children would be improbably vast'* (my emphasis).[43] To avoid becoming a social outcast Freud censored himself. A century later doctors found themselves

Saying no to Daddy

censored by government and healthcare authorities for their findings. Campbell's revised 1997 edition of *Unofficial Secrets*, published
exactly 100 years after Freud's recantation in 1897, identifies the ways
in which the government and health authorities covered up what they
knew to be the truth: 'that the doctors were probably right.'[44]

Augustine (Big Hysteria), Anna Furse

That Freud was also 'probably right' is an issue that attracted Anna
Furse in *Augustine (Big Hysteria)*. Freud has long been a subject for
or subjected to feminist dramatic treatment, most notably in Hélène
Cixous and Simone Benmussa's staging of *Portrait of Dora* (first performed in London in 1979), a revisioning of a Freudian dreamscape
to make visible Dora's, the patient's, viewpoint.[45] Similarly, in 1991,
Anna Furse gave a feminist treatment to the life of Augustine, star patient in Charcot's Salpêtrière clinic for hysterics in Paris in the 1890s.
The new writing company Paines Plough, of which Furse was then director, performed *Augustine* in 1991.[46] To the directorship of Paines
Plough, Furse brought her feminism and commitment to physical theatre, both of which she had previously explored in Blood Group, a
company she founded in 1980. Furse sought to identify new writing
less as a dramatic tradition than as total theatre in which language,
music, physical playing and the visual might all work productively
together.[47] Her feminism encompassed not just grassroots politics,
but was also concerned with a more philosophical line of enquiry: exploration into the possibilities of a 'feminine' language in the theatre,
broadly in line with Cixous's *écriture féminine*. *Augustine* is both reflective of Furse's total theatre approach and engagement with a style
of new French feminism.

Based on the real life case of Augustine, Charcot's star patient,
Furse developed a physical style of writing on the body; of playing
out, writing out, Augustine's role as abuse victim. Her production
variously made use of archival photographs of the real Augustine, projected at appropriate points on to the set (Augustine's hospital bed);
music, significantly in the form of Augustine's 'double', a violinist
designed to accompany Augustine and 'play'/speak her emotional language, and the symbolic use of sound effects.

49

In *Augustine* Furse brings together Charcot and Freud. While Freud did actually visit Charcot's clinic he would not have done so at a time when Augustine was resident. Furse imagines this three-way encounter, however, in order to find a theatrical moment in which to locate Freud's admission of the connection between hysteria and abuse, and his subsequent denial. This she does through the changing relationship that Freud has with Augustine: from being willing listener to Freudian doctor. In contrast to Freud's final diagnosis of Augustine – that she desired Monsieur Carnot, her mother's employer and lover – what is made clear to the audience through Augustine's body, her 'theatre of forgotten scenes', is that she was raped and repeatedly abused by Carnot. Elements of an abuse narrative surface: the 'failure' of the mother to protect her child; the references to oral, vaginal and anal abuse (which Augustine describes at one point as a rat in her bottom),[48] and the abuser's life-threatening demand for secrecy (tell and I'll kill you at knife point).[49] Yet to hear them requires someone to listen and to believe.

While stylistically very different to Daniels's more naturalistic register, Furse, like Daniels, has sought theatrical devices that both reveal an understanding of abuse and aim to bring the victim's story out of silence. The doubling of Augustine with the violinist is a means of giving expression to the child's tortured self/soul. Augustine is also represented as a 'child-woman': as a young woman haunted like Daniels's Evelyn/Eve by her abused child-self. This was evocatively and movingly signalled in the production's opening use of a young girl singing the tune of a German children's song: 'Ach, du liebe Augustine, Augustine, Augustine' (*Augustine*, p.17), a song that Augustine also later sings to herself. It is not just words that give expression to Augustine's story; the physical 'writing' of her body tells of her abuse. While Charcot shamanistically seeks to control, conduct and categorise her hysterical symptoms, he is blind to the emergent physical narrative that speaks her rage, shame, fear and pain. The actress's body that convulses and contorts through the stages of the *grande hystérie* 'performs' for Charcot, but also re-enacts the scenes of abuse – except that he refuses to see them.[50]

Charcot's treatment of Augustine takes the form more of abuse than care, in his insistence on being able to produce, through drugs such as amyl nitrate,[51] or through the horrific use of the ovarian compressor, Augustine's hysterical symptoms. When Freud also deserts her, stops listening, Augustine 'frees' herself from both doctors. Her final dream sequence suggests, as in the closure to *The Madness of Esme and Shaz*, the possibility of spiritual self-redemption. Kneeling in a praying position her vision is of God, hundreds of Jesus figures and the Virgin Mary who steps on a snake at her feet. 'Anything else you'd like to tell the audience?' asks Charcot at this point. 'She's talking to Magdalena! . . .', replies Augustine, 'AND SHE'S LAUGHING!!!' (*Augustine*, p.49). The intertextual referencing of Cixous and her manifesto for an *écriture féminine*[52] indexes a shared feminist viewpoint: woman must exit the patriarchal stage and take up her own place, her own body that, while she remains in the Father's house, cannot be hers.

Augustine's final appearance is in full colour: strong lighting to suggest that she has overcome the hysterical symptoms that have only allowed her to see in monochrome. She appears in order to disappear and exits Vesta Tilley style, dressed in clothes she has taken from Charcot and Freud (who are left seated on stage, vulnerable and childlike in their underwear). This is a tongue-in-cheek act of appropriation (this final appearance is, according to Furse's directions, performed vaudeville style). While she exits in the borrowed clothes of the masculine, Augustine also prophesies a future for the 'newly born woman' in which 'you [men] will put your tools down, you will listen, really listen, and you will believe every word I say . . .' (*Augustine*, p.49).

Male hysteria

Forcing Freud to listen to the truth he could not face was also the subject of Terry Johnson's *Hysteria*, performed two years later at the Royal Court (1993) and directed by Phyllida Lloyd. *Hysteria* offers a dramatic representation of an ageing Freud confronting his repressed views on child abuse and facing the possibility that his own father may have abused his sister. The play is both farcically funny and darkly sinister as the surface realism of the stage is transformed into an increasingly surreal landscape (encouraged by the presence of Salvador Dali)[53] of repressed anxieties. Freud's nemesis is Jessica, daughter of a patient whom Freud counselled for abuse, and then later told her she had not been abused. As a consequence his patient, Jessica's mother, committed suicide. Johnson leaves the dying Freud with Jessica as his recurrent nightmare. The play's closing image repeats her initial entrance: tapping on the windows to Freud's house, asking to be let in.

I include this brief mention of Johnson's production because his staging of Freud's hysterical reaction to abuse, chimes with contemporary male hysteria, of the kind expressed, for example, by David Thomas in *Not Guilty* (1993). Thomas hysterically insists that neither he nor anyone he knows is an abuser, and devotes a whole chapter to 'the myth of the bad man', in which he attempts to turn the tables on women.[54] By contrast, however, Johnson's play argues that it is not women's but men's behaviour that requires examination. Jessica's case is pressing: Freud, Father of psychoanalysis, must consider the possibility of what is hidden in his 'house'.

Abuse as cycle
Easy Access (for the Boys), Claire Dowie

Placing the therapist under scrutiny was to become a feature of the 1990s as therapists assisting patients with recovered memories of abuse found themselves under attack from outraged fathers and, in some cases, from patients themselves who subsequently decided they had been misled. High profile cases in America[55] and, by the mid-1990s, organisations in both America (False Memory Syndrome Foundation) and Britain (Memory Syndrome Society) contested the credibility of accounts of recovered abuse. From a feminist perspective this presented a very difficult issue. Views on the matter have ranged from Armstrong who is concerned that recovered memory has become a media circus belittling and denying painful realities, to feminists who resist and resent any suggestion that abuse has not taken place, and to others who question some of the therapeutic practices of recovered memory.[56]

Theatrically, the question as to who is telling the 'truth' – therapist, abused or abuser – lends itself to a thriller, suspense-styled, did-daddy-do-it drama, as for example in Kay Trainor's *Bad Girl* (Old Red Lion, 1992), or Mike Cullen's *Anna Weiss* (directed by Vicky Featherstone at the Traverse, Scotland, 1997). Similarly, suspense underlies Claire Dowie's *Easy Access (for the Boys)* (Drill Hall, London, 1998) where the question of what actually happened is hard to fathom. Except that Dowie's play counters gendered, feminist expectations by bringing the abused male, rather than female, body into the theatrical frame.

Easy Access takes the form of a video diary kept by rent boy Michael. Extracts from Michael's diary are video projected on to the stage and merge with live events. Intimate, private secrets, are, therefore, given a public screening. Dowie's stand-up style of theatre in which she usually performs her own dramatic monologues, also characterises the writing of *Easy Access* (which Dowie directed but did not appear in). The diary techniques enable a monologist style in which the audience is situated as (frequently uncomfortable) addressee. Thematically, too, the play echoes Dowie's earlier concerns for the lonely, unloved child at risk in her stand-up play *Adult Child/Dead Child* (1987), though in *Easy Access* she is more explicitly concerned about abuse.

Not that there is anything 'easy' about her treatment of this issue. Where Johnson took up the feminist line in his play, Dowie explores the complexities of abuse alongside homosexuality and male prostitution in hers. Michael's recovered memories of abuse are complex and ambiguous. Unlike his abused best friend, Gary, who hates his father for abusing him, Michael disconcertingly expresses a sexual need for his father that can be traced back to childhood abuse. Access to Michael's anus has been made 'easy' through successive relations with men, beginning with his father, the man, who as Gary describes, made his 'arse so easy access in the first place'.[57] While Michael protests, rather too fiercely protests paternal love[58] the difficulty that he experiences in his relations, particularly with his gay lover, Matt, suggests that the abuse haunts every other attempt at a relationship. Dowie encodes this visually through sexual sequences in which Michael's arousal happens only when Matt is 'replaced' by the figure of his father, Ed (*Easy Access*, p.8). The father figure is also complexly imaged. Unlike Gary's 'psycho' abusive father, Ed is portrayed as a liberal, non-authoritarian, 1960s, drug and Bob Dylan loving dad. Yet, as Daniels's theatre repeatedly demonstrated, appearances can be, and often are, deceptive.

The dangerous sexual tensions in *Easy Access* 'climax' when Ed has a young woman Ruth and her son Jake come to live with him. As Michael tries to expose the threat to Jake, which at some level is also a threat to himself, or to the belief in the relationship with his father as somehow special, Ed counters by making Michael appear the threat: the (potential) abuser. By editing Michael's video diary in such a way that it is Michael who appears to desire Jake sexually, and is also represented as a possible risk to Matt's young daughter Becky, Ed rearranges the 'truth'. Yet, the question still nags: what exactly is the truth? As an abused child, is Michael a risk to other children? The final freeze-framed image of '*Michael catching Becky jumping off a wall, holding her to him, both cheek to cheek, smiling into the camera*' (*Easy Access*, p.59) is frightening on account of the father's editorial control. Like Freud he gets to decide the public 'truth'. Yet, the possibility that this may image another 'truth' is also unavoidable, and deeply disconcerting. Moreover, Dowie's mediatised aesthetic also figures the way in which, during the 1990s, the Father's house no longer played out its secrets in private, but turned private trauma into public spectacle: child pornography broadcast for 'easy access' via the web.

Frozen, Bryony Lavery

The ambiguity of the abuser's identity is removed, however, in Bryony Lavery's chilling and emotionally charged play *Frozen* (Birmingham Repertory Theatre, 1998).[59] *Frozen* distils the terrifying subject of abduction, abuse and child murder into three voices, three characters.

As one critic noted, playing Birmingham's main (rather than studio) space, gave 'the idea [of child killing] space to resonate among a big audience'.[60] The narrative of *Frozen* unfolds through monologues delivered by the child's mother, Nancy; a professor of psychiatry, Agnetha; and, exceptionally, the killer himself, Ralph. Each of the three characters is in some way 'frozen': Nancy through the death of her child; Agnetha in mourning over the death of her colleague (briefly also her lover), and Ralph with his 'Arctic frozen sea' of a 'criminal brain'. Each of the three characters gradually 'thaws': Nancy as she eventually puts aside her anger and forgives Ralph;[61] Agnetha as she comes to terms with the death of her colleague; and Ralph who, through an interview with Nancy, discovers remorse, and (possibly) in consequence, takes his own life.

Although the play is not a 'thesis' play, it does contain a thesis, delivered lecture-style in Agnetha's academic presentation entitled: 'Serial Killing . . . a forgivable act?'[62] Based on psychiatric investigation, Agnetha's research proposes that child killing may not necessarily be a consequence of being biologically disposed to 'evil', but may be caused by injury to the brain brought about by repeated abuse in childhood. The responsibility for killing may shift, therefore, from an individual to a cycle of familial abuse, as suggested in *Easy Access for the Boys*. While a difficult topic to stage, it is characteristic of Lavery that, on the one hand, she does so with a sense of hope and optimism, even in the darkest of situations, and, on the other, that she touches, feels for a contemporary moment. Children who go missing and are later found murdered became a frightening feature of the 1990s. Lavery was influenced in her research by an account by Marion Partington about the murder of her sister Lucy by Fred West, and was inspired by the way 'she and her family had moved forward through love and intelligence'.[63]

In feminist terms it is important to note that the energies for moving forward in the play come from women, and especially from the mother, Nancy, an ordinary woman who demonstrates extraordinary energy in her ultimate forgiveness of Ralph and belief that 'nothing's unbearable' (*Frozen*, p.97). Both Nancy and Agnetha have public voices: Nancy through her campaigning for Flame (a self-help organisation that assists with the recovery of missing children and 'outs' paedophiles in local communities), and Agnetha through her lecturing. Both women have scenes in the play where they address an 'audience', and it is important, Lavery suggests, that public attention is paid to women's experience and knowledge.

From anus to vagina
The Vagina Monologues, Eve Ensler

The use of theatre as a forum for sharing women's experience and knowledge was characteristic of much feminist theatre in the 1970s, but was far less common in the 1990s. One high profile production, however, to engage in a sharing of women's real-life experience of violence emerged at the close of the decade when American Eve Ensler's *The Vagina Monologues* came to the London stage (King's Head, 1999). Ensler describes herself as a feminist. She has also revealed that her father sexually abused her.[64] Her political commitment and personal experience of abuse are brought to her one-woman stage show. The show is composed out of numerous interviews that she held with women about their vaginas, and is reminiscent of a 1970s style of feminist sharing (like Armstrong's *Kiss Daddy Goodnight*, for example). The published text of *The Vagina Monologues* is also endorsed by a foreword by Gloria Steinem, staunch feminist advocate of the power and veracity of women's recovered memories of abuse.

Ensler's monologues serve as a reminder that child abuse is just one form of violence against the (mostly, although not exclusively) female body, that also includes rape, female circumcision, gynaecological examinations, or, quite simply, the ignorance that women are kept in with regard to their bodies. One particular monologue, for example, is highly reminiscent of Churchill's closing monologue for Betty in *Cloud Nine*, focusing on the idea that women of certain generations were actively discouraged from touching themselves 'down there' (*Monologues*, p.25). The treatment of child abuse comes in an angry sequence mid-way through the show that includes accounts of the rape of Bosnian women. Exceptionally, Ensler's abuse monologue is delivered not by a white persona but in the persona of a 'southern woman of color', who relates bad memories of her 'coochi snorcher' that include being abused by a friend of her father's when she was ten years old. The incident ends in further violence as her father shoots her abuser (*Monologues*, p.79). These bad memories subsequently are redeemed, however, by pleasurable teenage memories in which the young girl, not unlike Daniels's young women, finds comfort and sexual pleasure through another woman. To include an account of abuse by a woman of colour is significant for the way in which it highlights that child abuse is more frequently perceived in terms of gender, rather than as a raced and classed issue. As Melba Wilson writes in her study, *Crossing the Boundary: Black Women Survive Incest*, 'information and analysis about the sexually abused child who is black and female is noticeable by its absence in current research'.[65] That said, it is also problematic in terms of its globalising and essentialising impulse: the desire to connect with damage done to women worldwide, but at the possible risk of erasing the different social, sexual and cultural circumstances. Unlike the anus (as previously noted) the vagina does signal the site of femininity, but, like its 1970s feminist antecedents, such as Judy Chicago's vagina-styled art work *The Dinner Party*, *Monologues* risks an essentialist reduction of women to Woman/vagina.

That said, *The Vagina Monologues* is one clear example of women claiming 'in-yer-face' theatre for themselves, with reviewers noting both the larger number of women in the audience (to which I would also add my own observation that women were attending in groups), and their greater enjoyment compared with the more uncomfortable male response. 'Not since David Mamet's *Oleanna* has a play so obviously split the genders', wrote the reviewer for *Time Out*.[66] More importantly still, it is an instance of theatre in the 1990s re-generating a grass roots feminist movement. Ensler's show has been instrumental in the founding of V-Day, an organisation aimed at ending violence against women and which raises funds by staging performances of the *Monologues*. The first British V-Day was held at the Old Vic, London, 1999. As a number of high profile actresses, including

Kate Winslet and Cate Blanchett, gave their support, it provided a modern echo to the moment almost a century ago in 1908 when theatre women, several of them stars from the West End stage, formed the Actresses' Franchise League to pledge allegiance to the campaign for women's suffrage.[67] In our contemporary moment, what brings together the playwrights I have been discussing here, notably Churchill and Daniels among them, with the V-Day project, is the shared desire for 'a world where women and children live free, safe, equal and with dignity' (*Monologues*, p.177).

4   Girl power, the new feminism?

Feminism: 'an adventure story' for girls

How can feminism interest young women today? Why should young women be interested in a movement that generally has such a bad press and is perceived to be 'over'? These are questions feminism currently faces. Researching past feminist literatures and publications, however, I was reminded that getting young women involved in feminism was also a problem that second-wave feminists faced. In her introduction to *Feminism for Girls: An Adventure Story* published in 1981, Angela McRobbie explains how, given the media depiction of feminists as 'dull, boring, and quite united in our lack of humour', it needs 'an adventurous girl to give feminism more than a second thought'.[1] In the 1970s McRobbie introduced her experience of and involvement with the lives of working-class girls as a research topic at the Birmingham Centre for Contemporary Cultural Studies (CCCS). Feminism as 'an adventure story', while an unlikely proposition, was one that promised the young women that McRobbie met and worked with a 'new kind of adventure', based on mutual (cross-generational) support, confidence, and knowledge about women's rights, situations, politics, and bodies.[2]

The idea of feminism as 'an adventure story' for girls was also adopted by second-wave feminist theatre-making. The first productions by The Women's Theatre Group, for example, consisted of devised shows specifically aimed at a schools' audience. The one published script from this period, *My Mother Says I Never Should*, exemplifies the educative principles of this work: a Brechtian, montage styled piece in which two schoolgirls get to learn about pregnancy and contraception.[3] In the course of the play, the girls are able to learn about their bodies, become more confident and see their lives opening up to opportunities other than teenage pregnancy.

If that was then, the question now is what happened to the idea of a feminist adventure for girls? What has happened to the lives of young working-class women? In her closing essay for an updated, second edition of *Feminism and Youth Culture*, McRobbie expresses a particular concern: the way in which sexual politics have been de-politicised and re-individualised as a consequence of the Thatcher years and the conservative media. Moreover, she claims that 'popular feminism' may not only be 'shifting to the right but actively re-energising the right through the seductions of individual success, the lure of female empowerment and the love of money'.[4]

The kind of 'popular feminism' that concerns McRobbie can be found in the style of 'girl power' promoted, from 1996 onwards, by The Spice Girls. Designed to give established feminism a 'kick up the arse' and to promote power through female solidarity,[5] 'girl power' seemingly offers a much more exciting, glamorous adventure story for girls than its earlier feminist model. Divorced from the political, however, it can only operate within a personal or individual frame of what young women want or want to be. It has no political agenda to change the social structures within which girls live their lives, and merely suggests that by taking an aggressive stance together, girls will get what they want.

Having the confidence to 'get what you want out of life' is something that 'new' feminists accuse second-wave feminism of taking away from women. As observed in Chapter 1, for example, Katie Roiphe accuses feminism of encouraging women to be fearful of sex, of equating sex with danger (Aids, rape, harassment) rather than pleasure.[6] Yet without mutuality and a feminist epistemology all that is left of the adventure story for girls *is* confidence. While young middle-class women like Roiphe[7] may be able to turn this to their bourgeois feminist advantage, the social reality for young working-class girls, as plays by Rebecca Prichard and Judy Upton in this chapter illustrate, tells a rather different story.

Both Prichard and Upton are concerned in their theatre with paying significant (although not exclusive) attention to the lives of young working-class women. In contradistinction to second-wave feminist theatre-making, their theatre is neither issue-based nor concerned with educating audiences with a particular feminist agenda. Rather, their drama story-tells the disjunction between the hardships facing different communities of young working-class women, and the right-wing discourses of 'girl power'. Where the first half of my chapter overviews the two women writers and their work, the second part shows more specifically how the gap between the idea of empowerment and the social reality of disempowerment, gives rise in the 1990s to a girl-gang culture, as dramatised in Upton's *Ashes and Sand* (1994) and Prichard's *Yard Gal* (1998).

'Essex girl': Rebecca Prichard

Rebecca Prichard launched her playwriting career in 1994 through the Royal Court Young Writers Festival. In that season's festival entitled 'Coming On Strong' she developed and wrote *Essex Girls*, a two-act play about teenage girls and single mothers. A published collection of work based on the 'Coming On Strong' festival includes *Essex Girls*,[8] in an otherwise 'boy' dominated volume: *Peaches* by Nick Grosso,[9] that follows Frank's encounters with 'peaches' (women); Michael Wynne's *The Knocky*, a story of hard times facing a family on an estate in Birkenhead, Liverpool, and Kevin Coyle's *Corner Boys*, based on his teenage experiences in Derry. All of these plays are characterised by a dramatic world in which people struggle to make sense and purpose out of difficult times or empty lives, though *Essex Girls* differs from the other plays in the volume on account of its all-female, young girl focus (being one of the post-*Top Girls* 'handful of all-girl plays' that Ravenhill alluded to). The gendering of the volume is particularly marked in the contrast between Prichard's 'Essex girls' and Coyle's *Corner Boys*. In *Corner Boys* the boys hang around on street corners, have girlfriends and get into street-gang fighting because there is nothing else to do and nowhere else to go; in *Essex Girls* boys are a subject of conversation, but the girls are the subject of the play.[10]

Prichard is resistant to the label of 'woman writer' though at the same time argues that she has drawn 'strength from working with other women and seeing what issues are particular to women'.[11] Important to Prichard is, she explains, 'the playwright's work as a voice of social criticism, and the audience's role as witness, which is one of the few things we have left that makes people feel responsible for others in society'.[12] While Prichard argues that she likes to 'write about people in extreme situations',[13] I would argue that she likes to write about young women 'in extreme situations', and that dramatising the experiences of young women is where she finds her 'voice of social criticism' as a writer. Like Upton in *Ashes and Sand* (see later), in *Essex Girls* Prichard writes out of a world that she is familiar with, drawing on her own Essex background and working with young women as a youth drama worker (arguably a theatrical equivalent to McRobbie's involvement with girls' youth culture in Birmingham in the 1970s).

The contemporary teenage world of *Essex Girls* is comic but hopeless. A first act set in the girls' toilets in a comprehensive school in which three girls are rivals over boys and looks, and argue about bodies, pregnancies and abortions is funny but bleak. Through comedy Prichard raises an awareness of young lives going nowhere. To reinforce this point, Act Two of *Essex Girls* focuses on a seventeen-year-old single mum in her council flat in Tilbury, Essex and her girlfriend who comes to visit. The lively verbal banter between the girls in Act One is replaced by a much more subdued tone, punctuated by the cries of the infant on the baby monitor. 'Life's an adventure, innit. To be lived,' insists Karen to single mum Kim.[14] However, the idea of 'adventure' for both of them, Kim especially, is hard to reconcile with the lack of opportunities facing the girls.

As a columnist in a *Guardian* feature on Prichard was later to reflect, the dramatist's own 'origins' were indexed in the title of her debut play,[15] but she has since been more widely identified with the so-called 'drama of disenchantment'.[16] Although Upton and Kane are more commonly associated with 'bad girl' theatre than Prichard, Prichard's own style of dramatic 'disenchantment' has kept to its disadvantaged-young-women focus. Her subsequent plays, *Fair Game*

(1997) and *Yard Gal* (1998), use violence and gang culture as part of a social exploration into the lives of teenage no-hopers.

Fair Game is an adaptation of a play by the Israeli writer Edna Mazya: *Games in the Backyard.*[17] The original drama was based on a real-life crime in which seven boys on a kibbutz imprisoned and raped a girl, but were acquitted at trial. Mazya's play was a protest against the male dominance of the courtroom drama and the acquittal, and her play, ultimately, helped to overturn the non-guilty verdict at appeal.[18] Prichard's adaptation omits the courtroom scenes and concentrates on the mounting tensions and rivalries produced by the introduction of a girl into a boys' gang, that lead to the boys committing multiple rape. Moreover, the boy who is goaded by the others to commit the first rape is the girl's step-brother. Insightfully, Prichard argues the difference between Mazya's original and her adaptation as the shift from Mazya's asking 'when does the rape end?' (given that the girl is 'raped' again in the courtroom), to her own questioning of 'when does the rape begin?' (dramatised through her focus on the gang behaviour of the boys).[19]

The play caused shock waves before it was performed: children's charities expressed alarm at the Court's plans to cast young teenagers in the roles, and pre-performance discussion began to link *Fair Game* with the Court's most controversial dramas – Bond's *Saved*, Kane's *Blasted*.[20] 'Shock' publicity, however, militates against the play's serious, political engagement with the masculinist culture that the boys 'buy' into and the consequential violence acted out on the female body. In a departure from earlier feminist dramatisations that opted for the stylisation of rape,[21] Prichard works through a realistic register that pulls spectators into the violence of the masculinist gaze: a 'drama with no exits – no "safe areas"'.[22] As theatre it plays like a 'game' the boys are out to 'win', not just against the 'girls', but also competitively, taking sides against each other. If there is salvation, it comes, as it does in Kane's theatre, through finding love or tenderness in a moment of abject horror: the rape between Prichard's step-brother and sister produces the play's one moment of tenderness as the step-brother kneels to comfort and cry with the sister he has raped.[23]

Fair Game adds testimony to Prichard's idea that a playwright should vocalise social criticism and aim to frame the personal within the political. Boy–girl relations in *Fair Game* are dramatised not as a matter of personal struggle but as part of a power struggle linked to gender concerns. More shocking than young people playing the rape was, I found, Prichard's account of researching and drafting the play in schools and her observation about the play's relation to the real experiences of young girls: 'taking the first draft into schools was frightening: teachers stopped them using certain girls to play the central character because it was felt the part was too close to their experience'.[24] The rape victim in Prichard's play who speaks and postures aggressively to get what she wants (to join the group and get the sexual attentions of one particular boy), highlights the 'gap' between image and reality; between the desire to be (and to have) one of the boys and the reality in which she becomes their victim. That this speaks to the real-life experiences of the schoolgirls Prichard met in the inception of her theatre project offers a telling and significant warning to Roiphe's advocacy of sexual empowerment, or the 'girl power' style of 1990s feminism.

'Seeing red': Judy Upton

Like Rebecca Prichard, Judy Upton is a dramatist who launched her professional playwriting career in the 1990s. *Everlasting Rose*, a play about the fear of ageing, was performed in 1992 at the New Play Festival, Old Red Lion, London. Upton has maintained her commitment to the London 'fringe', and proved a regular contributor to The Red Room's repertoire in the 1990s. Red Room director Lisa Goldman, is someone with whom Upton has found a rewarding artistic collaboration, with Goldman directing Upton's *The Shorewatcher's House* (1995), *Sunspots* (1996), *People on the River* (1997) and *Know Your Rights* (1998). Other studio spaces also housed her work in the 1990s. These include the Room at Richmond's Orange Tree which staged the *Temple* (1995) and *The Girlz* (1998); The Door at Birmingham Repertory Theatre (*Confidence*, 1998), and the Royal Court Theatre Upstairs, which staged *Ashes and Sand* (1994) and *Bruises* (co-produced with Soho Theatre Company, 1995). All in all, this constitutes a considerable body of dramatic work in the 1990s. It was

Upton's production of *Ashes and Sand* in the 1994–5 Royal Court season that brought her to critical attention (alongside Nick Grosso, Sarah Kane, Judith Johnson and Joe Penhall). *Ashes and Sand* was that season's winner of the George Devine Award for new writing and has been argued by some critics as the production that heralded the emergence of angry in-yer-face writing.[25]

Under Goldman's direction 'The Red Room has increasingly defined its role as a provocateur on the London new writing scene, pro-actively commissioning and developing political new writing.'[26] Goldman's commissioning for The Red Room's 1998 season 'Seeing Red', for example, required that she contact writers interested in social (socialist) change. 'In 1968,' Goldman explained, 'people had a dream that they could change things. That confidence has been crushed out of them. The writers I contacted had all been wanting to say something but felt that no one was interested in them writing political stuff any more.'[27] As one of those writers contacted and commissioned by The Red Room, Upton is identified as a dramatist interested in 'writing political stuff'. *Know Your Rights*, written for the 'Seeing Red' season, is a two-hander that looks at the social, legal, medical and benefit systems in place that mean that two women who might have been able to help each other through their respective personal difficulties (one a single parent, the other with a husband in care, suffering from Alzheimer's), end up estranged, attempting to sue each other, and in worsening circumstances. Similarly, in the Red Room's 1997 season on the media, 'The Big Story', Upton contributed *People on the River*, a play that takes a critical look at the role of the media and victim television (of the kind that Kane also re-visioned in *Crave*).

While her association with The Red Room characterises Upton as a political writer, her angry style has also earned her (in theatre journalism) a place among the 'boys'. Although for most theatre critics it was Kane who was the truly 'bad girl' of British drama in the 1990s, Upton's style of angry writing, and attention to violence – especially in *Ashes and Sand* and *Bruises* (which deals with cycles of abuse) – meant that her work has been grouped with the new angry young men's writing.

Interesting in this respect is Benedict Nightingale's representation of Upton. In 1996 Nightingale drew up a list of ten writers representative of the most exciting dramatists to contribute to what he called 'British theatre's writing renaissance'.[28] Of these, only two were women – Upton and Kane (the others were Samuel Adamson, Simon Bent, Simon Block, Jez Butterworth, Nick Grosso, Martin McDonagh, Joe Penhall and Michael Wynne). All of the writers, with the exception of Upton (listed as aged thirty-two) were under thirty. Like the Osborne generation before them, these writers were distinguished by their youth and anger. While Nightingale acknowledged the diversity and difference of the writers on his list, he proposed 'similarities of style and content', in so far as the dramatists 'express[ed] the feelings of a generation formed by the 1980s'.[29] This generation Nightingale also began to identify in his reviewing as dramatists of the disenchanted, or as he styled it, the 'new Theatre of Urban Ennui',[30] explained as theatre attending to the 'muddle of urban life today',[31] but without having a social or political agenda like earlier generations of writers. Nightingale also singled out socialist Royal Court director Ian Rickson, responsible for Upton's *Ashes and Sand* and Penhall's *Some Voices* in the 1994–5 season, as principally concerned with directing this new kind of theatre.[32]

While Nightingale's observations are broadly appropriate, he does end up eliding the way in which gender is a significant factor in the ways in which 'urban life' is presented. In Upton's theatre, what is significant is the attention that, like Prichard, she gives to the urban lives of young women. This is very different to the all-male cast of Simon Block's taxi-cab-drivers-cum-tennis-table-players in *Not a Game for Boys*, or Penhall's predominantly male exploration of schizophrenia in *Some Voices*. Women may 'figure' in these plays as part of masculine dysfunctionality (a girlfriend and wife apparently make and receive phone calls to and from their male partners in *Not a Game for Boys*; the schizophrenic Ray takes up with a girlfriend who has her own problems with a violent boyfriend in *Some Voices*), but they do not figure in their own right.

While London is a popular location for the expression of urban disenchantment (or rather, London's down-market, run-down, districts), Upton tends to set her work in southern seaside towns that are out of season or gone to seed: Hastings, Worthing, Brighton. The location is significant – not least because it layers in a complexity to the post-Thatcher geographical divide of a wealthy South and impoverished North. This is not to argue against the reality of an industrial North laid waste through the radical 1980s closures of mines, steel works or boat-building industries (as depicted in *The Full Monty*, for example) but to show that the prosperous Tory south also has its low spots, areas of poverty characterised by struggling local economies and dead-end jobs and lives.[33]

Seaside towns gone to seed are especially evocative of good times gone wrong; where the idea of having fun is undercut by the dysfunctionality of the 'popular' that no longer entertains, seems behind the times or out of season. They are further evocative of class: a sign of a working-class culture that, like the characters in the plays, is struggling to survive. In *Confidence*, for example, Ella argues that 'the pier's a big let-down' and the '"entertainments" at the Pavilion' need to go altogether.[34] Arcades are a particular favourite of Upton's: slot machines that promise a big win but rarely pay out, unless you fix them.[35]

In those plays, like *Ashes and Sand*, *Sunspots*, *The Girlz* or *Confidence*, where Upton pays particular attention to young women (the gang in *Ashes*, the sisters in *Sunspots*, the schoolgirls under pressure to conform in *The Girlz*, or Ella in *Confidence*) the seaside setting, figuratively, comes to stand for the unfulfilled promise of 'better times' for women. In *Confidence*, Ella, Madonna-style, uses all the men who come into her life (Dean who looks after the ice-cream kiosk, his older brother, Ben, who manages the seaside kiosks for their owner, Edwin, an ageing capitalist and conman) to try and realise her dreams of a materially better future. She has two things to trade: her body and, as the title of the play suggests, her 'confidence'. Ella is a 1990s refashioning of the 1980s material girl, typified by Madonna in the title role of the 1984 film *Desperately Seeking Susan*. Madonna plays the working-class girl who uses girlfriends and boyfriends, 'borrows' and steals to get by, and, in the end, gets to hang on to her man and is materially rewarded for her dishonesty (when she assists in the capture of a murdering jewel thief). The twist, however, in Upton's representation of Ella as a material girl in the 1990s is the 'trashing' of romance and wealth. The men Ella gulls are ultimately not reconciled to her cheating ways. She makes no female friends with whom she might share her hardships. Her schemes to make money all come to nothing and she ends up as penniless as when she started.[36] While quirky, fun to watch (especially in the way that she fools the men), Ella's 'confidence' and willingness to trade sex for 'business' is not enough for her to escape her material and social circumstances. Ultimately, she has nothing, not even her body, to call her own.

Finding or claiming a 'space' of your own was a marker of 1970s feminism, where 'space' might stand for a wide range of locational needs and desires, from the more literal (somewhere to live) to the more figurative (body as 'space'). Without a 'space' to call your own, independent ways of living and creating were compromised. With the shift in the 1980s towards 'top girls' feminism, came the idea that if you had no 'space' to call your own, you could take over other spaces. Without her own place in the city, Madonna/Susan in *Desperately Seeking Susan*, for example, makes the city her 'own': a public washroom turns into a 'private' bathroom, other people's homes, 'spaces', are ones you simply help yourself to. However, Upton's young women in the 1990s struggle to claim any kind of 'space' as their 'own'. The family home (where it exists at all) is seen as dysfunctional and/or problematic. The girls in *Ashes and Sand* spend a lot of time hanging around the arcade machines, and in *Sunspots*, Pola is actually living in an arcade (out of season), and has lied to her sister, Aimee, about having a flat for them all to stay in when Aimee and her boyfriend Sam come visiting. If you cannot lay claim to your own space then you can leave your signature on other public spaces in the form of graffiti; spraying your tag name as a sign of presence and of erasure; of protest and of displacement.

Dramaturgically, Upton achieves her critical take on the social realities facing young working-class women in the 1990s, through a technique of mimetic representation that gradually distorts and becomes less familiar; more surreal. Like the mirrors used in the set design for the Court production of *Ashes and Sand* (angled to show the inside and outside of a room), Upton's dramaturgical effect is of the familiar made alien. An ice-cream kiosk in *Confidence*, for example, not only has a stock of Cornettos and Calippos, but is also home to a frozen hamster (*Confidence*, p.25). Upton's techniques of distortion in which the 'real' becomes more and more unreal, links to the idea that lives are going nowhere. Fantasies (of better lives) never become realities, and the more frustrated and 'blocked' dreams become, the more unreal and violent life in turn becomes as a way of coping.

Girl gangs
Ashes and Sand, Judy Upton

In the mid-1990s girl gangs were headlining the news. Just a week before the opening of Upton's *Ashes and Sand*, actress Elizabeth Hurley was set upon and robbed by a girl gang close to her London home in Chelsea.[37] Upton's own research included 'newspaper reports about girl muggers on the Palace Pier' as well as her own teenage experiences.[38] In-depth articles on the girl gang phenomenon quoted statistics that showed a rise in serious offences committed by women: a rise of 250 per cent since 1973.[39] If feminism had previously concerned itself with male violence and abuse of women (as discussed in the last chapter) it now also had to address the issue of violence committed by women. Violence by young women was accounted for in different ways: it was seen as a way of coping with violence; as a result of the increase in violent role models for young women; or of the blurring of male and female roles, enabling women to be more masculine and more competitive.

Ashes and Sand exemplifies the idea of frustrated dreams turning to violence: a kind of gender-reversed *Brighton Rock* for the 1990s. Of the play itself Upton wrote:

> I was angry in the spring of 1994 when I wrote *Ashes and Sand*. The play just poured out. I was angry for myself and my friends, dragged, kicking and screaming through a hell-hole of a comprehensive school, to end up living lives that fell well short of our dreams. But seaside girls are fighters. We don't give up easily.[40]

The girls in the play, Hayley, Anna, Jo and Lauren, have dead-end jobs and little or no home-life. Their idea of a way out is to travel to somewhere exotic like Bali. Given their lack of money, crime is one way that they try to make their dreams come true. Their speciality is mugging and robbing young men on the pier. That they never get to far-away places is not only because their crimes get detected, but also because they betray each other. When Hayley, leader of the gang, is locked up in a police cell overnight, Jo and Lauren trash her house and steal the travel fund for themselves.

Interwoven with the narrative of the girls' gang, is their friendship with a young police officer, Daniel. Daniel, single and unclear about his own desires and sexuality, is also seeking a way out in the form of a job transfer to Gibraltar. Like the girls, Daniel does not get to leave. Caught up with them in a complex web of friendships and betrayals, he becomes the object of their hostility. In the play's penultimate scene they 'rape' him; holding him at knifepoint and covering his naked body with the women's cosmetics they have found in his room.

Summarising Upton's work, Nightingale argued that 'her characters might shock doctrinaire feminists, since she recognises what's destructive and self-destructive in women and men alike'.[41] Behind this statement, however, is an idea of feminism that is concerned to show that all women are victims and all men are the villains. But this is an outdated and oversimplified version of 1970s radical feminism. The shock for feminism in the 1990s (to take up Nightingale's view, but to take it in another direction), is rather the way in which the 'top girl' promise of empowerment gives way to violence when that promise is unfulfilled or broken. Violence, symbolically prefigured in Churchill's Angie who puts on her dress to 'kill' her 'mother', is actual and 'real' in Upton's girl gang setting.

Gang culture encourages the girls to be tough because their world is tough. Hayley thinks nothing of crouching down beside the headless corpse of a suicide car driver at the roadside scene that Daniel and his colleague Glyn are investigating.[42] In a world where, as Anna explains, 'Men always like to get together to slag you off' (*Ashes*, p.13), the girls group together in an act of resistance. Violence is a way of coping: 'I feel angry. If I don't hurt someone I don't know what I might do,' says Hayley (p.13). The girls steal because they cannot afford to buy the things they need or the things they want (see *Ashes*, p.31), and whatever they dream of, 'someone comes along and smashes it to bits' (p.46). At the close of Act Two, Upton demonstrates the perpetuation of violence and the shattering of dreams by counterpointing a male victim who turns would-be-rapist being knifed by the girls, with the image of Hayley, deserted by Daniel after her attempts at seduction, taking a knife to her pocket book where she writes down her plans and dreams (*Ashes*, pp.56–7).

Where material girl Madonna in the 1980s represented an image of the overtly or aggressively (hetero)sexual woman, her bad girl image was not one that extended to serious criminality or violence. In the 1990s, however, a number of more violent bad girl images began to emerge in popular culture. One in particular is interesting here, given that it also, like Upton's drama, has a seaside connection. Tank Girl was a late 1980s creation by the Worthing-based comic artists Jamie Hewlett and Alan Martin. Described as 'ferocious, foul-mouthed and sexy', the comic strip creation was turned into a movie, *Tank Girl*, in 1995.[43] In Upton's play, after Jo and Hayley have raided an off-licence, the girls make a comparison between themselves and another iconic representation of women and violence in the 1990s: Thelma and Louise. Ridley Scott's controversial 1991 film *Thelma and Louise* has been noted for its gender reversal of the male buddy film, tracking the adventures of two women who embark on a trail of robbery and violence against men. However, while the film sustains the friendship between the two women, Thelma and Louise, Upton's girls have trouble remaining loyal to each other. Internecine betrayals involve the girls stealing money or boys from each other. Violence is both directed outwards (at their male victims) and inwards (violence turning on themselves). The latter manifests itself not only in terms of the betrayals within the group, but also in the way that Hayley harms herself, taking a blade to her arm (*Ashes*, p.12).[44]

Gender roles, the play demonstrates, are indeed changing. The need for a girl gang appears necessary to a sense of female empowerment: to be empowered by an all-female gang, rather than marginalised (or, indeed, as *Fair Game* illustrated, victimised and brutalised) as a girl in a boy gang, and to take the place of a family. The girls play, tank-girl style, at the aggressive feminine and masculine aggressor. The play on gender stereotypes takes the male victims by surprise. They expect sex not violence from the girls. It is not only the girls, however, who are blurring gender roles in the play. In the figure of Glyn, Daniel's older work colleague, Upton represents a traditional husband and father figure who spends most of his time apparently envious of Daniel's single lifestyle and discontented with his traditional, familial role, while Daniel seems confused about his sexuality. He steals women's shoes, cosmetics and clothing – signs of femininity that he appears to feel both attracted to and violent towards.[45] In the course of his work as a police officer he has been attacked three times and in each incident his attacker was a woman. The idea of the man as the victim and the woman as aggressor is finally and forcefully imaged in the 'rape' scene and Daniel's breakdown.

Ultimately, this suggests that the aggressive girls-together style of 'empowerment' is actually a sign of disempowerment. In contradistinction to the Spice Girl myth of the ordinary girl turned superstar, the young women Upton depicts are unable to transcend the economic and cultural conditions of their social reality. In the absence of a materialist–feminist agenda working towards the transformation of social structures, the girls find their own way of manipulating, and, ultimately, violently breaking social rules and regulations. As Ian Rickson, director of *Ashes and Sand*, argued: 'Upton is concerned about how socially deprived her characters are and her plays build to a violent release of energy that is upsetting but also purging for the audience.'[46] I would argue, however, that it is less a question of 'purging' than provoking an audience into a social awareness of lives for young girls who, like their movie idols Thelma and Louise, are denied adventures, and through frustration, anger and violence, seek to make their lives their 'own'.

Yard Gal, Rebecca Prichard
In contrast to the girl and the boys' gang in *Fair Game*, Prichard's 1998 production of *Yard Gal*, like Upton's *Ashes and Sand*, dramatises

an all-girl gang. However, *Yard Gal* is set not at the seaside but in Hackney, East London, and portrays a group of young women who exist out in the margins of society; a group accustomed to a way of life that involves drugs, prostitution and violence. Commissioned by Clean Break, the play grew out of a period of extensive research and workshopping with women prisoners in 1997 at HMP Bullwood Hall, Hockley, Essex. Prichard used this research to create *Yard Gal* as a two-hander: Boo, who is black, and Marie, who is white, share the narrative of their Hackney street gang.[47] In Act One the girls introduce us to the different members of their gang. The act climaxes in the narration of the death of gang member Deanne who, high on alcohol and drugs, falls from the balcony of a deserted block of flats. Act Two describes the stabbing of Marie by a rival gang, and, in retaliation, Marie's stabbing of the rival gang leader. In Act Three Boo has been arrested and is in prison for her involvement in the gang's violence, while Marie is still on the outside, pregnant, and struggling to survive on her own, and, eventually, to make a life for her child.

Composed as a kind of duet between Boo and Marie, Prichard's story-telling register is important to the play's aesthetic and composition. As a shared, rather than single narration, *Yard Gal* moves away from the idea that this is going to be the story of one, individual young girl. That the story is in fact that of a community of girls, is underlined by the way in which narrating rather than mimetically representing action, requires the two performers to engage in multiple role play, playing all the members of their gang. The performers therefore have a number of functions to fulfil: playing all of the characters in addition to their own, establishing the various locations and recreating the different dramatic situations calls for energetic vocal and physical performance registers. The Royal Court production, for example, mirrored the austerity of the play's subject matter by using a non-realist, minimalist set – working with four steel boxes for props and specialist lighting effects to switch between streets, night clubs or taxis – and therefore putting a greater emphasis on the performers to vocally and physically set the location, principally through the use of the Cockney–Caribbean rhyme and slang which the girls share (irrespective of Marie being white and Boo being black), used in conjunction with high, physical energy. Stylistically, this performance register maps with the at-risk, 'thrill' of life on the edge. The 'gap' created through the reported role play of the dual narration, however, keeps an audience from being drawn into the pathos of the tragic and violent lives of the girls.

Having the girls give voice to their own uncensored stories means Prichard avoids lecturing her audience on the hardships of the yard gal. Boo and Marie are not victims, but, like Upton's seaside girls, are 'fighters': tough yard gals who won't take 'shit' from anyone. The opening also establishes that the girls are there to talk about life as it really is: 'we's from Hackney. People talk a lot of shit about Hackney when they ain't never been there, and they talk a lot of shit about yards when they ain't never met none. So me and Marie we come to tell you a story that is FI'REAL' (Yard Gal, p.6). This positions the girls as an authority on their subject and signals the gap between their lives and those of the predominantly (although not exclusively) white, middle-class audiences of theatregoers who are unlikely to have experienced the world they aim to present. In the Royal Court production this was reinforced by the convincing performances of Sharon Duncan-Brewster (Boo) and Amelia Lowdell (Marie) who, as Nightingale observed, came across as 'less the product of drama schools than of tower blocks, markets and alleyways'.[48]

In Ashes and Sand and, to give another 1990s example, in Judith Johnson's Somewhere, which also examines the dead-end lives of a mixed, boy and girl gang of teenagers (Liverpool Playhouse Studio, 1993), relocation, the notion of being 'somewhere' else, gives expression to the idea of a better life.[49] In Yard Gal, however, Prichard's young women do not desire or dream of leaving their street life. In their world, it is better not to dream; better, as Boo explains, to teach yourself not to want things (Yard Gal, p.31). When Nero, a black dealer who is both lover and surrogate father-figure to the girls, lectures them on the benefits of dealing as a way of making money to leave the area, neither Boo nor Marie pay any attention. On one such occasion, Boo's response to the idea of leaving is '"No-one ever get out the area"', adding, 'but inside I just thought "Why get out, I love Hackney man."' (Yard Gal, p.31).

Prichard's dramatisation of an all-female street gang, like Upton's, contrasts with the way in which, historically, urban street culture has been identified with working-class boys, rather than girls. Feminist analysis attributes this to the greater regulation of girls in the home.[50] The 1990s, however, has seen a continued trend in the decline of the traditional family unit and, therefore, of the 'home' as a regulating influence on young girls. In the play, the girls have no home: Marie has an abusive, violent father she is not supposed to see; Boo lives in a kids' home. Instead, the girls make the street and the gang their 'home'.[51] This functions in a contradictory way: as both empowering (as the girls claim a public space which traditionally has been a male preserve in working-class youth culture), and disempowering because it denies them the possibility of any private, personal 'space'.

In the absence of family, the girls come to depend on each other for support. Boo and Marie are introduced as 'best mates' and they describe the ways in which they look out for each other. Boo cares for Marie if she has one of her fits, and is the one who stays behind when Marie is stabbed, even though this means she ends up getting arrested. Prichard's dialogue indexes the idea of sharing in the way she shares out portions of the storytelling or the girls start and finish sentences or explanations for each other. The play begins with, and never loses sight of the fact that the girls need each other to tell their story; to back each other up. When one moment, the moment of Deanne's suicide, is too painful for Marie to carry on with the story, Boo picks up the narrative thread. Or, conversely, when Marie narrates how she stabbed the rival gang leader, it is Boo who goes silent.

Being supportive towards each other is, however, in conflict with the tough and violent image of the yard gal. Girl power is unrealistic and challenged in Prichard's play by the social reality of the yard gals that places cooperation or mutuality between women at risk in a community that requires them to be tough, competitive and violent in order to stay alive.[52] In effect, Prichard counterpoints two narratives: the friendship and affection between Boo and Marie, and the violent life of their all-female gang. The friendship between the two girls is constantly put at risk by the violence of the group, of which they are also a part. In performance the collision of the opposing forces of the friendship between two women and the violence of the group is made visible through the way in which the performers 'speak' both narratives: their own and that of their gang. This climaxes at the close of Act Two as Marie and Boo's quest to find each other is thwarted by Marie's stabbing of a rival gang leader. The violent crime that she commits on behalf of the gang, but for which Boo is the one who is imprisoned, effectively pulls the friendship apart.

In Act Three, as Boo and Marie keep apart from each other, the spatial arrangements between the performers signify the breaking up of their friendship. And yet, ultimately, something of their friendship does survive: in Marie's naming her daughter after Boo, and Boo's sense that 'every one you known stays inside you a bit' (*Yard Gal*, p.55). The sense that despite events the girls take away something of each other inside them closes the play in a spirit of survival. Traditionally, the idea of storytelling is linked to the idea of surviving, of staying alive. Scheherazade tells the emperor stories in order to entertain him and to avoid being put to death. *Yard Gal* tells a story in which the audience bears witness, listens, in order that the story of Boo and Marie, based on the 'fi'real' survives, lives beyond the moment of its telling.

Plays like *Ashes and Sand* and *Yard Gal* have earned the Royal Court a reputation for girl gang theatre.[53] Moreover, while the dominant tendency has been to review the anger of this drama within a male (Osborne) lead tradition, it has caused a few reviewers to question the gender effects of this writing. With plays like Upton's *Ashes and Sand* and Kane's *Blasted* appearing in the 1994–5 Court season, then, perhaps, speculates reviewer Sarah Hemming, 'the true inheritor of John Osborne's mantle is an angry young woman'.[54] The playwright as 'angry young woman' is taken up in the next chapter, which is concerned with the theatre of Sarah Kane.

5   Sarah Kane: the 'bad girl of our stage'?

Sarah Kane is the most controversial of playwrights to feature in this volume. She exploded on to London's Royal Court stage in January 1995 with her debut play *Blasted* that outraged theatre critics on account of its representations of a violent war, somewhere in Central Europe, but set in a hotel bedroom in Leeds. Exceptionally for a theatre production, the play featured on *Newsnight* and made tabloid headlines, with *Daily Mail* Jack Tinker's 'utterly and entirely disgusted' of 'Tunbridge Wells' voicing the view of a majority of critics.[1] *Blasted* joined the 'canon' of the infamous – Howard Brenton's *Romans in Britain* and Edward Bond's *Saved* (which Kane much admired). The Court was widely criticised for staging *Blasted* and the judgement of its artistic director, Stephen Daldry, was called into question.[2] Kane herself expressed 'genuine surprise that so much media attention could be devoted to a play in a 65-seat theatre in the same week that thousands . . . died in a Japanese earthquake',[3] and that 'a 15-year-old girl' was 'raped in a wood'.[4]

    The whole point of what is considered newsworthy, or not, and the way in which sensationalist reporting marginalises significant global events is thematically central to *Blasted*, though it was some time before reviewers were able to 'see' beyond their initial reactions to her theatre – reactions that were significantly modified in the wake of Kane's suicide in 1999, aged just twenty-seven years. Writing after her death, playwright and close friend Mark Ravenhill recalled his first preconceptions about *Blasted*. Given the play's reception and the way it had been described in the press, he, like so many others, had decided it must be 'terrible'. But he read the script and straight away revised his opinion: 'from the first few lines, I knew I was in the hands of a playwright with total mastery of her craft'.[5] 'Edward Bond was an obvious influence', Ravenhill continued, 'and there was quite a lot of Beckett in there as well. But as I read *Blasted* – with its great passions locked in a small room – I was constantly reminded of Racine.'[6]

The Racinian echoes detected by Ravenhill, 'grand passions' 'blasting' out of a 'small room', might also be used to describe her next play, *Phaedra's Love*. Kane's revisioning of the Hippolytus and Phaedra myth took inspiration from Seneca, rather than Euripides or Racine – a decision in part influenced by Caryl Churchill's version of Seneca's *Thyestes*, also for the Court (1994). Nevertheless, there is a highly Racinian feel to *Phaedra's Love*: the setting, the royal palace, functioning as spatial metaphor for Phaedra's inescapable passion, presented as a human rather than god-driven emotion.

Phaedra's Love was not only written by Kane, she also directed it at the Gate Theatre (May 1996), and went on to direct Buchner's *Woyzeck* at the Gate before the Royal Court staged her next work, *Cleansed*, this time on their mainhouse stage (while Prichard's *Yard Gal* occupied the studio space, 1998).[7] *Cleansed* is set in what appears to be some sort of clinic, punishment or correction centre for those who do not conform to an 'agreed' social, sexual norm. Like *Blasted* and *Phaedra's Love*, *Cleansed* makes significant technical demands on the theatre to stage its violent landscape. However, Kane went on to thwart the expectations of her critics with *Crave* (August 1998), minimalist in aesthetic and 'action' and in which four performers 'speak' for about forty-five minutes of their troubled loves and lives. Kane's own life was more and more troubled by depression and she took her own life in February 1999. Her final play, *4.48 Psychosis*, was drafted, revised and delivered to her agent, Mel Kenyon, shortly before her suicide.[8] The play was performed posthumously in the Court's Theatre Upstairs in June 2000.

Exceptionally then, Kane's entire canon of work is a canon of the 1990s. In this chapter I propose to focus on three of her plays: *Blasted*, *Cleansed* and *Crave*, treating them as a kind of cycle. Kane herself talked about *Blasted* and *Cleansed* as two plays in a possible trilogy about the 'nature of war'. James Macdonald, director of both plays, was more sceptical about the idea of a trilogy, although admitted

78

that there were 'links between the two' but that these were only 'thematic rather than narrative for the simple reason that everyone at the end of *Blasted* is dead'.[9] I would agree that continuity is not in the fictional worlds or characters, but in the way in which these plays show Kane's concerns for a contemporary world depicted as violent and damaging, and in need of change. It is a cycle that, in the final analysis, is not so much about war, but rather focuses on the possibility (however slight) of finding love in a loveless and violent world, or as Caryl Churchill specifically observed of *Blasted*, 'a tender play' for all its violence.[10]

There is a certain and, on my part deliberate, irony in presenting Kane in this study, given that during her 'public' lifetime as a playwright in the mid to late 1990s, she more frequently was grouped with male writers. Michael Billington's list of 'young guns of British drama', for example, groups Kane together with Jez Butterworth, David Eldridge, Martin McDonagh, and Joe Penhall.[11] Veronica Lee's list of 'young guns' (yet more militarism) challenging the 'straight drama', positions Kane alongside Mark Ravenhill, Patrick Marber, Ben Elton and Conor McPherson.[12] Just occasionally this kind of reporting on the new wave of writing, characterised as young and angry, gave a mention to Rebecca Prichard or Judy Upton, but almost invariably included Kane.[13] If women playwrights were frequently represented as marginal to a revival of all things masculine in the 1990s, as my introduction argues, Kane, exceptionally, was presented as included in, not excluded from, the male-dominated circles of the young and the angry.

There are some curious tensions in the image-making that surrounds Kane as a writer, tensions around issues of gender, age and the masculine. She variously was hailed as the 'bad girl of our stage',[14] 'the karate kid of the British theatre',[15] or, as one reviewer of *Blasted* wrote 'Kane has proved she can flex her muscles alongside the toughest of men.'[16] One of the ways of dealing with Kane's youth (she was twenty-three when *Blasted* was staged) and gender (apparently women are not supposed to write such violent plays)[17] was to represent her as an honorary male. I would argue that this also came about because of the staging of *Blasted* at the Court: widely acknowledged, in the wake of Osborne, as home of the 'angry young man' (see also comments in Chapter 4). *Blasted* was the production that revitalised the Court tradition of the young and the angry, and Kane (like Upton) was 'claimed' by that tradition. If the press created a 'ladette' of British theatre in the 1990s, then Kane was it. In interviews she talked about theatre in relation to football (which she was passionate about), and peppered newspaper articles with reports of excessive drinking bouts and a liberal use of swear words.[18] This, I suspect, was partly Kane's mischievous streak: exploiting the image that she had been given that was not of her choosing.

Like every other playwright in this volume, Kane had a dislike of labels. In her interview in the *Rage and Reason* collection, she makes it clear that she did not like the 'woman writer' label: 'I don't want to be a representative of any biological or social group of which I happen to be a member. I am what I am. Not what other people want me to be.'[19] At this point in time there has been relatively little feminist interest in her work. Michelene Wandor merits *Cleansed* with a scant entry in her revised, second version of *Look Back in Gender* in an analysis that suggests *Cleansed* offers a treatment of a violent and dysfunctional 'family',[20] and Kane is briefly discussed in the *Companion to Modern British Women Playwrights*.[21] Her theatre, as Graham Saunders argues, marks a break with a tradition of women's dramatic writing,[22] that generally takes the 'woman's side' (as observed, for example, in discussion of Sarah Daniels's plays in Chapter 3), and, arguably, is even somewhat removed from writers like Prichard and Upton whose stage pictures of urban violence concentrate on the damaged lives of young women. Instead, as Saunders observes, it is the damaging effects of a 'diseased male identity' that are central to Kane's theatre.[23] In bringing a feminist view to Kane's theatre in this study, it is her vision of a violent contemporary world and the underlying causal relationship this has to gender generally and a 'diseased male identity' specifically that is significant.

Moreover, I shall argue in this chapter that through performance Kane offers a new perspective to the Butler style of 1990s gender philosophising, one that contests the 'normalising' forces through which the sexes are kept in place, by making us *feel* the violence of the symbolic masculine. 'Dramatists' wrote Billington in his more generalist, 'young guns of British drama' article, 'are tapping into a generation's despair at our prevailing moral nihilism: as Jack Bradley said, quoting Chesterton on poets, "they make you feel what you already know"'.[24]

Blasted: 'perceptual explosion'

In 1990, just before the outbreak of war in the former Yugoslavia, I attended a women's studies conference in Dubrovnik. There were already signs of unrest: people were out protesting on the city streets. Political campaign posters were pasted up around the city walls. As a British visitor/tourist, it was impossible to understand what was going on, but also impossible not to feel the climate of growing unrest. Waiters that I had seen, all smiles and civility in the hotel, I also saw out on the streets hotly demonstrating among the crowds of people that gathered in the city for political rallies. When, some time afterwards, I next saw the hotel I had stayed in on that conference trip, it was as a mediatised image: part of a televised broadcast on the war in Yugoslavia. I recognised the hotel instantly, but was shocked by its new, war-torn appearance. Incredulity was an overriding feeling: the sense that a place, a city, so recently visited, could erupt into such a violent civil war.

Blasted captured a feeling of the Bosnian war. A hotel bedroom in Leeds, occupied by a couple, Ian and Cate, comes under fire as it is plunged into a European war. Britain's isolationist, island mentality is challenged through Kane's transition from the private, personal moment in the hotel bedroom to civil war, dramaturgically reflected in her shift from a recognisable 'real' in the first part, to an increasingly 'surreal' second half. Like so much of the playwriting considered in this volume, Kane is insistent in her play on the connection between the personal and the political; the intimate and the epic. Private lives and 'wars', as dramatised between Ian and Cate, are not to be divorced from the broader political canvas, but are very much a part of it.

Among her many hostile reviewers, Paul Taylor of the *Independent* reviled *Blasted*, describing it as 'a little like having your face rammed into an overflowing ashtray, just for starters, and then having your whole head held down in a bucket of offal'. The horrific acts in *Blasted* are only acceptable, Taylor argued, if 'you can feel there's something happening to your heart and mind as well as to your nervous system'.[25] The following year, Taylor was invited to join one of the Court's script meetings to report on how plays get selected and developed, and in the article detailing his experience of the meeting noted the ability of the Court's panel to 'remain open to the surprise of work that's struggling to articulate new patterns of feeling'.[26] This very strong echo of Raymond Williams (see Chapter 1, p. 9) is interesting both for the way in which it identifies the Court's particular concern with and feel for the 'new' and, thinking of Kane specifically, for the way in which while the Court had sensed the 'new patterns of feeling' in *Blasted*, reviewers, such as Taylor, had not grasped them at the point of production.

I would want to turn Taylor's original criticism of *Blasted* around to argue that it is precisely Kane's ability to touch hearts, minds and nervous systems that makes her writing so powerful. Those seeking to defend her theatre generally do so on the grounds that she shows violence not gratuitously, but purposefully to show a violent world; that she fights fire with fire. I want to present a related, but at the same time rather different argument: that her dramaturgical, political and aesthetic invitation is for us *to feel differently*. Writing on 'The Phenomenological Attitude' Bert O. States describes the art of the Impressionists as 'painting a perceptual critique of the real world'.[27] A phenomenological view, I would argue, is useful to bring to an understanding of Kane's theatre. As a dramatist she stages a 'perceptual critique' of our violent contemporary world, and the damaging consequences this has for gender relations (*Blasted*), exclusions (*Cleansed*) and desires (*Crave*). A complaint frequently made about her theatre is that it has no moral framework, but viewed in this way, Kane's theatre is highly moral in that its purpose is to connect directly with the horror of the world and its violence, so that 'we are compel[led] to feel that which we perceive'.[28] Crucially, in respect of this point, States argues that 'phenomenological criticism . . . posits a stopping place, as it were, *at* the starting place, not of all possible meanings but of meaning and feeling as they arise in a direct encounter with the art object'.[29] As Kane considered that contact with 'art'/theatre could bring about change, this meant that she worked with a view to theatre having a post-theatrical sequel: a reawakening of perception, an invitation to see differently. 'Art isn't about the shock of something new', she argued, 'it's about arranging the old in such a way that you see it afresh'.[30]

I want to harness the idea that Kane's theatre offers an experience of 'suffering' or feeling, to an argument I shall take forward through all three plays, that central to her 'perceptual critique' is an investigation into the violence of a contemporary world that produces oppressive gender positions. This is expressed differently in each of the three plays, beginning in *Blasted* with a focus on the gender binarism of the masculine and the feminine. In *The Newly Born Woman*, Hélène Cixous outlined the hierarchised opposites that underpin the symbolic systems through which culture and society are organised in the interests of the masculine.[31] Femininity, she explains, is identified with passivity; masculinity with activity. Cixous offers this as a starting point for transformation: as the moment 'to invent another history'.[32] This might seem an unusual point of reference to bring to *Blasted* (given what many feminists have identified over the years as the essentialist risks of Cixous's proposal), but interrogation of the masculine/feminine hierarchy is one that, nevertheless, I would argue, underpins the oppositional, gendered power play in *Blasted*, and begins an interrogation of the symbolic that haunts all of her subsequent work – *Cleansed* and *Crave* in particular.

The gender 'war' between Ian and Cate is played out in the first two scenes. Cate, retarded, jobless, prone to fits and suffering from a speech impediment when made anxious, is sexually bullied by Ian – a man more than twice her age and armed with a gun. The sexual bullying is skilfully orchestrated in these first two scenes to show the complexities of verbal and physical abuse – powerfully captured in the recurrent imaging of Cate sucking her thumb (underlining her child-like quality),[33] in the presence of her abuser.[34]

The collision of opposites works not just in terms of characters, but also in respect of the setting. While Kane specifies that the hotel location is Leeds, her directions also state that the *very expensive hotel* room . . . is so expensive it could be anywhere in the world' (*Blasted*, p.3). The universal language of the hotel room is what makes it locate and translocate: be specifically placed in Leeds and yet caught up in the Bosnian war. The 'language' of the hotel room is one of conflicting discourses: on the one hand, the room suggests the possibility of intimacy and pleasure (a double bed, flowers, champagne on ice, a mini-bar for drinks and a bathroom); on the other, the room has an impersonal quality as a space through which people pass, but do not belong. There is a parallel point to be found to this in the different attitudes that Cate and Ian express towards the room: Cate is *amazed at the classiness of the room*; Ian says dismissively 'I've shat in better places than this' (*Blasted*, p.3).

Although disadvantaged, damaged and victimised in the sphere of the feminine, Cate nevertheless is resistant to her oppression – specifically through her refusal to acknowledge the masculine. Her response to a naked Ian, commanding her to 'put your mouth on me' (*Blasted*, p.7) merely produces a fit of the giggles (also I noted, watching the revival of *Blasted* in 2001, shared by the audience). Her laughter is, however, the laughter of the hysteric. Kane's stage directions point to Cate's hysterical positioning: signed through her laughter and fits. As Cixous and Clément explain, the figure of the hysteric is marked by the duality of resistance and conservatism; of refusing the masculine even while oppressed within and by it.[35] The hysterical patterning of Cate's subordinate yet resistant position to Ian structures the first half of the play and 'climaxes' in the rape, that gives way to war, rape and violation of women and men on an epic scale.

After Cate is raped, a soldier armed with a sniper's rifle invades the hotel bedroom, and, overpowered, Ian now finds himself in the position of the 'feminine' previously occupied by Cate (who makes her escape via the bathroom window). Ian, in turn, is raped at gunpoint by the soldier, after which his eyes are sucked out and eaten, which is what, so the soldier tells us, happened to his girlfriend. Compositionally, then, the private, intimate scenes in Part One are juxtaposed with (and are a part of) the public atrocities of war presented in Part Two). Seen together in this way they create what States describes as a 'bridge of recognition': when elements work intertextually and allow for the possibility of seeing something new, or experiencing the *punctum* of something that has been '*overseen*'.[36] Read intertextually, or rather, I would argue, seen intervisually, Cate's rape re-circulates in the images of war that follow. As Kane herself explained:

> My intention was to be absolutely truthful about abuse and violence. All of the violence in the play has been carefully plotted and dramatically structured to say what I want about war. *The logical conclusion of the attitude that produces an isolated rape in England is the rape camps in Bosnia* [my emphasis]. And the logical conclusion to the way society expects men to behave is war.[37]

After Cate returns to the hotel (Scene Four, following Ian's rape and the soldier blowing his brains out) she and Ian begin to function rather like a Beckett couple. By Act Two in Beckett's *Happy Days*, Winnie is buried up to her neck in sand, while Willie (albeit on all fours) is still capable of movement. Here, Cate survives and is mobile, while Ian visibly disintegrates and is unable to leave the hotel room; is forced into the passive position of the 'feminine'. Immobilised and sightless, with just his head appearing above the floor boards, and unable now to cope on his own, he desires the 'end' that never comes. In the classical tradition, in *Oedipus the King*, for example, with the loss of sight comes insight, self-knowledge or wisdom, and *man* offers himself up to the gods as atonement for his sins. Despite Cate's objections, Ian argues that this is a godless world that makes no sense: 'No God. No Father Christmas. No fairies. No Narnia. No fucking nothing' (*Blasted*, p.55). In the absence of a spiritual world to make sense of living, Ian makes no apology or atonement for his actions. He does not speak of repentence, remorse or regret, but he is made to feel, to live the pain and damage of his actions, through which, finally, he is able to recognise Cate. Blind, he needs to hear Cate; to touch her, to feel her presence. In the final moments, as Cate pushes food and drink into his mouth, Ian addresses the last line of the play to her: 'thank you'. This is the final moment, but the first time that Ian really 'sees' her, and in this ending is imaged the possibility of another beginning – or in Cixous's terms, 'the other history'.

For Ian to reach this point of agnorisis requires, as previously stated, for him to live the pain and damage of his actions. The way that Kane realises this is through her overturning of the logic of the 'real'. Ian 'dies' only to find he is still alive. Spatially and temporally Kane shifts her dramatic frame out of the symbolic into the semiotic. 'You take me to another place' Ian says to Cate earlier in the hotel bedroom scenes, a remark that Cate de-romanticises through her reply 'It's like that when I have a fit' (*Blasted*, p.22). Now Ian 'lives' the time and space of Cate's hysterical fits, with suicidal thoughts, shitting, laughter, nightmares, tears and hunger.[38] It is dying without death. The shifts between light and darkness that Kane uses in the end sequence, should, according to convention, indicate the passing of time. Theatrically, however, the experience of this is not one of time passing, but of being stuck in time. As Cate explains about her fits:

> The world don't exist, not like this. Look the same but –
> Time slows down.
> A dream I get stuck in, can't do nothing about it.
>
> (*Blasted*, p.22)

Kane draws her spectators into this different temporal rhythm and spatial vacuum. A sense of a world 'other' than the one we know is heightened through her play with dramatic conventions, and in particular her disruption to the conventions of on- and offstage action and her play with registers of realism. The more that Kane insists on representing on stage (rather than off) the acts that the journalists listed as so shocking, which at the point of Ian's descent into living death include defecation, masturbation, and cannibalism, the more the apparatus of mimesis is made visible; the more the 'real' becomes 'unreal'. As a spectator I would not deny experiencing these events as shocking. However, I would argue that the 'real' force of their horror comes not when events are seen in their individual scenic moments, but through their visual cross-infection. For example, when, in the play's closure, Ian 'eats' the baby, and Cate returns to the hotel room with bread, sausage and gin, that she eats and then feeds to him, the *punctum* arises not at the point that Ian mimes the eating of the baby (a moment that we 'know' from all the review writing), but as the after-image of cannibalism re-circulates when the actress in the role of Cate, strict vegetarian, eats meat.[39] Similarly, when Cate buries the baby she has saved under the floorboards in the hotel bedroom and improvises a makeshift cross out of two bits of wood bound together with torn pieces of lining from Ian's jacket (see *Blasted*, p.57) the hotel bedroom becomes a graveyard. The 'overseen' image of the anonymous grave (made familiar, for example, through Second World War media news footage) is re-imaged through its hotel location as burial ground; not underground, but under floorboards. In turn, the image of the burial infects the hotel location, activating the anonymous, the impersonal feeling that characterises urban hotel life (such as that which Caryl Churchill dramatised in the second piece to her 1997 production of *Hotel*).[40]

Cixous's theoretical frame, sketched into this analysis of *Blasted*, does not, in itself, treat specific material circumstances of gender inequalities as integral to its critique of gender hierarchisation. The impulse behind Cixous's writing is philosophical rather than social. That said, it is important to note that Cixous was writing in the 1970s climate of feminist thinking, politics and culture. If it is possible to use this frame as an analytical lens for *Blasted*, as I am arguing here, then I must also ask what it means to do this in the context of the social and cultural climate of the 1990s and from a set of feminist interests (mine, not Kane's), some thirty years later.

As my Chapter 3 in particular signals, violence against women – child abuse, domestic abuse, rape – remains an on-going issue for feminism. While writers of the so-called ' new' feminism, like Walter, have tended to focus on the legislation needed to address the issue of violence against women, calls for legislative reform do not, however, address what my introduction also identified as an increasingly misogynist mainstream culture in the 1990s. *Blasted* ultimately takes issue with this masculinist culture, though ironically, in its original moment of production in 1995, it was in many ways, as the introductory comments to this chapter explain, seen as a part of it.

That this was a misreading can be further argued if *Blasted* is seen in the context of other representations of male violence from the

1990s. Turning briefly to British film in the 1990s, for example, Claire Monk persuasively shows 'a strand of male-focused films whose gender politics were more masculinist than feminist'.[41] Two films that Monk details in her analysis are particularly relevant to this discussion of *Blasted*: Mike Leigh's *Naked* (1993) and Gary Oldman's *Nil By Mouth* (1997). *Naked* portrays a serial abuser and rapist; *Nil by Mouth* includes a portrait of violent domestic abuse. The concentration on the masculine and the relatively unexplored position of women as victims of the masculine lays the films open to readings that are misogynist rather than progressive (*Naked* more so than *Nil by Mouth*). In the case of *Naked* specifically, Monk notes that very few critics pointed out the possible misogynist reading that arises out of the absence of any critical stance on Leigh's rapist.[42] This makes for a very interesting point of contrast with the widespread critical outcry against Kane, accused of not providing a moral line on the violence of *Blasted*.[43]

On the one hand, Kane shares some of the concerns to be found in these cinematic representations of violent masculinity – particularly, with attempts (albeit with various degrees of success) to show the damaging effects of violence to the male abuser, which she does in all three plays studied here.[44] In respect of *Blasted* specifically, Kane represents Ian as a masculine oppressor, damaged by the position he occupies. As a tabloid journalist (involved in the kind of 'filth' Kane ironically was accused of dramatising) with a rotting body (he has terminal lung cancer), one might read Ian figuratively as an embodiment of all-that-is-wrong-with-masculinity-in-the 1990s. Marked by racism, sexism, fascism, homophobia and a negative attitude towards disability, he signifies masculinity unreformed; untouched by the kinds of social and cultural changes that feminism argued for. All that he does – and this includes becoming some kind of killer for the state – he does because he 'love[s] this land' (*Blasted*, p.30). Yet this is a love built on a love of the self and not of the other whom he does not see, or rather, sees only through the gaze of oppressor. On the other hand, it is the way that Kane is not exclusively male-focused, nor exclusively focused on a disadvantaged male underclass (the implication being that there is less excusing of behaviours on grounds of social disadvantage), that makes her work different to the cinematic representations of masculinity that Monk describes.

The failure to 'see' Kane's critique of masculinity is also consequent upon an inability to read her new 'structure of feeling'. Although concerned with private and public worlds, the intimate and the epic, Kane departed from the recognisable style of a Brechtian-inflected dramaturgy, formerly used in feminist stagings of the personal as an epic and political concern. In its place is a formal interrogation of the real that is felt compositionally (the 'real' is blown away by the second, surreal half of the play) and through the performance style and energy this requires. The combined effect is one of an hallucinogenic spectatorship: a real made unreal, known and yet not known; a dramatic world that begins in a tempo commensurate with 'reality' and moves into a dislocated, monumental feeling of being inside–outside space and time. In this sense, Kane's theatre might be situated with other (male) writers of the 'so-called "ecstasy generation"'.[45] Yet what makes Kane's theatre different, and this becomes clearer as her canon develops, is that she does have a vision beyond a nihilistic view of 'masculinity in crisis', a vision that rests on the redemptive possibility of love.

Cleansed: gender punishment

The possibility of love as a means of salvation is central to *Cleansed*. *Cleansed* opens with a drug dealer, Tinker, shooting heroin into the eyeball of a drug addict, Graham. Graham's sister, Grace, comes looking for her brother, and stays on in what appears to be some kind of clinic or correction centre for young men (not without resonance of a boys' public school), in order to re-find her dead brother and ultimately to 'become' him. The clinic or centre is actually specified in Kane's directions as a university. The idea of a university as an institution that regulates, represses and regiments, rather than encourages the creative, the imaginative and the unorthodox, haunts the play's central concerns with the regulation of sexuality, staged through a series of encounters and love relations that unfold between 'inmates'.

In the second scene, gay lovers, Carl and Rod, sit '*on the college green just inside the perimeter fence of the university*' (*Cleansed*, p.109). On the other side of the fence can be heard the sounds of a cricket match. The fence at which Carl and Rod are positioned suggests a divide which was highly evocative of internment or the concentration camp.[46] Carl and Rod are the 'wrong' side of the divide; are locked away to be 'cleansed' in the interests of the 'healthy' citizens out on the other side of the fence. Using a cricket match to represent the world beyond positions *Cleansed* as a further (I would argue more complex and sophisticated) interrogation of the masculine that Kane began in *Blasted*. Most critics tried to position *Cleansed* within a political frame. Michael Billington, for example, wrote 'you never learn who or what lies behind Kane's hermetic chamber of horrors. If it is meant as a political metaphor, it remains an extremely shadowy one'.[47] It makes more sense, I feel, to argue *Cleansed* as a figurative dismantling of the psychoanalytical framework that endorses and produces 'a diseased male identity', one that punishes homosexual, same sex couples, and (as *Blasted* exemplified) is even damaging to heterosexual relations. In this respect, *Cleansed* is working in similar territory to Butler's gender theorising in the 1990s, albeit in a different medium.

In *Bodies that Matter*, Butler offers an explanation of the 'symbolic constraints under which becoming "sexed" occurs' which is helpful to discussion at this point:

> The symbolic domain which compelled the assumption of a sexed position within language was held to be more fundamental than any specific organization of kinship. So that one might rearrange kinship relations outside of the family scene, but still discover one's sexuality to be constructed through more deep-seated constraining and constitutive symbolic demands.[48]

What Kane makes visible in *Cleansed* are those abstract, invisible, 'deep-seated constraining and constitutive symbolic demands'. To make them visible and knowable in a way that is different to how they are already known, to make us *feel* them she turns them into a spectacle of punishment. She invites us to see the violence of the symbolic. The expression of love between Carl and Rod, for example, is quite literally hacked to pieces as Tinker, at different times, cuts off Carl's tongue, hands, feet and penis. Speaking love, writing love, dancing love and fucking are all 'silenced'.

To offer punishment as a spectacle risks, as Foucault explains in *Discipline and Punish*, the possibility of the punishment appearing more violent than the crime committed (hence its historical disappearance).[49] In introducing 'deviant' sex positions as crimes to be punished Kane highlights the comparative brutality of the symbolic domain, relative to the 'offence' of the 'offender', especially as those who 'offend' frequently are represented through visual and/or verbal discourses of martyrdom.[50] *Surveiller et punir* ('to watch and to punish'), the original French title of Foucault's study resonates throughout *Cleansed*. Tinker, a complex character who functions as drug dealer, doctor and torturer, takes on the surveillance role. He watches the lovers Carl and Rod, and what he sees he punishes. In this way, moments of private intimacy are shown as regulated, policed and punished, in the interests of a heteronormative gender economy.

As in all of Kane's plays, the ideological concerns of *Cleansed* are integral to theatrical form and to the techniques of staging that a particular form demands. In *Cleansed* the design of the playing space (by James Herbert in the 1998 production) was fundamental to the idea of punishment as spectacle. In addition to the perimeter fence setting of a university, there are also a number of interiors: rooms that function as torture chambers. Specifically these are the White Room (sanatorium), Red Room (sports hall), Black Room (shower room converted to peep-show booths) and Round Room (university library). Each has the 'power' to nourish the body: to keep it well (White), to keep it fit (Red), to keep it clean (Black) and educated (Round). Each, however, is re-designed to punish. The set also was physically difficult for the performers to negotiate: acting on a slope or a bed set at an angle, or having a body harnessed and suspended in the air, all of which worked as an externalisation for the difficulty of striving for a feeling, a love, that other (symbolic) forces seek to repress or to deny. Visually, therefore, the setting functions as an oppressive and repressive sight/site of torture – but one occasionally marked by an externalisation of a love that refuses to give in to punishment. Grace, after sleeping with Graham, for example, is beaten up and raped in the Red Room by an unseen group of men. The rape is followed by a round of gunfire as Graham rushes to protect her body. The back wall turns to blood (red paint bursting out of balloons). Yet despite the violence, the pain, their love survives: a shower of daffodils hits the stage.

As the figure of speech suggests, to be in 'unspeakable pain' is to be unable to give expression to the pain through language. Elaine Scarry explains that the body in pain cannot truly express what it feels in words, that pain has a 'language-destroying capacity'.[51] Torturing the body, subjecting it to pain, involves a reversion to a state before language; shows language in the unmaking or 'uncreating'. If I take Scarry's point and relate it to the challenge to the symbolic that I am arguing Cleansed performs, then by analogy, the bodies in pain contest the symbolic and propose an anterior, pre-symbolic state that allows people to desire differently: Grace to love Graham; Carl to love Rod.

If as Scarry argues, the act of torture produces a pain that is 'so incontestably real that it seems to confer its quality of "incontestable reality" on that power that has brought it into being', then it follows that 'It is, of course, precisely because reality of that power is so highly contestable, the regime so unstable, that torture is being used'.[52] While the institution 'houses', gives 'rooms' to all those who are positioned as marginal within the symbolic domain, these repressed, marginalised figures are also dangerous because they threaten to contest, to destabilise the very constraints and systems that seek to keep them in place. Just as Cate in Blasted is positioned as hysteric, and, as both conservative and transgressive, other figures in Cleansed are also victims and transgressors. Grace/Graham and the castrated Carl function as enactments of what Butler describes as 'two inarticulate figures of abject homosexuality, the feminized fag and the phallicized dyke'. The idea, as Butler explains it is that the 'Lacanian scheme presumes that the terror over occupying either of these positions is what compels the assumption of a sexed position within language.'[53] Even under the threat of punishment, however, Kane's figures disturb and refuse to occupy 'appropriate' gender positions.

The contestability of the symbolic domain is further underlined in Cleansed by the way in which Tinker, who punishes and tortures, also, like Ian in *Blasted*, damages himself, through the damage he causes to others. Tinker repeatedly visits the peepshow in the Black Room to watch, to objectify an anonymous woman who performs for him. He pays his tokens, she performs, he masturbates. Yet there is no feeling, love or even sexual satisfaction to be had here. Tinker has to stop his obsession with Grace, get her out of his sight before he can begin to see the woman in the peepshow properly; to arouse desire and love that acknowledges, sees the 'other', not just the self.

Not to be 'seen', not to be loved, makes life not worth living. When Grace fails to notice Robin, he dies. Without their loved ones, and with bodies mutilated and cross-gendered, Carl and Grace/Graham sit, desolate in the rain and in a patch of mud by the perimeter fence. Love is the only way of making sense of a life that is otherwise without meaning, is 'pointless'. Yet, like *Blasted*, *Cleansed* ends with a feeling of hope (however fragile); hope dependent on the possibility of love surviving a contemporary world represented as a violent, authoritarian 'wasteland'.

Crave: 'not what I meant at all'

In contrast to *Blasted* and to *Cleansed* and much to the surprise of reviewers, *Crave* had none of the violent acts or atrocities that everyone had come to expect from Kane. The project began '"by accident" to fill a gap in a rehearsed reading season set up by Paines Plough', for whom she was writer in residence.[54] Mark Ravenhill (then literary manager for Paines Plough) explained that the play was written under the pseudonym Marie Kelvedon: 'Marie gave her the licence to experiment with another part of her voice.'[55] The sense of a split identity, of working with 'another part of her voice' is represented in the double entry of biographical notes in the 1998 Methuen edition of the text that lists Kane and Kelvedon as writers. While the Kane biography constitutes a factual account of her theatre credits to date, the Kelvedon biography is a satirical invention that captures the mischievous note of humour to be found threaded through Kane's work (and in *Phaedra's Love* in particular).[56] While humour is present in the fictional biography published with *Crave*, it is mostly absent from the play itself. Bodies may not be hacked to pieces as they are in *Cleansed*, but, nevertheless, *Crave* charts a process of dissonance and disintegration; one that is arguably much bleaker than before.

Directed by Vicky Featherstone (director for both the original production in 1998 and the revival of *Crave* in 2001), *Crave* was minimally set with a row of four chairs, one for each performer. Accompanying the chair arrangement were just two tables, equipped with water and glasses for the performers to drink from. The set, in subdued colours (greys and blues) did not change. Very occasional lighting changes (quick flashes of light marking the opening, the moment of breakdown (see later) and the closure) accentuated a moment, but that was all. Each of the four figures – an older man (A), younger woman (C), older woman (M) and younger man (B) – were seated for the performance, and while vocally they performed certain kinds of interactions or moments of connecting up, there was no stage action and dramatic development in the traditional sense.

The majority of reviewers likened the style of *Crave* to Beckett – especially in respect of the rhythms of Kane's text and her 'characters' that I shall term speaking bodies. Kane herself explained that she thought of *Crave* as 'more as a text for performance than as a play', further expanding on the idea of performance as 'visceral', as enabling you to be 'in direct physical contact with thought and feeling', and the need for theatre to 'speak so directly to an audience's experience'.[57]

Featherstone's arrangement of the speaking bodies and Kane's style of composition work to suggest a confessional mode: four figures, each in their own psychiatrist's chair.[58] Much of the delivery was directed out towards the spectators (rather than the traditional turn-taking system of dialogue acted out between performers), so the audience is positioned as psychiatrist, as the one who listens. Writing about *Crave* after Kane's suicide, Paul Taylor commented (with a warmth rather different to his initial hostility towards Kane's theatre) on the way 'in which the characters sat on a line of swivel chairs like the guests on some metaphysically confessional TV show. The piece is Jerry Springer meets T.S. Eliot'.[59] The confessional TV chat show is an important point of reference, although Kane manipulates it towards her own, rather different ends. Where the TV show uses studio guests or specially invited audiences to confess to their pain and trauma, it is packaged in such a way for television broadcasting that there is a loss of feeling. The TV format offers a performance of trauma, but not in the way that Kane talked of performance as 'direct' and 'visceral', rather as histrionic or melodramatic in register, and reliant on foregrounding or presenting an individual as suffering subject.[60]

In *Crave* the visual regularity of the performers lined up in their chairs, is contrasted with the aural irregularity of the voices that, together, variously register emotional chaos. Psychology of character and development of narrative give way to individual outpourings in which, if anything is shared, it is the 'craving' for a centre or core out of which to make meaning. A talks of a 'hollow heart' (*Crave*, p.174). B speaks of centres and the lack of balance that arises 'when your sense of centre shifts' (*Crave*, pp.192–3). Language circulates in the already said: is replete with quotes from elsewhere (the Bible, T.S. Eliot, Shakespeare), with clichés, or fragments of popular songs. But language can only ever approximate the 'real'. 'Do you remember me?' M asks at one point (*Crave*, p.156). In response, subsequent lines delivered by different performers suggest a process of recollection, of remembering that is only by approximation: 'C *Looks like* a German,/A *Talks like* a Spaniard,/C *Smokes like* a Serb' (*Crave*, p.156, my emphases). At other times, to underline the feeling of approximation, of never really knowing someone, and never really being able to *say* what they are like, Kane quotes figures of speech from each of these three languages (German, Spanish, Serbo-Croatian). Language is not adequate to the task of 'speaking' love, and is completely inadequate when you find yourself without the love of the one you love. As B, echoing T.S. Eliot, states 'that is not what I meant at all' (*Crave*, p.192).

I would go further with this line of argument to suggest a shift in *Crave* that makes the play much bleaker than either *Blasted* or *Cleansed*. The glimmer of hope in *Blasted* as Ian comes into contact with the semiotic 'feminine', or the redemptive quality of love in *Cleansed* have all but gone. The loss of hope, love (and faith) is also marked by a repression of the Imaginary (and of the possibility of jouissance). The Law of the Father, so dangerous in *Cleansed*, is everywhere and ever present; inescapable and unavoidable, even when the child is in the womb, and most 'at one' with the mother.[61] *Crave* (and

95

we should note the active, rather than passive construction of the title, in contrast to *Blasted* and *Cleansed*) is a permanent state of being in exile from the pre-Oedipal or semiotic. The fantasmatic figure of the 'Good Mother' (à la Klein) is much sought after by the figures in *Crave*, but she is constantly elusive. The breast, the 'balloon of milk' (that in Cixous's, albeit somewhat essentialist terms, signifies the presence of the protective, nurturing, pre-Oedipal mother), two lines later, has become a 'bubble of blood' (*Crave*, p.177). Moreover, the breast that is described is the breast in the gaze of A, a self-confessed paedophile, and, arguably, is one of the most difficult of the 'love the monster' moments in Kane's work.

Not unlike Churchill's *The Skriker*, *Crave* is replete with memories, moments that hint at dangerous childhoods, or the child at risk. At one point, A actually describes an act of abuse against a child (*Crave*, p.158). I should stress, however, that abuse is not represented as it is in Sarah Daniels's theatre as a social issue (see Chapter 3), but as a contestation of the possibility of a place of safety; a place of well-being and being well. The life-giving, life-affirming properties of the fantasmatic mother constantly are denied. The possibility of refuge in the Other is repressed. 'You are dead to me', says C in a cyclical echo of her opening line to the play, repeated again a few lines down: 'Somewhere outside the city, I told my mother, You're dead to me' (*Crave*, p.155). Ultimately, there is no way out of the meaning-less, faith-less, being-loved-less state that *Crave* invites us to feel. No way out that is, other than death.

As the figures in *Crave* endure lives without meaning and live through, feel through, love through, black existential despair, it brings them to a point of breakdown – signified through an exiting of language as each figure *'emits a short one syllable scream'* (*Crave*, pp.186–7). Thereafter, the play appears to locate to some kind of psychiatric institution;[62] the point of breakdown leading ultimately to the release of death (suggested through the Lord's prayer styled ending). In one sense, one might argue that this end section provides an echo to *Cleansed*; shows the impossibility of surviving if you do not have love in your life. Why feed a body, why keep it alive, if it is not nourished through being loved (see *Crave*, p.187)? Looked at another way, this ending also prefigures Kane's final work *4.48 Psychosis*.

In the way I have presented them here, *Blasted, Cleansed* and *Crave* form a cycle of plays in the 1990s that variously treats and critiques the damaging and brutalising force of the masculine – not celebrates it. Kane was an avid football fan and drew a parallel between theatre and football: 'watching the actors perform is a little like watching [Manchester] United – when they fly, they take off together, and when they don't, the collapse is truly ensemble'.[63] But her analogy has everything to do with the physical energies and skills of a 'team' of performers, and not with a cult of the masculine, with which she was so inaccurately identified in the 1990s. Kane was looking for a football style of performance energy to 'play' love and, ultimately, to show how lost we are in a contemporary world without it. Cate, though she tries, cannot 'save' the baby from the military in *Blasted*. In *Crave* the child is again at risk; the damage of the militaristic masculine poignantly marked in A's recollection of the photograph of the Vietnamese girl on fire that shocked the world: 'her entire existence given meaning and permanence in the thirty seconds she fled from her village, skin melting, mouth open' (*Crave*, p.180). In *Cleansed* Grace and Karl manage to survive the institutionalising forces of the symbolic through love, without which their lives would otherwise be 'pointless'.

To survive the brutality of a damaged and damaging world, requires a love that is absolute, is extreme, because without it, as Kane showed in the taking of her own life, we may not survive.

6   Performing identities

Ideas of 'inappropriate' bodies, challenged by Kane in *Cleansed*, circulated in the 1990s: a decade that inherited the homophobic panic generated by the Aids crisis of the 1980s. In the popular imagination, fuelled by media representation, Aids had renewed the idea of homosexuality as a disease, a 'disease more dangerous than diptheria' as Clive claims in Churchill's *Cloud Nine*.[1] 'Healthy' (heterosexual) citizens needed to be protected from the (gay) disease; the family needed to be kept safe from 'contagion'. In 1988 the government passed the anti-gay legislation popularly known as Clause 28: legislation that prevents local councils from funding work perceived as promoting homosexuality. As legislation it creates, as one analyst explains, a 'structure in which an otherwise unspeakable "private" concern can be brought into the public sphere and given a proper place in "public" official discourse'.[2] In brief, Clause 28 legitimised homophobic fears.[3] Among lesbians and gays that only fuelled the desire to see an end to discrimination and for greater recognition in all walks of life. Arguably the decade did give way (albeit grudgingly) to more liberal views though, despite the election of the New Labour government in 1997, Clause 28 has yet to be repealed in England.[4]

   Views on identity also shifted among lesbians and gays themselves. A younger generation advocated queer politics: looked to more flexible views on identity, ways of crossing a range of identities, rather than occupying just one. In terms of a lesbian politics this involved a shift from the desire to claim a lesbian identity to a questioning (or queering) of identity that involved the interrogation of the category 'lesbian' itself. In theoretical terms, the issue is the difficulty (or not) of accepting a lesbian subject position, given the essentialist claim this implies: an identity category that as Sue-Ellen Case explains, 'posits the formation of the subject position as prior to other social constructions – possibly even determining them'.[5] In consequence, queer politics emerged in the 1990s seemingly as a 'corrective' to lesbian identity politics, and ideas of gender-bending performativity (à la Butler) challenged the ontological claim *to be lesbian*. The problem with the queering of identity, on the other hand, is that it risks the possibility that 'anything goes' and makes likely the evacuation of a contingent feminist position, so central to identity politics.[6] For many theorists the answer has been to invoke the category at the same time as insisting on its contingency: taking 'the essentialist risk'[7] of performing lesbian, at the same time as desiring beyond the limitations of identity politics.

In her study of lesbian theatre from the 1970s to the 1990s, Sandra Freeman devotes a chapter to 'a handful of authors', specifically, Nina Rapi, Phyllis Nagy, Bryony Lavery and Sarah Daniels.[8] Freeman makes the important point that while these writers engage with 'images of lesbians on stage', it does not mean that they 'necessarily see themselves as part of lesbian theatre in England, nor even call themselves lesbian playwrights'.[9] Freeman stops short, however, of teasing out the complexities of lesbian naming. As Butler argues, 'identity categories tend to be instruments of regulatory regimes', either, she explains, in the interests of oppressive 'normalizing categories', or 'as the rallying points for a liberatory contestation of that very oppression'.[10] The 'certainty' of a writer's sexuality, when it informs critical approaches to their writing can prove reductive either way: as a homophobic denouncing (as has happened in the case of Sarah Daniels), or by making the work 'fit' the lesbian 'cause'.[11]

Bearing this difficulty in mind, I present a chapter on identity that seeks to pull in different directions, to name and to un-name. The two playwrights whose work is under discussion, Bryony Lavery and Phyllis Nagy, come from different theatre generations and diverse cultural backgrounds, and variously engage with a politics of identity. Lesbian representation has claimed Lavery's attention over many years of writing for and performing in gay and feminist theatre communities, while Nagy, on the other hand, tends to contest gay and feminist orthodoxies in the interests of stirring up gender trouble. Her theatre is less about claiming an identity than exploring the possibilities that arise when identity gets displaced. Given this point of contrast, what this chapter will show, in line with shifts in thinking in the 1990s, is the desire for more flexible views on identity, both within the work itself and ways in which the work is critically approached.

Bryony Lavery: another love story

Bryony Lavery has produced a prolific body of work that, in addition to the lesbian feminist theatre for which she is best known, also includes plays for children, cabaret shows, and radio and television drama. Les Oeufs Malades, a group she formed with friends, staged early pieces, and feminist theatre influences in the 1970s came from working with companies such as Monstrous Regiment and The Women's Theatre Group. She was an artistic director of Gay Sweatshop from 1989 to 1991, and has performed in and also written for the gay pantomimes at London's Drill Hall. Despite this volume of work, and a career that, like Churchill's, began in the late 1960s, Lavery has not achieved comparable public attention. In contrasting Churchill's playwriting career with Lavery's, Mary McCusker of Monstrous Regiment noted that Churchill had come to attention through her relationship with the Royal Court, whereas Lavery 'has suffered from lack of public profile'.[12] That said, Lavery's relationship with the Birmingham Repertory Theatre in the 1990s, especially her production of *Frozen* in 1998 and *A Wedding Story* in 2000, has since enhanced the attention and recognition that her work deserves.[13]

At the start of the decade, as a well-established writer of gay and feminist plays, Lavery was situated in a theatre context that was struggling to survive. As one of the artistic directors of Gay Sweatshop (along with David Benedict and Cordelia Ditton), Lavery created *Kitchen Matters* that toured in 1990–1. The publicity I kept from this show states: '*Kitchen Matters* – possibly Gay Sweatshop's Last Supper'. The play, a Greek epic based on *The Bacchae* and set in a kitchen, offered a defiant comedy in response to the Arts Council's threat to cut the company's funding. The cultural and political climate post Clause 28, as explained in my introduction, meant that gay work was under renewed threat, but all the more precious and necessary because of this. The recollection I have of this show was of an anarchic, celebratory performance, adored by the Sweatshop audience; an event where people could come together to commiserate and to celebrate.

Her Aching Heart

At the same time as *Kitchen Matters*, Lavery also produced the hugely successful *Her Aching Heart*, for the Women's Theatre Company (Oval House, London, 1990; revived in 1991). Hard times were facing the Women's Theatre Company too, although at the start of the 1990s WTG was more fortunate than Gay Sweatshop, having secured a three-year funding deal with the Arts Council. As in *Kitchen Matters*, *Her Aching Heart* drew attention to the squeeze on theatre funding and the published playtext is replete with Lavery's wickedly funny stage directions that point to the way in which, as a two-hander, the performers are required to multi-role-play: '*Betsy enters: Although in these penurious times she may seem physically similar to Molly Penhallow . . . she is a completely different character.*'[14] *Her Aching Heart* was also, as director Claire Grove explained, a response to Clause 28: '*Her Aching Heart* is a lesbian historical romance. We decided that we hadn't done anything for a lesbian audience in response to Clause 28 so we wanted very much to re-affirm our commitment to our lesbian policy.'[15] The way that *Her Aching Heart* makes its response is to explore the inside/outside dialect that Diana Fuss, in her introduction to the seminal *Inside/Out: Lesbian Theories/Gay Theories* (1991) states underpins the heterosexual/homosexual binary.[16] *Her Aching Heart* turns heterosexuality 'inside out'; celebrates the possibility of a lesbian 'inside' by dramaturgically overplaying or citing (and so calling into question), the heterosexual as 'normative'.

Briefly, *Her Aching Heart* parallels two lesbian love stories. Molly and Harriet in the present cure their aching hearts by falling in love with each other. At the same time, they are reading a lesbian historical romance that recounts the thwarted love affair between Lady Harriet of Helstone Hall and Molly Penhallow. Much of the play's abundant comic energy comes from Lavery's multi-role composition and attendant performance register that gender-bends performatively to border on the frantic, the hysterical. Ideologically this hyped-up style of theatricality serves to highlight what Lynda Hart describes in *Fatal Women: Lesbian Sexuality and the Mark of Aggression* as the '*paranoid* nature of heterosexual patriarchy', 'linked to the disavowal of homosexuality'.[17] The play provides a dramatic tracing of the historical 'disavowal' of lesbianism, as Lady Harriet and Molly cannot, for several scenes, or rather, for most of the play, admit to their feelings for each other, largely because same sex desire is deemed (in the interests of heteropatriarchy) not to exist. Moreover, animosity between the women is fuelled by class, so that they are also kept apart by material, social and cultural factors. As women they have little in common.

The monologue form is generally a strength and dominant characteristic of Lavery's playwriting. In *Her Aching Heart* specifically, Lavery intersperses the dialogues between the Molly/Harriet couples with monologues. The monologue form allows for the revelations of thoughts and feelings to the audience. In terms of a lesbian aesthetic, it allows for the telling or making visible of a repressed sexuality, and is typical, for example, of coming out plays, such as Jill Posener's seminal *Any Woman Can* 1975.[18] As Hart argues, coming out functions as a 'de-secreting' or 'disclosure of a homosexual identity' that is potentially disruptive of dominant social and cultural systems that demand the 'fictional coherency of a symbolic order'.[19] That Molly and Harriet in the historical romance find it difficult to come out to each other is testimony to the force of the symbolic fiction. This speaks directly to the play's moment of homophobic (post Clause 28) cultural production and a need for Lavery's anarchic and celebratory play in which lesbian desire bursts on to the stage, as a refusal of the heteropatriarchal fiction that gives lie to lesbian lives.

Lavery's use of the 'lesbian historical romance' serves to historicise or to rupture the heteropatriarchal. Central to this rupture is Lavery's construct of Lady Harriet, represented after Freud as narcissistic woman. When Lady Harriet first appears in *Her Aching Heart* she makes it clear she has no interest in men, family or society. Hers is the 'lovely countenance' of femininity, that she gazes on in the mirror, a 'countenance', however, that also registers 'a devil of discontent' (*Her Aching Heart*, p.90). This does not mean that Lady Harriet represents a deviant sexuality, rather the 'devil of discontent' is contained within the feminine; is already dangerously present. Harriet's escapades mobilise the 'devil of discontent', to the extent that she is prepared to 'kill' (or think she has killed) twice in the interests of self-preservation and the avoidance of marriage.

Paralleling the two stories involves working across two different temporal modes. The historical romance temporally works back through a time that has already been. As an echo to Daphne du Maurier's *Rebecca*, Molly, from the past, enters with the line: 'Last night I dreamt I went to Helstone Hall again' (*Her Aching Heart*, p.88).[20] In retracing the romance between Harriet and Molly in the historical, fictional frame, the play moves forward to a conclusion that is a given: is already known, has already happened. Their love has no 'future'. By contrast, in the contemporary moment, love between Molly and Harriet is at the beginning of its 'future', one that, as it were, looks beyond the fictional frame, to the possibilities of a love to be. The (present/future) moment of being in love is on the one hand intensely private and personal, and on the other links, frequently via the songs that connect one 'time' to another, to a public social and cultural history that locates the personal within a complex matrix of oppression.

Lesbian does not figure in 'straight' opposition to the heterosexual but rather troubles the hetero–homo binary by having to pass through it in order to become visible. This is less a mode of establishing an alternative, radical, sexually defined category of lesbian (in opposition to the dominant), than lesbian defined as an *act of appropriation*. In an attempt to make the historical romance lesbian, to make it their *own*, for example, Molly and Harriet appropriate and impersonate the figures and conventions of the genre and 'ownership' is, therefore, a matter of 'theft'. Lesbian as thief mobilises the sign of the criminal, the deviant that attaches to her figure. As such, she is constantly under threat of punishment and may not, as the outcome for Molly and Harriet shows, survive the 'compulsory' fiction of the heteropatriarchal. 'I am not myself again', is the opening line to the song, 'In Love Again' (sung as a reprise at the close of the play), reinvesting the heterosexual cliché of the 'abnormal' state of being in love, with lesbian traces of instability, loss, and lack of (self) recognition. While fragile and vulnerable, however, lesbian love is worth the repeated 'offence'.

Nothing Compares to You

While Lavery continued her commitment to writing within and for a lesbian/gay defined context in the 1990s, she also worked in venues that are not associated with lesbian theatre (as are the Oval House and Drill Hall), but might be better described as 'gay friendly'.[21] *Nothing Compares to You*, *Frozen* and *A Wedding Story* were all commissioned by the Birmingham Rep. (which also in the 1990s developed a relationship with Tamasha Theatre Company, see Chapter 7). Where *Her Aching Heart* was a response to Claire Grove's 'brief to write a "two-hander exploring sexuality and gender"', *Nothing Compares to You* was a commission from Gwenda Hughes to write a '"small, girls' love story . . . something light, something gothic"' (Preface, *Plays 1*, pp. xii–xiii)'. What emerged was another, albeit rather different, love story to *Her Aching Heart*, and a large (eight person) cast for the studio stage.

Nothing Compares to You takes its title from the Sinéad O'Connor track and Sinéad tracks are used to thematise or to punctuate a particular moment. Act One predominantly works through monologues to present a seemingly disconnected group of people. Gradually, detective style, the play offers clues and clarifications as to the connections between people, building into a more interactive second act. Connections surface as a consequence of another Lavery device: the accident or tragic event. So many of Lavery's plays involve an accident that is the catalyst for (life-affirming) realisations among a surviving group of people.[22] In *Nothing Compares to You* the play opens with the death of Mary, dying in a car accident, caused, it is revealed only in the play's penultimate scene, by John, driving recklessly in a suicidal state of panic after his wife has left him.[23] The monologues in Act One gradually reveal Mary's friends, her lover, Lily, and Rachel, the woman she has secretly begun an affair with, to establish a gay community of whom it is said Mary's family have no knowledge.

Characters in *Nothing Compares to You* are already 'out', but what is disruptive in this drama is the idea that a play based on a friendship circle, like the popular 1990s television series *Friends*, for example, is set in a gay, rather than heterosexual group of friends and lovers.[24] Generic expectations of the friendship drama's heterosexual representation and attendant themes and concerns (boyfriend–girlfriend romances, engagements, marriage, etc.) are upset. The familiar is, therefore, made unfamiliar.[25] Not that Lavery's circle is exclusively gay: there is Miriam (Rachel's mother) and the quest for her lost cat; John whose wife has left him and causes Mary's accident, and Joy, who as her name suggestions embarks on endless quests for happiness, sought mostly through a combination of one-night stands (with men), booze and drugs. While Lavery's theatre is less 'extreme' than Kane's, what might be observed is that her characters, like Kane's, desire to be loved and to be in love. *Nothing Compares to You* shows how the 'life' goes out of people's lives when relationships (even with the cat!) go wrong.

Act Two uses the device of a New Year's Eve party to suggest the possibility of people on the eve of changing their lives, although not without quarrels, disappointments and betrayals.[26] For those for whom life does not renew, come the haunting figures, or death portents, the fylgias, drawn from Norwegian folklore. Like Churchill's *The Skriker*, *Nothing Compares to You* has its own kind of 'underworld', the haunting world of the fylgias, made physical by two performers in the production. As with the fictional device of the historical romance in *Her Aching Heart*, the play with the mimetic in *Nothing Compares to You*, where the dead do not stay dead and spiritual creatures haunt the stage, is designed to alter our vision. In this instance, it works rather like a Lacanian 'fishing' for happiness. Fishing is a physical, visual motif of the fylgias who hook-up (love) objects and trash; beauty and detritus. The parallel is made between 'joy', ecstasy or the sublime, and death (for Freud, the ultimate object of desire). Mary, her body sliced in two, an 'open' wound, comes finally to a moment of death that is also a final, ecstatic call upon the 'present joy' of loving (*Plays 1*, p.209). In the context of the play, *Nothing Compares to You* equates nothing/death with the moment of absolute desire, of loving another, beyond which there is, as Mary cries, 'Nothing more'; 'Nothing after' (p.209).

A Wedding Story

Lavery's relationship with Birmingham Rep. continued to endure, with *Frozen* produced on the main stage in 1998 under Bill Alexander's direction (see Chapter 3). With Birmingham she had found a 'home', one in which she felt very 'included', quite literally because she actually lived in the theatre flats during production projects. Artistically, it also gave her the opportunity to work with and for a particular space.[27] In November 2000, Birmingham premiered *A Wedding Story* that, along with *Frozen*, figures as her most critically successful work to date. Directed by Annie Castledine in a co-production with The Sphinx Theatre Company, *A Wedding Story* twinned Lavery's feminist theatre-making career with her Birmingham 'home', before transferring to London's new writing (and newly opened) venue, the Soho Theatre in 2001.

A Wedding Story is a story of two 'marriages'. One is the story of Evelyn and Peter, mother and father to Sally and to Robin. Evelyn and Peter's marriage undergoes a transformation as it becomes understood that Evelyn is suffering from Alzheimer's. Interwoven with the narrative of Peter and Evelyn's marriage is their daughter Sally's relationship with Grace that develops during the course of the play from a first sexual encounter (at a wedding) to their 'marriage' in the final scene. Both narratives therefore focus on a transformational moment in two different kinds of relationships, one heterosexual marriage near the end of its 'life'; the other a same-sex relationship that is just beginning. As in *Her Aching Heart*, uncertainty colours the possibility that the relationship between Sally and Grace will endure beyond the initial moment of sexual attraction.

Also framing *A Wedding Story* is Lavery's introduction of a cinematic text: *Casablanca*. *Casablanca* is Evelyn's favourite film and, with the onset of Alzheimer's, provides a touchstone of recognition. She can react (with joy) to a detail from the film, but she no longer grasps the whole 'picture'. In her disintegrating, rapidly fading memory, the film, a fiction, is as real to her as her family. As the illness advances she may fail to recognise her husband, yet at other times, encouraged by her son Robin (a lecturer in film studies) she has no difficulty in entering into, acting out the fiction of the film.[28] Lives are increasingly mediatised Lavery's play suggests (wedding videos being a case in point).

The narrative doubling of *A Wedding Story*, the cross-infection of the stories, means that the idea of marriage, the wedding, is 'contaminated' by a celebration of same-sex relations. I suggest the idea of contamination as an echo to Mary Douglas's thinking about pollution and taboo in her seminal study, *Purity and Danger*. In Douglas's analysis of social schemata, dirt, defilement is a way of signalling 'matter out of place'. 'Our pollution behaviour', Douglas explains, 'is the reaction which condemns any object or idea likely to confuse or contradict cherished classifications.'[29] Yet, as Douglas observes, the 'cherished' systems of classification, regulation or order depend upon an idea of what is not classifiable, is irregular or disorderly. What is 'proper' may therefore be 'defiled' by what is 'improper'.

At the heart of the play's disorder is Evelyn. Her illness marks her out as an irregular body: a figure displaced from her social roles as wife and mother and her professional role as a doctor – a role that serves to heighten the tragedy of her condition, given that as a doctor she understands the illness, but is unable to treat herself. Ultimately, there is nothing she can do to prevent the illness taking away her memory, her identity. Gradually, the 'proper' body gives way to the abject body that hiccups, farts, shits in public (at her daughter's 'wedding'), and speaks out of turn. It gets harder and harder as the illness progresses for the family to 'police' this body, to keep it in 'order'.

Yet through the disorderly comes the possibility of seeing differently: of seeing beyond the 'cherished' order that keeps things (people) in their place. Evelyn's disintegration, the unravelling of the person she was – still is, but yet is not – marks her out as in a state of transition. In such a state, Douglas observes, 'the person who must pass from one to another is himself in danger and emanates danger to others' (*Purity and Danger*, p.97). Between the life she once had and the death that awaits, Evelyn creates the space for herself and those around her to be displaced. Such a shift may, for example, be detected in the contrast between the opening wedding occasion (narrated by Peter and then by Sally) from which Evelyn has been excluded on account of her illness, to her inclusion, her presence, at the 'marriage' of Grace and Sally. As a figure on the margins, evacuated from her professional and domestic roles on account of her illness, Evelyn is reclaimed and repositioned within the family who have learnt (painfully and hysterically) to include rather than to exclude her.

Paralleling Evelyn's 'outside' to 'inside' trajectory, is that of Sally and Grace, who start out at the table of misfits at the opening wedding and end up enjoying a 'wedding' of their own. Like her mother, Sally is an irregular figure, one infected by the madness of love. As her father quoting, lecture style, from medieval literature (his specialist subject) declares, love is a 'wondre maladie' (*Wedding Story*, p.32); it also has the power to change lives, to turn them upside down. Like Evelyn's illness, the madness of love infects the play and in particular challenges the 'cherished' image of the pure, white (heterosexual) 'wedding story', by conjuring up the unruly body that desires and lusts; a Rabelaisian body that delights in sex, farts and defecation. Usually this is edited out of the 'wedding story' that refuses bodily functions, sexual drives, and so forth, through the (heterosexual) romancing of bodies that are pure, bound, not messy and not interested in sex.[30] In Lavery's play wedding clichés get 'roughed up' by events. An engagement, for example, is not a proposal to marry, but is used to describe (as a scene title) the first sexual encounter between Sally and Grace in a ladies toilet. When Sally instructs Grace about courtship, she uses the *Gestus* of a whoopee cushion: the farting object is used to illustrate and to deflate the idea of how people only reveal their good points in order to gain the affection of the one they love. (It is also used to demonstrate kissing, mounting passion and orgasms, see *Wedding Story*, pp.37–8).

That the whole family is transformed by Evelyn's illness, is suggested in Lavery's scripting of the piece, specifically her use of incomplete sentences throughout; sentences without punctuation that allow for 'gaps', silences to breathe new meanings into 'forgotten' words.

Hence it is not just Evelyn's language that breaks up, but the language of every character in the play; it is her 'world' that disorders the speech of the others, inviting them to think, see and feel differently (an invitation that also extends to the audience). Dramaturgically, therefore, Lavery finds an aesthetic for performing, for communicating the illness, and carries this through to the visual setting for the play that also suggests fluidity, a breaking up, a state of liminality. Though set at a wedding marquee in the production, the setting loses definition, is transformed through the play of light and fog. Like Casablanca in the film setting, it is a space in limbo: a place where people wait for their passage out. In Evelyn's case, the stage space is evocative of being in between the life she once had and the death to come.

Also like Casablanca, amidst a world at war and in chaos, this is a space for romance. For Sally and Grace it sets the scene for desire, romance, courtship and 'marriage', all of which is not without danger: risks (like Evelyn) a loss of self. In psychoanalytic terms, Peggy Phelan explains the encounter between self and other as both 'alluring and violent'. The violence we know about through feminist analysis of visibility and representation she explains, whereas the 'profound romance' of the encounter is something she argues that 'we still have relatively little knowledge of'.[31] In desiring a recognition and love of the other based on mutuality and equality, Sally and Grace challenge the dangers of a violent (heterosexual) economy, of self and other, yet at the same time violence to the self constantly haunts the possibility of a more equal exchange. When Grace presses Sally for her commitment, Sally complains she feels trapped, that she cannot breathe and an imaging of bars cut through the proposal. 'Can we open the window?/Escape' Sally asks as a plane passes overhead (*Wedding Story*, p.56). To be together, but not chained or coupled, looking 'out' rather than 'in' (p.71), is the challenge their relationship faces.

Issues of identity are further raised through Alzheimer's. Loss of self is not restricted to Evelyn as her failure to recognise, to acknowledge others, in turn produces anxiety in those she can no longer 'see', precisely because they cannot then see themselves. This is particularly acute in the case of the child denied the gaze of the mother. Both Sally and Robin find this hard to cope with and infantilise themselves

in attempts to reclaim their identity as Evelyn's children, or fantasise themselves committing matricide, releasing them all from the
pain of Evelyn's (maternal) disintegration. The position of the child,
however, is one that Evelyn, because of her illness, has 'claimed' for
herself. The battle over roles is hilariously, hysterically and movingly
staged in Scene Twenty where it takes the united efforts of the family to change an incontinent, protesting Evelyn, determined to escape
their administration. The overall effect is one of parents struggling to
deal with an unruly, difficult baby.

This scene also marks the transgressive shift towards the possibility of pleasuring in less restrictive behaviour, in a wedding story
that in Sally's words is 'bizarre', 'odd', 'unreligious' and 'unblessed'
(p.89), and loudly punctuated by a beatific, defecating Evelyn. As is
typical of Lavery's theatre, the darkest of moments are tinged with optimism, with hope. The alchemisation of Evelyn's illness from something that is base into something that is precious is also relevant to
or mixed up in her daughter's love story.[32] To be 'out' in one story,
is to be 'in' the other and while queering romance may risk assimila-
tion into an heterosexual economy,[33] it also figures the possibility of a
way out, where 'everyone finally gets some sort of exit-veezays . . . it's
where every one *flies*' (*Wedding Story*, p.91).

Phyllis Nagy: performing gender trouble

New York City born Phyllis Nagy settled in London a few months after attending a two-week residency with the Royal Court in 1991.
Arriving in Britain on a writer's temporary permit, Nagy chose
to stay and now holds British citizenship. Like Wertenbaker (see
Chapter 8), issues of citizenship and nationhood not surprisingly,
therefore, haunt her playwriting. Unlike Lavery, Nagy's English career
was instantly high profile as the Court launched her with a production of *Weldon Rising* (1992), a play that she wrote in the months
prior to coming back to London for good and that had the backing of in-
coming Court director, Stephen Daldry. Gay Sweatshop, now with rev-
enue funding and under the dual direction of another American, Lois
Weaver (of Split Britches), and James Neale-Kennerley, commissioned
and toured *Entering Queens* (1993). A further two plays that she had

actually written before coming to London, but had not had produced, were staged: *Butterfly Kiss* (Almeida Theatre, 1994) and *Disappeared* (Leicester Haymarket, 1995).[34] 1995 also saw the premiere of her most ambitious play to date, *The Strip*. This was followed in 1998 by the equally complex *Never Land* (co-production, The Foundry and Royal Court), and her adaptation of the Patricia Highsmith novel *The Talented Mr Ripley* (Palace Theatre, Watford), marking a shift towards the European within a matrix of cultural, social and sexual identities.

Nagy's reception as an American, feminist and 'out' lesbian playwright on the English stage has been beset by the difficulty that reviewers have had in trying to categorise her work. In the introduction to the first collection of Nagy's plays, theatre critic Michael Coveney explains that 'She [Nagy] has not (obviously) been lumped in with the new laddish and loutish drama . . . Nor does she quite tally with the feminist writers of the Royal Court in the 1980s, many of whom bit the bullet on sexual politics, parturition and mother–daughter relationships without really challenging ideas of form and style.'[35] Coveney's statement is interesting both for the way in which it signals the general reliance on labels in theatrical reception, and for the way in which his qualifiers – 'not (obviously)' and not 'quite tally[ing]' – imply that there might be hints of both laddism and feminism to be found in her work – though, perhaps, not quite as we might expect to find them. Not 'obviously' a new lad, and not 'quite' a feminist suggests traces of both, while firmly 'belonging' to neither.

However, it is the desire to resist categorisation that might be argued is a signature of Nagy's theatre. Like Butler, Nagy is keen to make gender (and other kinds of) trouble. Her characters appear as 'foreigners' to sexual, social, cultural and national systems that seek to fix or locate them. They do not embrace an identity so much as pass through a series of dis-identifications; desire to be 'other' than they are – though not to be 'othered'. Such a view is also Nagy's as a writer, 'out' as a lesbian writer, but desiring not to be contained by that identity in ways that counter the transgressive and contestatory impulse of her work.[36]

In terms of concerns that might be identified as feminist, since her arrival on the London stage Nagy has been particularly outspoken about the greater opportunities available to men (straight or gay), and the laddish culture of the British theatre in the 1990s. In an article for the *Guardian* in 1995 co-authored with her literary agent Mel Kenyon, Nagy expressed her disappointment over the backlash against feminism. Of feminism itself, Nagy and Kenyon wrote that 'in a world where fashion counts for everything, feminism is the mink stole of the nineties: we may secretly want one but we're damned if we're going to admit it'.[37]

While pointing out the gender inequalities of the theatre industry, and of society at large, Nagy is, at the same time, critical of a certain kind of woman-centred theatre-making. In her interview in *Rage and Reason* she identifies this kind of theatre as 'wombic': as essentially concerned with a 'narrow, domesticated' view of women's lives.[38] The kind of theatre she is drawn to making is illustrated in this brief comment from the *Guardian*, in which she describes the two scenes from contemporary drama that have inspired her to write for the theatre:

> Betty's masturbation monologue from Caryl Churchill's
> *Cloud Nine* and the scene in which Liz Morden is measured
> for her hanging from Timberlake Wertenbaker's *Our Country's
> Good*. Though different in their stylistic concerns and
> methods, Churchill and Wertenbaker point the way forward
> by their daring, passion and elegance. Their work is a constant
> inquiry into the ways in which form and content must
> respond to the time in which we live. Miles ahead of us all.[39]

Like the two scenic examples she cites, Nagy's own playwriting connects to concerns of gender and sexuality on a broad canvas of social and cultural issues, and through a dramaturgical frame that seeks to politicise through formal experimentation.

Weldon Rising

The expectation that as a lesbian writer Nagy would confine herself to a lesbian-identified position troubled both of her first playwriting experiences in London: for the Court with *Weldon Rising* and for Gay Sweatshop with *Entering Queens*. *Entering Queens* was an unhappy experience for company and writer given the clash between the company's brief to perform gay identified theatre and Nagy's more radical contestation (rather than celebration) of identity politics. With *Weldon Rising* Nagy upset the expectation that as a lesbian playwright, she would deliver a treatment of gay issues. While *Weldon Rising* deals with a community (or, more accurately, the lack of community) between various gay characters, she does not present 'gayness as an *issue*', which upset the gay (although not the mainstream) press.[40]

Set in New York City's meat-packing district, *Weldon Rises* centres on reactions to the murder of a gay man, Jimmy, by a passing stranger whom Nagy calls the 'Boy'. Working with flashbacks, the play operates through a number of different perspectives on the murder: the different views of the characters (Jimmy's lover, Natty Weldon; the lesbian lovers, Jaye and Tilly, and Marcel, a transvestite) and the ways in which the murder changes all of their lives. The piece has an apocalyptic feel: the setting is represented as getting hotter and hotter, creating the effect of a world that is reaching the point of melt down.

In brief, inspired by her own feelings about the growing violence in New York and her inability to find a safe environment, even in what she describes as 'the hitherto gay-sympathetic enclave of far West Village'[41] *Weldon Rising* confounded the expectation of the gay play. Yet it is precisely in the way in which Nagy shows that a gay community can no longer exist as an 'enclave' that her work connects to the contemporary moment. What she explores are positions of marginality and oppression matrixed within the dominant, rather than represented as a sub-set or enclave. *Weldon Rising* is, I would argue, at a crossroads where a contemporary feminist past meets a present that is looking to move out of the recognisable structures and arguments of identity politics, whilst not losing touch with the political impetus of its 'past'. In this respect, it is significant that *Weldon Rising* was the last play to appear in the last volume of the Methuen 'plays by women' series.[42] Its presence in the volume contests the homogeneity of the series label, at the same time as signalling the relative paucity of play publishing opportunities for women playwrights that make the homogeneity necessary – and, finally, in 1994, unsustainable.

Butterfly Kiss and Disappeared

If *Weldon Rising* is illustrative of Nagy's move beyond the recognisable concerns of a lesbian-identified, gay theatre, *Butterfly Kiss* is a heightened example of her resistance to a 'wombic' style of feminist theatre. Performed at the Almeida Theatre in 1994 (though written much earlier), *Butterfly Kiss* dramatises a maternal line across three generations of women: grandmother (Sally Ramona), daughter (Jenny Ross) and granddaughter (Lily Ross). Unlike Charlotte Keatley's *My Mother Said I Never Should* (1987) – a three-generation-mothers-play, that typifies the acceptable face of bourgeois-feminist mother–daughter theatre – Nagy's *Butterfly Kiss* re-presents the filial/maternal as a site of violence and murder. Nagy explains that she is looking for more honesty in her treatment of mother–daughter relations: 'I'm so tired of seeing mother–daughter plays where they're all so nice to each other'.[43] *Butterfly Kiss* has nothing at all to do with mothers and daughters being 'nice to each other'. The trail of violence that passes from mother to daughter and the act of matricide, while psychologically compelling, is ultimately political in its imaging of a violent exit from the familial.[44] The play exposes the fictions and forces that keep women 'inside' kinship structures of family and nation and their social regulation of sexuality, all of which militates against their desire to live and to love differently.

In the opening lines to *Butterfly Kiss*, Sally recollects telling her 'pregnant and screaming' daughter to 'bite the bullet of motherhood' (*Butterfly Kiss*, p.51). What is figuratively stated in the opening is literally enacted in the play's closure as Lily puts a gun to her mother's head and pulls the trigger. As the ending is already figured in the beginning – the crime committed and Lily locked up in her jail cell – dramatic attention focuses not on the crime itself, but on the motivation. In contrast to *Weldon Rising*, which examines a murder from different viewpoints, *Butterfly Kiss* concentrates on Lily's story, as events and relations unfold through her memoryscape. Lily's memoryscape does not produce a linear, cause and effect narrative, but works laterally and associatively and is visually represented through the staging of the play in Lily's cell. It is only in the 'secure' site of the cell, that memories, with no 'place' of their own, are unlocked.

Dramaturgically the play works through two different registers: direct address, that is used mostly by Lily, Lily's lawyer, Jack Trouver, and her lesbian lover, Martha McKenzie, and the scene-based fragments of family drama, as seen through Lily's eyes. It is significant that the lawyer and the lover, the one paid to listen and 'fact' find, the other listening because she cares (and is the only person in Lily's life to really care), are positioned to help with the storytelling and storyfinding.[45] In contrast, the blood relations – grandmother, mother or butterfly collecting father – have no direct address contact with the audience.

That organisations of kinship impose damaging constraints on women's lives is represented visually through Nagy's black comic device of having Jenny's body permanently hooked up to a blood pressure taking unit (signifying an entire body/life disorder). The desire for a life more exciting than married, family life, that has left her with a demanding mother and disinterested husband, also is suggested through Jenny's identification with Tallulah Bankhead. Tallulah, as Lavery's biography of the stage and screen actress reveals,[46] was a woman committed to behaving 'badly' and to sexual crushes and affairs that did not recognise boundaries – marital, sexual or otherwise. The figure in Nagy's play that approximates this is Christine, Countess Van Dyne, mistress to Lily's father, an exotic creature (Christine is always slipping into French) who has turned her back on motherhood. Lily is attracted to Christine, finds her 'beautiful', but is also resentful of the attention she receives from her father.[47] Moreover, the duality of Christine and Jenny, mistress and wife/mother, is a damaging consequence of social boundaries that legislate for what women are or are not allowed to be.

Through its portrait of the Ross family as cruel, violent and dysfunctional, *Butterfly Kiss* challenges the myth of the all-American family with 'two and a half kids, a mortgaged home approximately twenty miles from a major city' (*Butterfly Kiss*, p.83).

This is underlined by the numerous familial murder stories that are narrated throughout the play. In the Almeida production, the violence of nation, family and home was heightened through the projection, at the start of scenes, of red, white and blue colours.[48] In brief, it is the (American) family that emerges as the site of violence, the scene of crime, in *Butterfly Kiss*. All of Lily's attempts at friendships and relations (with Teddy, Martha or Christine) are haunted and damaged by it (and by the figure of her father in particular).[49] Lily would like to go travelling in Europe with Martha. This, though, is unlikely, not just because she is locked up for murder, but, metaphorically, because she needs to be free from the damage of the familial past in order to be able to 'travel' to a new future. Such an exiting, of mother and daughter, in the interests of a different life, a different 'future', necessarily will, Nagy signals, be a violent one.

The idea of exiting is central to *Disappeared*, Nagy's next play to be produced on the English stage (by the Leicester Haymarket and Midnight Theatre Company, February 1995; Royal Court June 1995). More conventional than *Butterfly* Kiss (both formally and ideologically) *Disappeared* focuses on the idea of a murder that may or may not have taken place as travel agent Sarah Casey 'disappears' after an evening spent in her local bar in Hell's Kitchen, New York City. She was last seen in the company of bartender and friend, Jack Fallon, and a stranger, Elston Rupp (manager of a thrift store, but posing as an entertainment attorney, Timothy Creighton). Rupp is the prime suspect, but was Sarah murdered, or did she walk out on one life to find another? It is perhaps not so much the idea of disappearing, but the idea of becoming someone else that Nagy explores in this play (and repeatedly explores in other plays, especially in her adaptation of Patricia Highsmith's Ripley novel). In *Disappeared* events are never proved one way or the other, and Nagy, as in *Butterfly Kiss*, leaves her spectators with ambiguity and questions, rather than clarity and closure.

The Strip and *Never Land*

'Utter tripe.' 'Pretentious bilge.' 'Ridiculous New Age freak show.' 'Would-be cool absurdist firago.' 'Watching it is rather like trying to wade through a lake of syrup.' These quotes are just a selection of the negative press review comments that were heaped on Nagy's production of *The Strip* in 1995.[50] Despite praise from a few critics, such as Michael Billington, Michael Coveney and Paul Taylor, in general the reaction of the press was negative and hostile. My argument here, however, is that *The Strip* is Nagy's most complex dramatisation of gender trouble to date and I therefore position it as central to my discussion of her work in this chapter.

Nagy primarily upset the theatre critics by making it virtually impossible for them to come up with their usual style of plot summary.[51] Though difficult to summarise, *The Strip* goes something like this. Ava Coo, a woman who works as a female impersonator, auditions for a spot in a Long Island nightclub, in front of the owner of the club, Otto Mink (also known as Mr Greene) and Calvin Higgins, a man who has come to repossess her car. Ava does not get the job, but Mink sends her off to audition at another club, Tumbleweed Junction, which she has to find herself. Calvin, falling in love with Ava, does not repossess her car, but accompanies her on the quest for Tumbleweed, which is where, unknown to Ava, her mother Tina is working as a cleaner. Other characters are variously caught up in Mink's transatlantic loop between Vegas and London: an American family, Lester and Loretta Marquette, and their baby Ray, dressed in a Ku Klux Klan hooded robe, are on the run and awaiting instructions from Mink in London. (Lester, a pawn in Mink's plan, has unwittingly blown up a bus full of Baptist ministers before the play begins.) Mink has designs on Loretta, but these are thwarted, however, by her befriending of Tom Warner, who looks after Mink's pawn shop in London, and his friend, astrologer Suzy Bradfield. While Loretta and Baby Ray take up with Tom and Suzy, Tom's gay partner, Martin, (also Calvin's brother), encounters Lester and the two engage in a macho/gay power play. On her travels, Ava meets up with reporter Kate Buck (who is actually hunting for Lester, and has also had letter contact with Suzy), and Kate falls in love with her. Complications follow complications, until, one way or another, all characters end up in Vegas in an apocalyptic styled finale.

What this description shows is that it is impossible to give an overview of events in the play, without hitting upon some of the 'crazy' feel to the piece (though note that this is not the same as saying, as several critics did, that the play suffers from Nagy's inadequate handling of her craft).[52] Moreover, the complexities and complications that are woven into the fabric of Nagy's writing made it harder still for reviewers to offer some explanation as to the play's meaning. Benedict Nightingale, for example, complained that he felt as though 'Nagy was playing computer games, and I could not join her because nobody had given me the password.'[53]

The idea of needing a 'password' is particularly revealing: one (magic) word to open up a whole new screen full of meaning. Yet Nagy's way of working is to propose an interactive and interrogative 'playing' that is not about accessing one game, but playing several. As one of her characters comments in the play: 'I prefer jazz to pop. It resists false notions of a single shared experience and is therefore unsentimental' (The Strip, p.200). The reference to jazz is also indicative of Nagy's own musical training which she brings to the composition of her plays. As director Steven Pimlott, who first worked with Nagy on Butterfly Kiss and was the director for The Strip (and subsequently for Never Land) observes: 'musical metaphors really apply in her [Nagy's] work – it is as if there are leitmotifs and rhythms. You have to hear her plays.'[54]

In contradistinction to the widely held critics' view of The Strip's 'narrative incoherence' or lack of 'dramatic sense', like Pimlott, I would argue Nagy's dramatic form as highly structured:[55] one that is working on and through several different levels and in a style of composition that arguably has more in common with Shakespeare than with contemporary writing.[56] Structurally The Strip echoes multi-stranded plays such as As You Like It or Twelfth Night, plays in which, through a series of apparently unconnected events and actions, characters re-locate their lives – geographically and sexually – and begin to make connections. That said, Nagy and Shakespeare are also worlds apart, or rather, each are dramatising very different world orders. Where Shakespeare's comedies move towards the restoration of a harmonious social order (however provisional that order may seem), Nagy moves towards connections that disconnect, re-connect, or connect up again, but differently. Fate or fortune in Shakespeare's time belonged to a very different belief system to that of The Strip where the 'wheel of fortune' now figures more literally in the gambling houses and casinos of a postmodern, transatlantic landscape, than as a force in the Elizabethan imagination. However, the idea of fate still has currency in Nagy's theatre and is central to an underlying thematic: the tension between essential and existential forces – especially in respect of social and cultural identities. One way to begin to understand this is through looking at the opening sequence to *The Strip*.

The play's slowly unfolding, opening tableaux (visually emphasising Nagy's multi-layered structure) includes the tableau of Tina-Coo, a forty-something mother, feeding coins into a one-arm bandit in Vegas that does not pay out. This immediately is followed by a sound-image: '*the music fades into the sudden sound of a progressive slot machine jackpot being hit. Bells and sirens. A river of coins dropping out of slots. The sound is overwhelming. Everybody listens to the phantom jackpot hit*' (*The Strip*, p.183). At one level this imaging reads easily as a late twentieth-century fantasy of the big win (on the pools, horses, lottery, etc.). More complexly the 'phantom jackpot hit', that captures the attention of 'everybody', juxtaposed with Tina's loss at the one-arm bandit, 'ghosts' in a belief in the controlling forces of 'fortune', at odds with a self-defining, existential, postmodern present. The difficulty for the characters in Nagy's world is negotiating the tension between an essentialist, direction-giving-force – whether it comes in the shape of the mysterious, *deus ex machina* figure, Otto Mink/Greene, zodiac charts, ouija boards, or the luck of the casino – and an existential desire for self-definition. Nagy describes this tension in her own words as a contradictory belief in coincidences and the belief that there is no such thing as coincidence.[57]

There is a parallel case to be made here for the tension that exists between the desire to self-define identity and sexuality, and the gender 'plan' that exists, as Butler and others argue, through citational practice. Ava Coo is a particular example of this. With 'tits' that 'look fake', and a body that means she does not 'really look like a girl' (*The Strip*, p.185), Ava positions herself in the feminine through impersonation; as a woman who plays a man who plays a woman. After her failed audition for a spot in Mink's nightclub, Calvin compliments her by saying 'I couldn't tell that you were a woman' (*The Strip*, p.187).

The effect of Ava's female impersonation (done badly) is to denaturalise the signs of femininity; to question the representational frame to which the real body is supposed to bear likeness.[58] Only with a shift in the process of viewing will Ava 'appear' to be a woman: 'I figure, the TV camera doesn't lie but maybe a smoky suzzy club full of drunken queens will.' (*The Strip*, p.185).

All of Nagy's characters in *The Strip* have to live through second-hand identities that inadequately stand in for who they really are. While this is a conditioning force in their lives, they still have the freedom to be performative; to become other than they are. Tina fantasises that she has a real life with her husband and real contact with her daughter; Loretta transforms herself into Lady Marquette and takes off with Tom and Suzy. Significantly, the reviewing 'body' criticised Nagy's characters as 'freaks', and took against the over-the-top, cartoon-style register of playing that the performers variously adopted for their roles. Yet, it is in the exaggerated style of playing that Nagy locates a sense of the performative; the freedom to play out roles that exist in tension with, but are other than, the social identities assigned to them.

Characters in *The Strip* tend to get into trouble when they get 'fixed' ideas about who they are, who they desire, and where they are going. Lateral, rather than literal ways of thinking and being are called for,[59] and this produces some strange relations, illustrated most clearly in the 'odd' coupling of Lester and Martin. In the opening act, from the viewpoint of his hotel room, Lester has spied on Martin and Tom in their home (private space), as 'a couple of homos living across the airshaft' (*The Strip*, p.191). Yet when Lester meets Martin in the public, all-male space of a gay bar, he is unable to read the signs of homosexuality. Lester views the bar, the leather gear, and so on, through his own fascist, homophobic, misogynist gaze as a woman-free zone. To disempower and to shift Lester's 'gaze', Martin engages him in contests of strength – arm wrestling, work-outs in the gym. At the close of Act One, squeezing his balls tighter and tighter, Martin instructs Lester to 'close your eyes and think of England' (*The Strip*, p. 226). He has Lester trapped in the submissive, heterosexual position of the feminine. The power play between the two men does not stop there, however. In a tableau that echoes the biblical betrayal of Jesus by Judas, Martin kisses Lester, and later sneezes three times. It is Martin who gets ill, however, or is contaminated after the mouth to mouth contact; a kind of inversion of the contamination motif in which the 'plague'/Aids appears as a heterosexual, not homosexual 'disease'. Martin's (false) 'god', the temple of the body through which he has defined and empowered his existence (bullying not only Lester, but also his partner, Tom, and friend, Suzy) gradually, then massively, collapses.

This power-play of the masculine, that cuts across sexuality, points up one of Nagy's feminist concerns with the way in which women, lesbian and straight, have been disadvantaged: 'The recent fascination with and adulation of the male body has led to an unprecedented popular interest in the art of gay men. And that art is not always sympathetic or even generous to women.'[60] This further connects to the way in which those figures in *The Strip* who are most disadvantaged are the wives/mothers, Loretta and Tina. Loretta has been forced to live Lester's fugitive existence, and Tina is materially disadvantaged by her absentee husband. There are no all-female spaces serving as a refuge to these women. Even when Tina cleans the ladies toilets in Mink's nightclub, Mink, as the owner, is empowered to walk right in.

Looking beyond the frame of gender identity and sexuality, *The Strip* makes a broader intervention into late twentieth-century capitalism and its bankrupt culture. Mink may be some sort of capitalist 'god', offering 'booze' . . . 'car stereos' . . . 'fax modems' in the apocalyptic closure (*The Strip*, p.263), but mostly he trades in taking away, rather than giving. It is an economics of loss not gain: cars are there for repossession; goods in the pawn shop are second-hand. All of this was reflected in Tobias Hoheisel's set design for the 1995 Court production that included a mock-up of the Sphinx and pyramid – copied not from the Egyptian wonder of the world, but the replica to be found at the Luxor Hotel, Las Vegas. This is the realm of Baudrillard's hyperreal, in which notions of origin and authenticity are eradicated through the process of copying what is already a copy. There is no access to the 'real', only the re-circulation of what has been as something other than what it was. For example, *The Strip* is replete with biblical allusions, though often mediated through another frame of cultural reference, such as the 1970s musical, *Jesus Christ Superstar*. As the world is experienced as some kind of simulated display, a kind of global Disneyland, then it is no longer possible to distinguish the real and the fictional. Ava, on her road movie style quest with Calvin, for example, refers to the 'loony tunes' towns they pass through – a generic (Disney derived) term she variously uses to include an Amish village and Brighton Village (a reproduction of an early American settlement). Other ritualised markers of a symbolic past are on the point of vanishing. The law courts in Liverpool that Loretta, Tom and Suzy enter are disused. The eternal flame marking the tomb of Kennedy that Calvin (out of respect for history) goes to see at the close of Act One goes out. And if history is barely circulating through the contemporary fictions of postmodernity, then the only other form of contact with it is through a written, and therefore ideologically constructed, version of the past – the kind we see Loretta teaching Baby Ray.

To achieve any meaningful connection to the past, and therefore to a future that is other than the apocalyptic final scene, in which a hitherto silent Baby Ray wails in the stillness, requires breaking out of personal and historical patterns; making new connections, looking to new possibilities. The difficulty of achieving this, however, is imaged in the final tableau of Baby Ray in the arms of Tina. While Tina speaks of 'chance' and of 'endless possibilities', she also reinvents the past: taking up the position of mother again, naming the baby Marshall after her estranged husband (*The Strip*, p.263). The world has and has not changed; has shifted and yet stayed the same. As Lester says of the pawn shop 'we got other people's sad old stuff all over the place. It's like limbo'(*The Strip*, p.260). How to transform lives out of the 'sad old stuff' we have to live through and with is one of the key questions that Nagy's theatre poses.

The hostility of the press towards *The Strip* was a major disappointment for Nagy. So much rides on having a Downstairs (main house) success at the Court. Her next play, *Never Land*, however, brought her (through a curious route) back to the Court, where she chose a studio, rather than main house production.[61] Freeman offers Nagy's view of *The Strip* as the end to a first cycle of plays and speculates on *Never Land* as a new departure (*Daughters*, p.154). On the one hand one might argue *Never Land* as turning to Europe: to a new location (and, therefore, to new possibilities) of performing identity (also a feature of her adaptation of the Ripley novel). On the other it connects to and continues Nagy's enduring concern with family and nation as an oppressive 'block' to identity and to desiring differently.

In *Never Land* the 'sad old stuff' of the bourgeois-realist, family drama gets turned inside out to make visible the danger that is sanctioned through structures of familial kinship and nation. Set in the home of a French family, the Jouberts – father (Henri), mother (Anne) and daughter (Elisabeth) – Henri is obsessed with all things English. He plans to move the family to England to manage a bookstore in Bristol, owned by his friends the Caton-Smiths. In Act Two, however, Henri's plans are upset: Heather Caton-Smith visits Henri in his work place (Albert Montel's perfumery), to tell him that her husband is withdrawing his offer. In Act Three, Anne anxiously awaits the return of Henri who is missing after the disappointment of losing the job opportunity in England and events move towards the tragic closure that involves the death of the entire family at the hands of the father.

Henri's nationalism, made strange through having a Frenchman obsess over Englishness, foregrounds the racial prejudice that circulates within a nationalist discourse. To keep the family safe from a criminal element, safe from the 'menace', is Henri's self-appointed task. His friends the Caton-Smiths typify middle-class Englishness that, despite the comedy, is dangerous for the national, racial and class-based prejudice that their views embody – exemplified as they join Henri at the close of Act One in acting out a scene from *Fawlty Towers* (a BBC comedy series resourced by humour reliant on national stereotyping).[62]

The idea of 'undesirables', of a criminal element, gets more firmly focused on Elisabeth's new boyfriend Mickey – a black American lavatory attendant in a casino. The encounter with Mickey creates a kind of European exposé of the American film *Guess Who's Coming to Dinner*, where a white affluent American family politely airs its reactions to their daughter's black fiancé.[63] By contrast, in Nagy's play the 'dinner' encounter (Elisabeth and Mickey have actually eaten the family picnic and had sex before mother, father and the Caton-Smiths come home), stirs up prejudice, positions Michael as the 'menace' and creates chaos not harmony.

In terms of gender, where Nagy makes trouble in *Never Land*, it is to show the violent exchange of women in matters of romance, love and marriage. 'Speaking' desire is necessarily marked by the violence of 'othering' (as argued earlier). When Elisabeth fantasises a romantic encounter with and marriage to Mickey, it is marked by the reality of a sexual encounter that climaxes to a point of violent harming (Mickey is poised to cut Elisabeth with a broken bottle). Anne's recurrent dream/nightmare, that begins as a romantic fantasy dominated by one of three boys with strawberry blond hair, turns into a scene of rape and violation. Nagy freezes action at the point of violence. 'Cut the vision into me' cries Elisabeth, while Michael is frozen, immobilised, about to cut her face with the broken bottle (*Never Land*, p.31). He desists. The moment passes, but the vision is 'cut' into the gaze of the spectator.

The most striking instance of the 'marriage' between love and violence comes in the final scene as Henri, having shot Elisabeth (offstage), returns to shoot Anne. In the Court production Sheila Gish's Anne figured as a kind of mesmerising masquerade of femininity: dishevelled, alcoholic, machining suits for Henri and, at the point of being shot, struggling through the love lyrics of a Dusty Springfield song. Anne dies for her performance of femininity; for loving Henri. In this moment too Nagy tackles the myth-making that turns patriarchal failure into heroism (Willy Loman style), by blowing the family clean away; out of existence. The 'menace' that Henri looked for, sought to keep the family safe from, is inside not outside. It is a matter, Nagy argues, along with so many of the playwrights presented in this volume, of pulling down borders, of seeing across divides in the interests of (be)longing and desiring differently.

7 Feminist connections to a multicultural 'scene'

The 'violence' of naming, of being known as a 'woman playwright' or a 'lesbian writer', gets further complicated for those writers who find themselves labelled as a 'black woman playwright'. As Winsome Pinnock, the first of the black and Asian writers and companies to be discussed in this chapter complains: 'When I started writing I was constantly being asked whether I considered myself a black playwright, a woman playwright, a black woman playwright or just a playwright – as though I could choose different identities!'[1] Writing in a post-1970s period, however, it was often necessary to choose between race and gender: between writing for a black company, not necessarily concerned with gender, or a women's company, not necessarily interested in race. To get a play published might mean inclusion in the Methuen *Plays by Women* series, or, later on, appearing in the *Black Play* volumes, edited by Yvonne Brewster, director of Talawa.[2]

As a response to this, and given the then funding opportunities for forming small-scale companies, some black women practitioners set up their own groups, such as Theatre of Black Women or Iamni-Faith.[3] Such companies devised, wrote and performed work that gave expression to socially and culturally neglected experiences of black women. At the same time, some of the established women's companies, notably The Women's Theatre Group, gradually began to recognise the need to transform the all-white composition of their membership.[4] WTG introduced its multi-racial policy in 1985 and in 1988 commissioned Winsome Pinnock's *Picture Palace* (which treats the subject of male violence against women, especially in the media), and *Zerri's Choice* by Sandra Yaw in 1989. As The Sphinx Theatre

Company, the group has commissioned plays by Jackie Kay (*Every Bit of It*, 1992) and Amrit Wilson (*Chandralekha*, 1994).

It would be wrong, however, to suggest that the 1980s was a time of cultural and racial integration, feminist or otherwise. Beatrix Campbell talks of the 1980s as 'the riotous decade' in her documentation of the disturbances and rioting in Bristol, Brixton, Toxteth, Tottenham and Birmingham.[5] Economic factors of material deprivation in the Thatcherite 1980s were 'lost' to a public imagination that dwelt on rioting as a matter primarily of race. Lord Scarman's report after the Brixton rioting in 1981 pressed for a policing that showed greater sensitivity towards 'the difficulties, social and economic, which beset the ethnically diverse communities'.[6] Such communities, tended, however, to be perceived as problematic rather than in need of support and protection: '[Police] commissioners appeared rather like great white settlers doomed to preside over territories teeming with what must have seemed to be restless natives'.[7]

White colonial, patriarch, Clive, 'father to the natives' in Caryl Churchill's *Cloud Nine*, knows that his subjects are getting 'restless'.[8] In staging her critique of heterosexual normativity against a colonial, African background, Churchill was visually demonstrating that sexual difference also needed to be considered as a matter of 'whiteness'. As post-colonial critic Gayatri Chakravorty Spivak later observed, 'the constitution of the sexed subject in terms of the discourse of castration was, in fact, something that came into being through the imposition of imperialism'.[9] Yet, as a consequence of its white, middle-class, heterosexual thinking, feminism, as it entered the 1980s, was essentially driven by sexual difference, in a way that failed to include other sites of difference (see also last chapter). Those women who felt 'othered' and excluded by this, began to organise and to theorise around their exclusions. While necessary to defining a black feminist position and to offering a challenge to a white feminist politics that might, in the event, become more rather than less inclusive, the exclusionary practice of identity politics created difficulties and tensions between women. As Heidi Safia Mirza, editor of the *Black British Feminism* anthology (1997), explains, 'the more marginal the group the more complete the knowledge' and 'black women, being the victims of 'triple oppression [race, gender and class], were the keepers of the holy grail'.[10] Activist and writer, Pratibha Parmar, observes that what was needed was a process of re-conceptualisation from '*all of us* engaged in political struggle' in order to achieve a 'movement away from intransigent political positions to tentative new formulations'.[11]

'Tentative new formulations' emerged in the 1990s through the need to think beyond the boundaries of nation. In order to find a way out of the white paradigm of international feminism, which, from the vantage point of the West, continued to reinforce hierarchical concepts of centre and margin; of 'First' and 'Third' worlds. Hence, in the 1990s, proposals for a transnational, rather than (white) international, feminism began to provide some exciting ways of formulating feminism differently. As exponents of a transnational feminism, M. Jacqui Alexander and Chandhra Talpade Mohanty explain that this involves thinking globally but in conjunction with different, local geographies; understanding 'the local in relation to larger, cross-national processes'.[12] Critical understandings of race and capitalism are essential to this feminist conjunction of the global and the local if the possibility of a genuinely democratic, cross-border collaboration between women is to be achieved.

This chapter examines black and Asian work that variously critiques the limits of an originating, white mode of 1970s feminism; desires beyond the fragmentation of 1980s identity politics to seek an understanding of black British experience that operates diasporically within and across cultures and geographies. What characterises the theatre examined in this chapter is, as Pinnock signals in her comment about labels, the need to understand identities not as distinct or separate, but as convergent, or interlocking. Subject positions are dramatised as multiple, transformative and historically located, rather than singular, essentialist and universal.[13] Such theatre moves beyond a representational 'othering' of black women, to making visible the complexities of what Alexander and Mohanty identify as 'citizenship machinery' and the basis on which exclusions (of gender, race, class and sexuality) are made in the interests of imagining the possibility of a democratic, multi-racial, feminist future.[14]

The chapter begins with some general observations on black women playwrights and moves more specifically to an examination of two 1990s plays by Winsome Pinnock: *Talking in Tongues* (1991) and *Mules* (1996). Both plays contribute in different ways to what, broadly, might be read as an evolving transnational feminism: *Talking in Tongues* on account of the ways in which the play takes issue with a separatist (black and white) politics, and *Mules* for its critical take on global capitalism. The chapter continues by looking at playwriting in a company context: at productions by the Asian and women-led company Tamasha that invite a re-conceptualisation of the family through issues of race and nation. It concludes with an examination of two solo performances: SuAndi's *The Story of M* and *Goliath*, based on Beatrix Campbell's *Goliath: Britain's Dangerous Places*. The presentation of this work is deliberately diverse: discussion of Tamasha includes consideration of *East is East* by Asian actor Ayub Khan-Din, rather than a woman playwright; SuAndi's work crosses theatre and performance art, and *Goliath* was a collaboration for a women's company (The Sphinx Theatre Company) that operates a multi-racial policy. In brief, crossing borders, making connections, is not just a concern of the work itself, but is also reflected in the contexts of theatrical and cultural production.

'Breaking Down the Door'[15]: black women playwrights in the 1990s

Pinnock argues that 'despite the marketing of "Cool Britannia" as a new and exciting multicultural society' it is the case that 'the multicultural is notably absent' from theatre, a view shared by many other black and Asian practitioners.[16] For playwrights like Jenny McLeod seeking to consolidate a writing career in the 1990s, or recently emergent writers, like Tanika Gupta, experiences have varied between feeling used by a venue as the token black writer (McLeod), or finding it difficult to get through the door at all (Gupta).[17] Gupta complains specifically of being patronised, of literary managers constantly wanting to 'develop' her work, but not actually get to the point of staging it.[18] 'Most theatres don't take risks on black playwrights, or on women playwrights' argues McLeod, 'Winsome [Pinnock] and I can write as many plays as we can write, and all of them can get put on, but it is still not enough'.[19]

Like 'women playwrights' who desire beyond a reductive identification with 'women's experience', black women playwrights do not wish exclusively to be identified with staging the black experience. At the same time, their theatre is variously shaped and touched by experiences of growing up as black women in Britain. Pinnock's 1987 production of *Leave Taking* (Liverpool Studio Theatre),[20] for example, offered a cross-generational and cross-cultural staging of differences between an immigrant mother and her two daughters, struggling to make sense of their lives in contemporary Britain. McLeod historicised black, British, female experience as one of social and cultural alien-nation. *Raising Fires* (Bush Theatre, 1994), set in an Essex village in 1603, has only one black character, Tilda, blamed and ultimately sacrificed by the village for all its social ills and problems, cast out, at the end of the play, to appease an angry mob.[21] For another playwright Bonnie Greer, who, like Nagy, is an American who has moved her theatrical home from New York to London, giving expression to the experience of growing up black surrounded by white culture is also significant. Greer's portrait of American art expert Anna Eastman in *Munda Negra* (1993) images an angry black woman who has to confront her own childhood internalisation of a desire to be white.[22]

Despite the problem of labels, Pinnock acknowledges that her early career was helped 'by women within theatres and by institutions that primarily existed to promote *women writers* [my emphasis]'.[23] The first full production of *A Hero's Welcome*, set in the West Indies in 1947, took place at the Royal Court in 1989 through the auspices of the Women's Playhouse Trust (the play had had a rehearsed reading in 1986). *A Hero's Welcome* was later published in the first British anthology of contemporary *Black and Asian Women Writers* (1993), along with scripts by Maya Chowdhry, Zindika, Meera Syal and Trish Cooke.[24] McLeod too had support from the women's company Monstrous Regiment who staged *Island Life* (1988), a play about the relationships between three women in an old people's home and the 'lies' they tell themselves to make their lives bearable.

McLeod's *Island Life* is so called because a high wall surrounds the residential home that the women are placed in, figuratively 'imprisoning' the women in a world of their own, removed from the world at large. 'Me never see no wall so big till me come a England' complains, Jamaican-born resident, Emmy.[25] In the 1990s, England's 'island mentality', as playwright Judith Johnson describes it in the process of writing *Uganda*, a more expansive (racially and sexually) representation of family life in contemporary Britain, needs to be challenged.[26] Crossing-borders, crossing cultures with a view to performing a feminism for the twenty-first century is important to much of the theatre discussed in this and the following chapter, and exemplified in Pinnock's Royal Court production of *Talking in Tongues* (1991).

Talking in Tongues, Winsome Pinnock
Talking in Tongues is a drama about healing: of finding ways of criss-crossing the matrix of heterosexual, racial and material oppressions in the interests of sexual, cultural and social fusions that are less damaging to individuals and to communities.[27] Composed in two acts, *Talking in Tongues* translocates between a New Year's Eve Party in London (Act One) and a holiday in Jamaica (Act Two). At the London party, tensions within a multi-racial group of friends erupt when Leela and her girlfriends Claudette and Curly are witness to Bentley's (Leela's partner) affair with Fran, a white woman and partner to his best friend, Jeff. In order to recover from the discovery of Bentley's infidelity, Leela takes a holiday in Jamaica with Claudette. In the Jamaican setting, Pinnock introduces another multi-racial grouping (doubling performers from Act One): Diamond, Sugar and Mikie, all Jamaicans 'serving' the tourist industry, and a white brother and sister, David and Kate. Kate is in self-imposed exile from England, choosing to live as a gardener on the island, while David is visiting. In moving from the claustrophobic interior of the London setting, to the outdoor beach setting of Jamaica, Pinnock signals the need to broaden the horizons of diasporic thinking. As Pinnock herself explained: '[*Tongues*] was about exploring the changing nature of cultural identities and the collision or clash of cultures;

it was about the beginning of something new and the potential for change'.[28]

One of the ways that Pinnock signals the desire for 'the beginning of something new' (beyond the thematics of her play), is through her dramaturgical composition that draws on a tradition of stage naturalism, but whose Eurocentrism is in collision with the need to give voice and representation to the multi-racial. Pinnock explains that she writes 'within a tradition of European playwriting, but about subjects that take in my own heritage, my own past'.[29] In *Tongues*, the play's naturalism marks the intransigence that Parmar identifies (see earlier): the inability to shift out of old (white) towards new (multi-racial) ways of thinking. Characters, from their different ethnicities, gender, sexualities and class collide and clash through a formal dramatic arrangement that can no longer contain them. As Leela complains, negotiating the world in a language not her own makes you feel invisible, 'only half alive . . . because you haven't the words to bring yourself into existence' (*Tongues*, p.195). Formally, the play shares the yearning for a coming 'into existence' that signifies more than, or breaks up, the realist tradition of the English family drama; creates a 'new structure of feeling'. As Meenakshi Ponnuswami argues, while the widespread use of realism among black women playwrights, may seem conventional and 'a repudiation of post-modernism', realism, nevertheless, is transformed through the diasporic context of black experience.[30] Not only is realism racially marked as a white dramatic tradition, but the narrow, private confines of the domestic, the familial, are opened up to epic questions of race, nation and capital, central to the conceptualisation and realisation of a future, feminist citizenship, a 'politics of inclusivity across racial and national lines'.[31]

Through the figure of Claudette, Pinnock dramatises the difficulty of a separatist politics in which all white women are seen as the enemy: as women who see black women as 'inferior' and who 'steal' black men for their lovers. To be consumed by such hostility is also, however, to be damaged by it; to be marked out as angry, inferior 'other'. Annoyed on behalf of Leela at Bentley's infidelity, Claudette's body is literally convulsed with anger. Her body suffers, symptomatically producing and making visible an internalised politics of rage

(*Tongues*, p.203). To think only in terms of being the racially marked other to the white woman's standard of beauty, as the black women do at the London party, is to be driven away from their bodies; is to 'block' freedom of movement (dance), speech and sexuality.

Carrying the trauma of racially marked relations does not, Pinnock argues through her dramatisation, constitute a progressive way forward.[32] This requires more cross-cultural understandings and less entrenched divisions, as illustrated in the play through Leela's ultimate ability to release rather than hang on to her pain which is achieved through an act of violence. In a reversal of Act One, where it is Leela who is betrayed, in Act Two it is Claudette who loses her Jamaican holiday lover, Mikie, to the white woman, Kate. In response to Claudette's pain, Leela joins her in an 'attack' on Kate's femininity, grotesquing the white woman's make-up and cutting off her ponytail while she is asleep on the beach. Sugar is blamed for the attack and is dismissed from her job. Yet it is to Sugar that Leela confesses her 'crime' and through confessing begins to talk in tongues as her repressed anger, rage and hatred spew out of her body.

In the play's prologue, Sugar narrates a childhood memory of Jamaican women who found a way of letting go of the pain of their oppressed lives. One of the women in Sugar's tale is described as a mute, who, through an hypnotic state would astonishingly come out of silence and into voice, talking in tongues, in 'a language that go back before race' (*Tongues*, p.174). This suggests a different mapping to the contestation of 'naturalised' gender identities explored by Butler in *Gender Trouble*, published close to the time of Pinnock's play.[33] Where in *Gender Trouble* Butler restricts herself primarily to categories of sex, gender and desire, Pinnock layers race into the categories of contestation.[34] This is not to propose the primacy of race over gender as *the* language of oppression, but to fuse race into the categories of division that hinder the 'speaking' of desires. Pinnock gives visual representation to this in the figure of Irma, a party guest in Act One possessed of an hermaphroditic body; two sexes in one. Though played by a woman in the Royal Court production (Ella Wilder), Pinnock instructs that the role can be taken by either a male or a female performer (*Tongues*, p.172). Leela encounters Irma after witnessing Bentley's infidelity. As she cries, Irma laughs, explaining that she laughs at everything (*Tongues*, p.193). 'Laughter in the face of serious categories is indispensable for feminism' argues Butler (*Trouble*, p.viii), beautifully staged by Pinnock through her representation of Irma. With her two-sexed body and her bald head (product of a hairdressing disaster), Irma's category-defying presence signals the possibility of release from the trauma of heterosexual coupling and the construction of the feminine. Further, as a black woman(man) who laughs rather than cries, Irma prefigures the release into a language 'before race' that Leela so desires.

For women to 'find our way back to each other', as Pinnock argues (*Tongues*, afterword, p.226), to find points of commonality rather than difference, depends on exploring the possibilities of a 'language' that desires to communicate across cultures; seeks connections, fusions, rather than difference and containment. To connect is to resist the boundaries that keep white upon black in place. As a site of international tourism, Jamaica also refuses the binarism of black islander and white holidaymaker. Leela and Claudette do not go back to Jamaica to find their 'roots', their homeland, but they go back as tourists, as holidaymakers who also demand the services of Diamond, Sugar and Mikie. Any desire to re-figure the various and multiple inequalities that this produces must necessarily take account of the colonising effects of international capitalism, as Pinnock highlights in her 1996 production of *Mules*.

Mules, Winsome Pinnock

Mules dramatises women who traffic in drugs. As a Clean Break commission, the play is the dramatic outcome of research Pinnock undertook among women prisoners in London and in Jamaica. Like *Talking in Tongues*, *Mules* translocates between London and Jamaica, but with an emphasis on capital, rather than on multi-racial relations. The set design for the Royal Court production involved grey suitcases that would locate a scene by opening up to show a brightly coloured view of Jamaica or London. The idea of the suitcase suggested travel and the excitement of foreign locations. Yet the idea of London as a capital of corporate success, or Jamaica as exotic holiday destination, is undermined by the play's re-configuration of these international destinations through the part they play in the business of drug smuggling: the harsh social realities of each location that women struggle to escape.

The street girls in London and the sisters, Lyla and Lou, selling second-hand underwear, in Kingston, Jamaica, are all so poor that they get recruited by Bridie as mules, drug traffickers. Pinnock's dramatisation of the traffic in drugs, an illegal trade, serves to historicise the effects of late twentieth-century capitalism. The illegal, illegitimate international drugs business indicts the 'criminality' of 'legitimate' capitalist trading responsible for hierarchies of oppression and the poverty of Jamaican women like Lyla, who ends the play working in a ganja field on slave labour wages. Through her research with the women prisoners, Pinnock explains that she learnt and became interested in the way that poverty motivated 'criminality': 'a lot of the women, so-called criminals, were actually taking action to provide for their families, in the way they knew how'.[35] The drugs trade, therefore, becomes a means of agency for these women; a means, as Pinnock argues, of refusing poverty, of 'escaping being victims' (ibid). As a mode of transgressive agency it also afforded a certain kind of spectatorial pleasure: 'the joy of transgression, the joy of criminality, and however dangerous that was, we found that people identified with it'.[36] Set against the thrill of whether or not the women would get through with the drugs, however, is the recognition of the risk to the woman's body. Smuggling the drugs inside the vagina marks the body as a site of capitalist injury: links to the commodification and consumption of the female body and to women in the sex trade where the vagina is penetrated for business, not pleasure.

For the production of *Mules* three performers had to take on all twelve roles for the rapid, short, swift-changing scenes. The quick change, multi-role playing meant that any one performer had to switch between dominant and subordinate positions in the capitalist system. Clare Perkins as 'top girl' Bridie, also, for example, took on two street girl roles and played a landlady. The effect of the performers crossing between materially empowered and disempowered roles was to make visible to spectators the inequities produced by a capitalist system. Moreover, it suggested the vulnerability of persons within the movement of capital, where no position is secure (even Bridie is brought down, possibly killed), and reinforced the idea that each gain is haunted by a loss. Bridie gives up her luxury home because it is haunted by the soul of a poor dead girl.[37] Allie, a runaway to London, rents a room frequented by its former occupant, Olu, who can no longer afford to pay the rent, and the street girls, dispossessed and homeless, 'cruise' around to thieve from middle-class homes and families from which they are excluded (*Mules*, p.37).

A celebratory dinner in Act Two of *Mules*, hosted by Bridie for her two right-hand women, Rog and Sammie, may be read as the nemesis of Marlene's dinner in *Top Girls*. Like Churchill's agency women, Marlene, Win and Nell, Pinnock's Bridie, Rog and Sammie have 'achieved', but at a cost to themselves and at the expense of other women. Written off like Angie as non-achievers, these women have 'succeeded' outside of the law, and ironically are in a position to 'buy' into the very system that had rejected them. Rog enjoys being able to buy clothes that shop assistants think she cannot afford; Sammie is able to fund her own private collection of original works of art, and Bridie 'enjoys' a luxury style of hotel living. As Pinnock comments, these women were 'sticking two fingers up at the [capitalist] system, in terms of being involved in crime and on the other hand being totally immersed in it; in its values of consumption and exploiting people who are weak'.[38]

The operations of capitalism make it impossible for there to be any real solidarity between women. It is not possible to have friendships; there are only transactions, which leave no room for 'pity'. What appear to be selfless acts of 'kindness' turn out to be disguised forms of selfishness: Allie is seemingly befriended by Pepper and Piglet who actually drug her and steal her money, and Bridie who claims she will look after the girls, does not rescue Allie and Lou from prison after they get arrested for drug smuggling. While the strongest bond in the play is that between the sisters, Lou and Lyla, the relationship between the two is damaged by Lou's imprisonment. Trying to find a way out of their poverty drives them apart. Reunited at the end of the play, in the ganja field, the sisters are brought full circle, back to the poverty where they started. While there is hope in the renewal of affection between them, in Lyla's baby, and resilience in their sense of humour, Pinnock's final imaging of the two women working the fields without hope of an alternative future, makes a chilling comment on a capitalist landscape that demands the women's subjugation, or, as Alexander and Mohanty, terms it, their 'recolonization'.[39]

As an all-female play, originally conceived for a mixed race cast, but in the event played by an all-black female cast, the play was critically received as a 'black play'. As Pinnock notes, a black cast generally means a play will be received as 'black'.[40] Coveney described *Mules* as 'a fascinating, kaleidoscopic look at black female drug smugglers' and David Murray detailed the smuggling as a movement from 'some third-world country to a western capital'.[41] 'Black female' and 'third-world', 'western' suggest, however, an 'othering' of the play as black and female, from a white, western vantage point, that does not allow for the possibilities of 'seeing' Pinnock's play, not just in terms of race and gender, but as detailing an overarching narrative of global capitalism, networking and intersecting with local geographies of oppression. This is a play that is not about being black and female, but about the way in which 'mules' as stateless citizens figuratively come to stand for the way in which women, across nations, face a variety of exclusions on account of their material, gender, racialised and sexualised states. To refuse to be positioned as victim, to transgress in the interests of a feminist agency may, in the end, Pinnock's play suggests, require women to break the 'law'.

Tamasha

Black women's theatre groups, like so many of the 'alternative' companies, tended not to survive the severe funding cuts of the 1980s and early 1990s. A few black companies managed (always with difficulty) to survive: Jatinda Verma's Tara Arts (formed in 1976) and Black Theatre Co-operative, set up in 1979, renamed Nitro in 1999, remain ongoing.[42] Exceptionally, one female-led company, Talawa, established in 1985, not only survived, but in 1991 secured its own building base at The Cochrane Theatre. Talawa (meaning 'small but powerful women' in Jamaican) was originally headed by a team of four women: Yvonne Brewster, Carmen Munroe, Mona Hammond and Inigo Espejel. Yet despite this all-female direction, ironically the company could not find plays by women that suited the 'epic' style that Brewster, as director, was keen for the group to develop. Not until 1992 did it perform a first piece by a black woman writer: Ntozke Shange's *The Love Space Demands*.

In 1989, at the close of the decade, an Asian company, Tamasha (Hindi for 'commotion') was founded by two women, Sudhar Bhuchar and Kristine Landon-Smith. Initially the women formed the company to adapt Mulk Raj Anand's novel *Untouchable*. Adaptation has remained a strength and interest of the company's work, that has included productions that examine gender, race and family issues (see later), alongside more epic styled pieces, as in *A Tainted Dawn: Images of Partition* (1997) that dealt with the 1947 partition of India. Whatever the production, what is important to the company is that it reflect Asian experiences, both of the Indian sub-continent and of Asian life in Britain, through theatre that is considered not as marginal, but as *central* to the stage, culture and society. Like other touring companies, Tamasha has sought co-producers for their work and has regularly collaborated with Birmingham Repertory Theatre Company, building up a strong multi-cultural following in the Midlands city.

Women of The Dust and *A Yearning*

Unlike Talawa, which struggled in the early years to find women's plays that would suit the company's style, Tamasha staged two woman-authored productions: Ruth Carter's *Women of the Dust* (1992) and *A Yearning* (1995). Both plays place a particular emphasis on social realities for Asian women, in India and Britain.[43] *Women of the Dust* examines a community of oppressed Rajasthani women workers, who have left their villages where the harvests have failed, to labour on a building site in Delhi. Their task is to head load baskets of bricks and this backbreaking work continues even if the women are pregnant. After giving birth, they carry on with their babies and young children alongside them. As one young Indian mother explains: 'When they're born on sites they are lost children. The only mother's song this baby hears is the cement mixer.'[44] What helps these women to survive is the support that they offer to each other, through laughter, tears and understanding.

This is a rather different sense of community to that portrayed in *A Yearning*, where the central figure, Amar, increasingly finds herself isolated from the women of her Punjabi community in Birmingham, England. As an adaptation of Lorca's *Yerma*, *A Yearning* transposes the rural Spanish village and setting into an urban, British Asian community, and takes as its dramatic focus the arranged marriage of Amar and Jaz, a Glaswegian, Punjabi owner of a mini cab firm. As a Glaswegian and Punjabi Jaz signals the complexity of racial identities: Scottish and Asian, both 'subjects' of colonial English oppression.[45] Though Glaswegian born, Jaz also identifies with a traditional India embodied in the figure of his bride. These cross-cultural tensions and collisions produce a fatal outcome. After the style of Lorca's play, *A Yearning* ends tragically as Amar kills her husband out of anger for the child he would not, could not, give her.

Carter's drama and Tamasha's staging of the play captured the pressures facing young Asian women caught between the traditional ways of India and living in a multi-cultural Britain. It is an example of what Jatinder Verma describes as a 're-invention' of a classic text: 'a deliberate attempt to confront the specificities of a particular theatre text with the different specificities – in time, place and cultural sensibility – of its performers'.[46] Carter's dialogue weaves the figurative style of Indian speech with the vulgar, harsher registers that index English city living. The staging combined minimalist suggestions of what were mostly domestic interiors (plus Jaz's office and a city park), with the colour and textures of Indian saris and fabrics (especially in the closing festival scene). In theatricalising this hybridity, *A Yearning* refused the simplistic, imperialist even, suggestion that 'West is best'. Amar's move to Britain is not represented as an 'advance' on a 'backward' Indian home, rather the play shows the complexities of a cross-cultural, inter-national oppression that ultimately positions Amar as isolated, friendless and desperate.

While the women of the Punjabi community begin by feeling compassion for Amar, they distance themselves as the 'madness' of her inability to conceive takes over. Separated from her own family in

India, Amar is not helped by her husband's family in Britain. Rather, Jaz installs his two sisters to spy on her to ensure that she does not bring dishonour on his family. Jaz fails to understand, however, that the sense of honour instilled by her Indian upbringing, prevents Amar from taking a lover or another partner. Confined to the home, that is not a home because it contains no 'life', there is no way out for Amar. As Pragna Patel, Asian activist of the Southall Black Sisters group, explains, 'the choice for women who dare break out of the very narrow confines of the roles prescribed by religion and culture is stark; either they remain within the parameters of permissible behaviour, or they transgress and risk becoming pariahs within their own community'.[47] In brief, the dramatisation of Amar's situation is a reminder to feminism, especially as it struggles with the issue of infertility (see Chapter 8), to recognise that women do not have equal access to or choice over reproductive rights.

Jaz's impotence (the reason for Amar's 'infertility') is figured through his exclusive concern with reproducing capital and not family. British born, Jaz is a product of the Thatcher years and has internalised the entrepreneurial drive to succeed in business. As Amar cynically observes to her cousin Arvind, 'money breeds money' (*A Yearning*, p.40). To work solely for financial gain is, the play suggests, dehumanising. Amar, unable to fulfil her social role as mother, is merely a prized possession, the watched over 'pot of gold' (p.32) whose feelings, emotions and needs are considered to be an irrelevance. Exemplary conduct is required of Amar, not just in the interests of family honour, but because it is good for business. 'My regular customers, they're not friendly like they used to be with me', complains Jaz of Amar's 'bad' behaviour (*A Yearning*, p.45).

The damage done to the Rajasthani women workers in *Women of the Dust* on account of capitalist interests ('Modern India has been built on their backs', p.27) is glaringly visible in the play's scenes of physical hardship and material deprivation. *A Yearning*, however, makes visible *hidden* pressures facing young Asian wives in Britain and offers a rather different image to the concept of the 'family business'. To summarise, Carter's play provides a dramatic echo to the words of Kiranjit Ahluwalia. Ahluwalia is an Asian wife who was

convicted in 1989 for the murder of her violent husband. In 1990, campaigning for her release, she spoke out about the silenced suffering of
Asian women:

> My culture is like my blood – coursing through every vein of
> my body. It is the culture into which I was born and where I
> grew up which sees the women as the honour of the house. In
> order to uphold this false honour and glory, she is taught to
> endure many kinds of oppression and pain, in silence. In
> addition religion also teaches her that her husband is her God
> and fulfilling his every desire is her religious duty. A woman
> who does not follow this part in our society has no respect or
> place in it. She suffers from all kinds of slanders against her
> character. And she has to face all sorts of attacks and much
> hurt entirely alone . . . I have come out of the jail of my
> husband and entered the jail of the law.[48]

Ahluwalia's words might serve well as an epilogue for Amar after the
'killing' of her husband. In life and in dramatic fiction, these two law-
breakers are testimony to the (violent) desperation and disempowerment that may be the hidden experience of some Asian women in
their different (family) communities.

East is East

Given the company's emphasis on adaptation, there arguably has been
less space for original new writing, which up-and-coming writers find
difficult. Tanika Gupta, struggling to find outlets for her work in the
1990s, commented that 'Asian theatre companies like Tara Arts and
Tamasha really only develop writers on a small scale.'[49] One exception to this, as Gupta notes, is Tamasha's success, indeed huge success,
with East is East: a comic drama about a British Asian family, by actor,
Ahub Khan-Din. Premiered at Birmingham Repertory Studio Theatre
and the Royal Court Upstairs in 1996, East is East transferred to the
Theatre Royal, Stratford East and the Royal Court Theatre Downstairs
in 1997, toured a number of cities (including Salford, where the play
is set), and subsequently was made into a screen version (Channel 4/
Miramax Films, 1999). As a new writer, Khan-Din had the benefits

of a workshop jointly organised by Tamasha and the Royal Court to which experienced practitioners and writers (who included Winsome Pinnock and Phyllis Nagy) contributed advice and skills. As a production *East is East* benefited from Tamasha's skills as an Asian and gender aware company, with, for example, direction by Kristine Landon-Smith, and Court actress Linda Bassett in the role of Ella.

Set in Salford in 1970, on the eve of the war between India and Pakistan over the independence of East Pakistan, *East is East* examines life in the Khan family: George (Pakistani) and Ella (white) and their children: Abdul, Tariq, Maneer, Saleem, Meena and Sajit.[50] Life for the Khan family centres on the running of a family business: a fish and chip shop in which all the family are expected to help out. 'The Paki family who run the chippy', as Maneer describes the family,[51] indicates the fusion of East and West, visually encoded in the play's set (a split-level design to show both domestic life and the chip shop), and unfolding through the play's dramatic action. Familial tensions ultimately explode when George attempts to arrange marriages for Abdul and Tariq to the daughters of a local businessman, Mr Shah.

There is much that might be discussed about *East is East*, especially given the screen version, of a growing Asian presence in popular culture[52] that is beyond the scope of this volume. This is distinct, however, from the success of *East is East* in the theatre, which as Pinnock and others observe, is not significantly multicultural. Considered in a feminist frame, the play claims my attention on account of the way that it maps and interrogates race, nation, class, gender and sexuality. Specifically, there are three key observations I wish to make: the representation of sexual difference as racially marked; the Asian child as a figuring of the tensions and complexities of a multi-cultural Britain, and the role of the white mother in a mixed race family.

Dramaturgically, Khan-Din, like Pinnock, draws on a western tradition of realism. In subjecting conventions of domestic realism to comic play through a British Asian lens, however, the tradition of the familial stage drama critically is exposed as quintessentially white. Moreover, in terms of composition, *East is East* plays on the regulation of sexual difference: the binarism of male and female. Composed in two acts, each act is structured in terms of the male (Act One) and the female (Act Two). Sajit's belated circumcision and castration anxieties 'climax' in Act One. In Act Two, arrangements for the marriages are upset through a series of comic interventions that hilariously conclude in a model of the female vagina (made by trainee artist Saleem, as an artwork depicting female exploitation) being hurled into the parlour and ending up in front of Mr Shah. While male and female structure the comedy, Khan-Din makes a serious point by showing that sexual difference is not the only difference to come into 'play', but rather converges with differences of class, race and religion, all complexly figured through the hybridity of British–Asian identities, cultures and experiences. Identity in *East is East* is also shown to be a matter of dis-identification. The sons are unable to identify with the father on account of his tyrannical and violent behaviour, particularly towards their mother. At the same time, dis-identification of father and family, in turn allows for feelings of social alienation to surface as the boys find it hard to 'belong' to the white working-class culture of Salford. To 'belong' to this culture, requires that they 'pass' as white: join in the racist jokes against themselves; dis-identify with their Pakistani origins.

While all of the sons and the daughter Meena, who has to fight for her freedom against Pakistani traditions of passive femininity, explore and experience the mixed-racial 'belongings' differently, the crisis of identity crystallises in the figure of youngest child, Sajit. From inside the hooded parka coat that he refuses to take off, Sajit is onlooker to the familial arguments and the violence of the father towards the mother. As a traumatised observer, a child who walks around corners miming the cutting of an imaginary string (umbilical cord) out of his back, Sajit is considered by the family as a 'problem' child, as possibly backward. Figuratively, however, he signals the harm done to the child who is witness to violence. Not unlike Churchill's Joan in *Far Away*, Sanjit, as a child who sees and keeps silent about the violence in the home, is also the child who 'carries' that violence into the world. When Sanjit finally takes off his coat it is to beat his father in defence of his mother.

Khan-Din's autobiographically drawn *East is East* places a much greater emphasis on explorations of masculinity, than femininity, when compared, for example, with either of Carter's plays. Reactions to the arranged marriages are those of Abdhul and Tariq; Mr Shah's daughters 'enter' only as framed images. That said, Khan-Din offers a lively and resilient role through Meena's tomboy character, and, more importantly still in feminist terms, is his portrait of Ella. As a white mother of mixed race children, Ella is a transgressive figure because she crosses the reproductive binary of white and black. Racial 'othering' that confirms white as the dominant, is upset, 'polluted' through Ella's cross-racial marriage and, in consequence, her 'white' maternal body suffers the same racial abuse as that of her family. Ella has to fight for her family not just in terms of race, but also class.[53] In the white urban terraced housing of Salford (introduced into the domestic interior of the set through exterior shots of terraces), without the material advantages of middle-class living, Ella works for (serving in the fish and chip shop) and raises her family of seven.

Moreover, the extent to which Ella is either empowered or disempowered varies according to social context. In the eyes of the British state she is more acceptable than her Asian, Muslim husband. Within the Pakistani community, on the other hand, Ella is disadvantaged in terms of race and gender. Disempowered in negotiations with the Shah family, Ella performs whiteness (speaks 'posh') in her attempts not to be outmanoeuvred. The heightened performativity of her role at this point signals the way in which Ella's position, as it shifts and intersects with family, community and state, is a matter of constant negotiation. As Pinnock observes, it is Ella's experience of a 'mixed race' marriage that 'has altered her own view of herself as an Englishwoman and of the children, the products of an interracial marriage'.

Theatre as cultural weapon
The Story of M, SuAndi

In the final analysis, however, Ella's 'story', the mother's story, is less central to *East is East* than that of the father and his children. For treatment of a white mother of a mixed race family as the 'subject' of a performance, I turn to SuAndi's *The Story of M*. As freelance Cultural Director of Black Arts Alliance (based in Manchester)

SuAndi campaigns internationally on matters of culture, race and gender. Although conceived for a live arts context (ICA Live Arts commission, 1994), her solo performance, *The Story of M*, has exceptionally played performance art venues like the ICA, alongside theatres, festivals and conferences in the UK, Europe and USA, and has also found its way into print culture.[54] The crossing of performance contexts is important for the way in which it signals a resistance to categories of 'writing', a practice that SuAndi shares with other black women artists/writers – Jackie Kay and Maya Chowdhry among them. In contrast to the revisioning realism strategies discussed in the first part of this chapter, such practitioners look for other ways of 'writing': through poetic texts applied to different performance contexts (Kay), or presenting the 'self' in a visual exploration of racial, social and sexual identities (Chowdhry).[55] *The Story of M* combines the use of dramatic monologue with the presence of the writer/performer; the character 'M' is Margaret, SuAndi's mother, played by SuAndi, daughter, performer. This 'heightened form of writing', as Catherine Ugwu describes it,[56] is one that compositionally and aesthetically 'writes' a story that has not been told: a story that 'locates' in the 'space' in between black and white.

What the performance tells is the story of a working-class mother to a mixed-race family. *The Story of M* begins at the end of Margaret's life. 'I've got cancer' (*The Story of M*, p.2) is Margaret's opening line as she begins her life story, not in any strict chronology, but through the lateral, associative surfacing of memories. The piece is simply staged: hospitalised, Margaret sits in her chair to reminisce, alongside projected slides that image 'scenes' from her life. It is not until the last slide is shown, and the audience sees a photograph of Margaret for the first time, that it is clear that Margaret was white. At this point, SuAndi steps out of character, takes off the hospital gown to appear as 'herself' to explain that mixed up in her African ancestry, inherited from her Nigerian father, is her white, Liverpool, Irish, Catholic, mother. For the spectator, especially the white spectator, what is demonstrated through the *Gestus* of the slide is an assumption that the victim of racial abuse must be black, not white. As Ugwu explains: 'By examining inter-racial relationships and experience, her work extends black tradition to embrace a wide range of black experience, challenging the propensity of black as well as white to confine the experience.'[57] The dramatisation of private, personal memories of Margaret, as remembered by and told 'through' her daughter, make public an 'invisible' twentieth-century history of race, gender and class relations in which the maternal 'white' body is racially marked.

Racial abuse in the monologue frequently is described as an issue of pollution or contamination. Margaret's two children, SuAndi and her older brother, Malcolm (lost to a life of crime), are too 'dirty' to be playmates for children of white families. Through the abuse can be heard the fear of contamination: black mixed up in white, refuses the boundary of the 'pure', uncontaminated, dominant, white imperialist body. Like Ella, Margaret racially is marked through her choice of black relations and mixed-race children. 'Punished' for her transgression, Margaret's laugh, her 'dirty cackle', heard and shared through her daughter's laugh, is a laughter, which like Irma's in *Talking in Tongues*, suggests a time 'before race'; an ancient laughter that cuts through the violence of racist discourse.

The police figure in several of the memories, though not as protectors of the community, but as racially abusive. They bully Malcolm and target Margaret's home, raiding the house at night looking for drugs or other signs of criminality, but finding nothing, remove SuAndi, aged only seven, alone while her mother is out working with her brother supposedly minding her. As Kum-Kum Bhavani and Margaret Coulson have observed 'black and white mothers may have completely different experiences and perceptions of the oppressive nature of the state. The worries black mothers may have about children being late home from school can be as much to do with fears of police harassment as with fears of sexual assault.'[58] Except that, as the figure of Margaret shows, the binarism of black and white does not obtain when 'white' is also 'othered' by mixed race relations. In terms of the policing authorities, Margaret is also viewed as a 'black' mother.[59]

The daughter telling the story of an 'ordinary', albeit courageous, mother is interesting in feminist terms for the way in which it challenges recognised conventions of biography as concerned with the one great, famous person. Like Carolyn Steedman's *Landscape for a Good Woman*, *The Story of M* is '*a story of two lives*': 'M' stands for Margaret, for mother, and, as SuAndi explains at the close of her performance, 'And now M for me' (*The Story of M*, p.18). SuAndi's project shares with Steedman's, the need to look at 'lives lived out on the borderlands'.[60] Margaret's 'borderland' life is given a public, cultural presence through the performance. Out of the personal testimony – Margaret's stories, re-shaped and re-told by her daughter – emerges a political landscape of social, racial violence. Told with affection and humour, the laughter of *The Story of M* is more dangerous than that of *East is East*. At the very moment of laughing, Margaret/SuAndi directly challenges the spectator as complicit in racism: if, deep down, the stories are not actually funny, then why are we laughing?

Goliath, adaptation Bryony Lavery
Racism in the police force and the racial tensions in urban communities that *The Story of M* describes happening in the post-war years are not, at the century's end, resolved. The case of Stephen Lawrence, teenage victim of a racist murder in 1993, gave rise in 1997 to a judicial public enquiry into the police handling of the case, staged in a documentary at the Tricycle Theatre, London: *The Colour of Justice – The Stephen Lawrence Inquiry*.[61] In 1991, an uncanny ten years after the rioting in Brixton and Toxteth, urban unrest produced rioting across three cities: Cardiff, Oxford and Tyneside. Documented by Beatrix Campbell in *Goliath: Britain's Dangerous Places*, the riots were also 'staged' in a production by The Sphinx Theatre Company of *Goliath*, directed by Annie Castledine, and adapted by Bryony Lavery (see Chapter 6) from Campbell's study (Newcastle Playhouse, 1997, and national tour). As a collaboration between Castledine, Lavery and Campbell, *Goliath* offered a feminist treatment of social violence that was male-authored and, largely, although not exclusively, racially motivated.[62]

Aside from her interest in the collaboration with Lavery, and the influence of Campbell's study, Castledine's inspiration for *Goliath* came from Anna Deavere Smith's performance of *Fires in the Mirror* brought to the Royal Court in 1993.[63] Briefly, *Fires*, which has been widely documented by feminist theatre scholars, is based on the Crown Height Riots, in New York's Brooklyn Heights, home to communities of African-Americans and Hasidic Jews. Like the British rioting, these communities erupted into violence in the summer of 1991, after the death of a black child, run over by a car in a motorcade of an Hasidic, spiritual leader, and the subsequent stabbing of an Hasidic scholar by African-American youths. Deavere Smith's performance is collaged out of taped interviews that she conducted in the aftermath of Crown Heights. As a one-woman play, Deavere Smith acts out living testimonies taken from the scene of events, in order that her audiences bear witness to them.

Taking her inspiration from Campbell's *Goliath*, Lavery created a one-woman show that was performed by Nicola McAuliffe.[64] The play opens with the death of a joyrider, Gary, and moves into sequences covering each of the cities and the events that lead to the rioting: fighting between youths and police outside a Pakistani-owned grocer's shop in Ely, Cardiff; clashes between police and 'joyriders' in Blackbird Leys, Oxford, and gangs and police fighting in Meadowell, Tyneside, that put Asian communities at risk. McAuliffe's characters therefore ranged across policemen, residents of the different estates, Asian traders, community leaders, joyriders, angry young men and grieving mothers.[65]

The disjunction between the single woman's body on stage and the acting out of the 'Goliath' of social violence visually reflected the disempowerment of women in the estate communities. As Campbell notes, in the outbreaks of violence, women across different communities, black and white, had least recourse to authority; 'had no agency, supported by the state, to share their grievances about the hazards of everyday existence'.[66] Especially poignant is Maureen's story in the Meadowell section, which narrates the story of her son Gary (the dead driver imaged in the opening of the play), like Maureen's son Malcolm, lost to a life of crime. 'The women in *Goliath* have no weapons, apart from the little stories of persistence and good will', explains Lavery, but their stories (like Margaret's) are to be celebrated for their courage and 'heroism'.[67] Storytelling in both performances is used as a cultural 'weapon'.

The Story of M and Goliath point towards the necessity, as Pinnock argued, for moving beyond discrete labels or identities of black, woman and playwright. To identify separately is to resist the need for making feminist connections. Moreover, this chapter shows that feminism can no longer afford to be as exclusively or predominantly concerned with matters of sexual difference as it once was. At the century's end, women can no longer stand as 'woman alone'.[68]

8   Feminism past, and future?

Timberlake Wertenbaker

In this chapter, I return to two key areas of debate: the relevance of feminism to women's lives at the close of the twentieth century and the 'crisis in masculinity' that I outlined in Chapter 1. To generate general discussion on both of these points, I specifically turn to another established and high profile playwright of the contemporary English stage: Timberlake Wertenbaker.

Like Caryl Churchill, Timberlake Wertenbaker has had a long and productive career on English and international stages. Also like Churchill, Wertenbaker benefited in her early writing years from support from a women's company,[1] and from a sustained relationship in the 1980s with the Royal Court and its director Max Stafford-Clark. The 1990s, however, were more difficult for Wertenbaker. Along with other playwrights in this volume, she felt marginalised by the 'rush of plays by male dramatists'. 'I don't think women have ever been a welcome voice', she explained, 'You sense a relief that we can shut those women up and get back to what really matters, which is what men are saying. . . . We talk about women dramatists, but it's significant that "woman" becomes the compound whereas "male" is the noun'.[2] Moreover, while the Royal Court was her 'home' in the 1980s, in the 1990s Wertenbaker found herself 'homeless': partly due to Stafford-Clark's departure in 1993 to go freelance and partly due to her resignation from the Royal Court Board, over the Court's drive towards private sponsorship which Wertenbaker saw as detrimental to new writing.[3] While still produced at the Court and still able to work with Stafford-Clark, the point is that these are now rather different, less secure, working conditions to those of the 1980s.

The issue of 'home' is interesting in Wertenbaker's case given her mixed cultural background. Anglo-American in origin, but raised in the French-speaking part of the Basque country, Wertenbaker, like Nagy, regards herself as 'something of an outsider in the British theatrical establishment: a tolerated guest rather than a permanent resident'.[4] More specifically she argues her 'outsider' status as partly due to cultural identity and partly due to gender: being a woman in a male-dominated profession. Michael Billington's comment in response to this – and this is a comment that is frequently made about Wertenbaker's work – is that 'the very qualities that make her an outsider are also the ones that have made her a good writer: an ability to view British life from a critical distance'.[5] The 'ability to view British life from a critical distance' is something that connects to other major concerns in Wertenbaker's work that I would argue include her desire for the epic, her concern with gender, and her belief in theatre as a redemptive and socially transformative force. These are all enduring characteristics of her work, though they shift constantly in response to political, social, cultural and theatrical change.

Wertenbaker has always been attracted to the idea of tackling 'big subjects', frequently turning to classic myths or plays and giving them a contemporary twist, as, for example, in *The Love of the Nightingale* (1988), or, more recently, her radio play, *Dianeira* (1999). The epic offers a way of resisting the received view of women's writing as somehow confined to and concerned only with domestic, 'female' environments. *The Love of the Nightingale* situates the rape and silencing of Philomele in a Greek tragedy, rather than a realist (home) setting.[6] Isabelle Eberhardt, a dramatisation of the nineteenth-century traveller in *New Anatomies*, and Mary, a fictional character in the eighteenth-century London setting of *The Grace of Mary Traverse* (1985), are both examples of women who abandon the confines of the domestic; take on male disguises and embark on epic journeys of personal, social, sexual and cultural discovery. Isabelle and Mary are women seeking adventures, and adventures, Wertenbaker argues, are still difficult for women to have, even at the close of the twentieth century.[7]

Although her first play of the 1990s, *Three Birds Alighting on a Field* (Royal Court, 1991) is very much a play about the 1980s: a savage critique of the Thatcherite legacy in Britain, figuratively represented through the art world with, as Wertenbaker explains, 'money being the only recognized value' (*Plays 1*, p.ix). This retrospective critique of the 1980s performed at the start of the 1990s is rather different, however, to the way in which subsequent plays become increasingly marked by Wertenbaker's insistence that we look critically at Britain in relation to Europe. More specifically, and in the context of this chapter, more significantly, is the way in which she makes important connections between issues of European citizenship and contemporary feminism.

Abel's Sister: a feminist past

An emergent feminism in Wertenbaker's theatre can be traced back to a relatively little known, rarely discussed (significantly, unpublished) play: *Abel's Sister*,[8] staged in 1984 in between high profile plays such as *New Anatomies* (1982) and *The Grace of Mary Traverse* (1985). *Abel's Sister*, a collaboration with disabled writer Yolande Bourcier, was Wertenbaker's first Royal Court production.[9] Wertenbaker worked on poems, stories and notes by Bourcier to script *Abel's Sister* and to map disability with feminist concerns. Briefly, Laura, married to Howard, is represented in *Abel's Sister* as a feminist intellectual and bourgeois feminist masquerading as a socialist feminist. Laura has ideas about a perfect world, a new world. She talks about this a lot, philosophises, but her words do not translate into lived realities. Sandra, Howard's sister, on the other hand, is disabled. She has a cyst in her brain and is a living critique of Laura's 'perfect world': someone who is not perfect, does not fit in, is not seen by the world as someone who can have a home, relationships, family, children. Sandra does imagine the world differently, but her perfect world is one which is flat – flat so that wheelchairs can get around.

Two issues are specifically highlighted in this dysfunctional landscape: motherhood and Englishness. Laura's feminist 'rational' self made the decision to get herself sterilised, but she is now suffering a so-called 'irrational' ache to have children. Sandra would like to have children but nobody thinks of her as a potential mother and anyway, as she puts it, her children might come out 'wonky'. Motherhood, therefore, emerges as an unresolved feminist issue, while Englishness is critiqued for its colonialist (reference is made to the then recent Falklands war), isolationist, island mentality: a life denying, rather than life affirming force, echoed in David Roger's set design of 'dried heather and artificial rocks, as unmistakably lifeless as the mounting for stuffed animals in a glass case'.[10] Howard and Laura's closest neighbour is Chris, actually some way off in his thatched cottage, an American who, but for Sandra, the English would not speak to. In brief, *Abel's Sister* dramatises a sterile, non-reproductive, non-communicating and selfish world, in which a less able 'sister' cannot have adventures.

On the one hand, Wertenbaker identified the 1980s as a decade without hope, a decade of despair; a time of feeling that the world might as well end, that humanity had forfeited its right to survive. On the other hand, she saw feminism as responsible for bringing some energy into the world.[11] Her concern, however, was whether this energy would last. In *Abel's Sister* feminism is represented as a rather fragile source of energy, that to survive must aim to be inclusive rather than exclusive; must move beyond the bourgeois feminist model of privilege and look to the transformation of family and nation.

The Break of Day: a feminist future?
These are all issues to which Wertenbaker returns in her mid-1990s play, *The Break of Day*. The play was directed by Max Stafford-Clark and performed by his newly formed theatre company Out of Joint. Wertenbaker had previously worked in this way with *Our Country's Good* that Stafford-Clark paired with George Farquhar's *The Recruiting Officer*. *The Break of Day* premiered in 1995 with Chekhov's *Three Sisters*, the same year, coincidentally, that Scarlet Theatre Company premiered their reinscription of Chekhov's play, *The Sisters*.[12]

In contrast to Chekhov's three sisters, Wertenbaker's three 'sisters' at the close of the twentieth century have had adventures in their lives and have been 'successful' women. Tess, Nina and April are women whose lives intersected with and were influenced by the feminism of the 1970s. Each woman chose a 'top girl' career-job: Tess is now the high-flying editor of a women's magazine; Nina is a singer–songwriter, and April lectures in classics at a university. Like Laura and Sandra, these three women are childless: April by choice, while Tess and Nina have discovered that they cannot have, though both desire to have, children. All three women are dissatisfied with their personal and professional lives.

In the mid-1980s, Laura's feminist vision, however inadequate, was at least a vision. In the 1990s, Tess, Nina and April struggle to find feminism relevant to their lives, or, more specifically, to view it as an energising force. In the opening act, they talk about their feminist past as an empowering moment that enriched their lives. Now Nina has no words for her songs; April's work has become an endless round of filling in forms, rather than teaching, and Tess's glossy magazine is divorced from the reality of women's lives. It is not just their own lives that generate a feeling of disempowerment, but the overwhelming sense of England as in a state of collapse – a country in which social and cultural systems (hospitals, schools, theatre) are underfunded and failing. How to find a way forward and out of this moment of social and cultural despair is a question the play poses.

Tess's idea in bringing the three of them together in her country home to celebrate her fortieth birthday (analogous to Irina's name-day in *Three Sisters*) is to look back at their feminist past and re-live that moment of empowerment. Conversely, however, Wertenbaker shows that the way forward lies not in the past but in making new, cross-border, feminist connections in the interests of securing a less selfish and more democratic future. Where *Abel's Sister* posed reproduction and nationhood as problematic (and as yet unresolved) issues for feminism, *The Break of Day* explores these further through the possibility of transracial adoption.

The adoption narrative is staged in Act Two as Nina and her husband Hugh leave England for Eastern Europe (exactly where is never specified), in order to adopt a baby girl.[13] The adoption is beset with difficulties that arise out of the social, medical and juridical chaos of an Eastern Europe that has abandoned communism for capitalism. Nina and Hugh are helped by Mihail and Eva from the East.

The ultimate success of the adoption depends on the cross-border collaboration of the two couples; their willingness to take risks and to find ways to circumvent, to manipulate and to resist the bureaucratic, medical and legal obstacles in their way. Eventually, what they find is that others are also willing to help; to transgress rather than to uphold state and international law. One way of characterising this cross-border collaboration is as a dramatisation of what M. Jacqui Alexander and Chandra Mohanty describe as a 'transborder participatory democracy' that is 'one in which it is not the state but people themselves who emerge as the chief agents in defining the course of the global economic and political processes that structure their lives'.[14] Out of the 'transborder participatory democracy' in *The Break of Day* comes the possibility of a more hopeful future, imagined through the figure of the cross-border child. In a monologue towards the close of the second act, and at a point where the adoption, after all the setbacks, is almost secured Mihail explains:

> Now it [history] will be in the hands of the children, possibly
> most of all, these cross-border children I have helped to get
> out. Born in one country, loved and raised in another, I hope
> they will not descend into narrow ethnic identification, but
> that they will be wilfully international, part of a great
> European community . . . We must not go into the next
> century with no ideal but selfishness.[15]

The cross-border child represents a concept of the family based not on nation, but on a transnational community: one that crosses borders and involves the collaboration between two sets of apparently outmoded beliefs, Western feminism and East European communism, both struggling to find ways of shaping the future; of struggling to find a selfless way forward in a world which, as Mihail describes, has 'no ideal but selfishness', where 'people talk freely, but only about money' (*The Break of Day*, p.86).[16]

There are three locational shifts in *The Break of Day*, each of which is significant in terms of the cross-border project. When the play opens, like *Abel's Sister* it is set in the English countryside – more precisely in an English country house, where the characters gather,

Chekhov style, to drink coffee, and talk 'post-feminist' lives. It marks a moment of stasis; of lives stuck, going nowhere; of disillusion and discontent. To move out of or beyond this millennium moment of despair and hopelessness, requires re-locating from the country house setting in England, to Eastern Europe in Act Two. Act Three re-locates to England, but not back in a 'home', a domestic, conventional, familial space. Characters re-unite backstage in a theatre dressing room for a touring production of the *Three Sisters* in which Robert, Tess's husband, is playing the part of Vershinin. The conditions of small-scale touring theatre mean that your 'home' is the company of like-minded people you work with. Your touring life keeps you moving, mobile, passing through different spaces, different communities with whom you seek engagement, with whom you hope you have something in common – or can persuade your audiences of points of commonality. Moreover, there is a parallel to be drawn between the small group of people involved in the cross-border adoption and the small-scale touring company: both situations involve groups of people committed to social and cultural 'causes' based on selfless rather than selfish principles.

Juxtaposed with the narrative of the cross-border child in Act Two is Tess's narrative, which details her infertility treatment at a London clinic. The short scenes in which Tess seeks treatment from the ironically named Dr Glad punctuate the scenes in Eastern Europe, so that the stage takes on a crossing-borders aesthetic. As this Act, in contrast to the registers of realism used in the first, is composed as a Brechtian montage it is designed to politicise, rather than to psychoanalyse. It demonstrates the risk to the maternal caught up in bourgeois feminist models of privilege in which control over reproductive rights is handed over to male-dominated biotechnology: to capitalism and to patriarchy. In contrast to Nina's way forward, Tess relinquishes her opportunity to shape, to participate in the 'moment', rather than allow herself to be shaped, defined by it.

You do not have to cross countries to see differently; to initiate social change. Laura's vision of a perfect world failed in *Abel's Sister*, because it did not look to ways of 'seeing' her less abled, less advantaged 'sister', who visits her 'home'. In *The Break of Day*, Tess employs

Natasha, possibly a Bosnian refugee, to clean her house. Nobody really knows where Natasha is from or who she is, and nobody thinks
it important to find out. Not to ask and not to attempt to understand,
however, means that violence and oppression continue. This point is
reinforced when a neighbour makes a brief appearance at the close of
Act One. Tess's neighbour in the English countryside is a widower
whose French–Jewish wife was exiled to Britain in the War to escape
the Nazis. He explains:

> She [his wife] died, three years ago just when the war in
> Eastern Europe started. I watch the television all the time
> now. And I see them, I think I see her. People with suitcases,
> walking, walking with their suitcases. I thought we'd never
> see those images again . . . I'm going to march with my
> suitcase every day for the rest of my life. I'm going to protest
> against history.
>
> (*The Break of Day*, p.46)

This speech and the powerful parallel drawn between the holocaust
and the war in Eastern Europe, finally prompts Nina to ask Natasha
where she is from. As in Kane's *Blasted*, *The Break of Day* encourages
'spectatorship' of a history of world events where people are invited
to feel affected and not disaffected by what they see.

The Break of Day and the critics

Like Nagy's *The Strip*, *The Break of Day* stands in Wertenbaker's
canon as the play that the critics least understood and were the most
hostile to. However, the negative press reviews are worth analysing
for the attitudes that they reveal towards feminism and for the possible misunderstandings of the cross-border feminism that I am arguing for here. My argument rests on seeing the possible connections between Wertenbaker's dramatisation of the political debates
about Britain in the 1990s and the feminist ones. Where, for example, Michael Coveney saw *The Break of Day* as a play 'torn between
two plays a state-of-the-nation talk-in, and an examination of selfish
parenthood',[17] I propose that nation and family are both a part of imagining the possibilities of cross-border citizenship. Or, where David

Nathan argued that the 'play edges to the conclusion that, whatever the public squalor, the gift of hope depends on personal fulfilment'.[18] I would maintain that the play shows that the personal is a part of a socio-political matrix: that a more hopeful future is not dependent on 'personal fulfilment', but on the agency to transform the social, economic, cultural and geographical structures within which the personal is sited. The personal lives of the three 'sisters' are a part and (potentially) a hopeful part of the epic political struggle to define a better future.

Secondly, *The Break of Day* was variously read by critics as a backlash against feminism play. Paul Taylor described it as an illustration of 'how the maternal drive can cause women to betray orthodox feminism' and Nicholas de Jongh concluded 'that for all the cut and thrust of feminism, Miss [*sic*] Wertenbaker believes women need motherhood'.[19] This shows how hard it is to engage in debate around reproduction without it being read as advocating a biologically determinist view of women's lives. It is difficult, as Susan Bordo acknowledges, engaging in a feminist debate around birth and pregnancy for 'fear of the conceptual proximity of such notions of constructions of mothering as the one true destiny for women'.[20] While Bordo argues that the time has come to have 'a public, feminist discourse on pregnancy and birth rather than leaving it in the hands of the "pro-lifers"',[21] the reception of *The Break of Day* demonstrates this may be hard to achieve. Nevertheless, through theatre, the play makes public the demand that feminist attention be paid to the maternal, as an unresolved issue, rather than as the (backlash) solution to women's discontent with working lives.

Thirdly, there is a less than sympathetic view of infertility in the theatre reviews. Comments range from de Jongh's dismissive and offensive description of Tess as 'poised to set out on an egg and sperm race'[22] and Charles Spencer's complaint that having personal knowledge about the 'agonies of IVF treatment' he was actually annoyed that this play left him 'dry-eyed' rather than 'reduce[d] to tears'.[23] Wertenbaker's aim, however, is to politicise (rather than to personalise or 'emotionalise') reproductive technology: to press home the point that if formerly feminism was concerned with contraceptive technology, it now has to address the issue of how, or indeed whether, women can take advantage of the new reproductive technology, without themselves being taken advantage of (emotionally, economically and medically).

Despite my very different reading of *The Break of Day* to those critics cited, I would not, on the other hand, wish to argue that the play is completely without fault. In terms of a proposal for a cross-border politics, there is a difficulty, I would suggest, between narrativising the play from the British viewpoint, at the expense of the Eastern European. The dispossessed and oppressed figures such as Natasha, or the neighbour's wife, whilst situated as critical points on the English landscape, do not have, but are in need of, more attention. Charlotte Canning has noted the 'imbalance between the specificity of England's political and social problems . . . and the vague difficulties caused by the end of communism for former Soviet bloc nations'.[24] Arguably, the most pressing issue is the absence of the Eastern European mother. Her absence hints at the very real difficulty of negotiating cross-border citizenship given the unequal positions that people, women especially, may be starting from.

Feminist connections: *Shang-A-Lang*, Catherine Johnson and *The Positive Hour*, April de Angelis

The Break of Day offers a cross-border feminism as a glimmer of a more hopeful twenty-first century. It is, however, only a glimmer in an otherwise dark picture of social and cultural despair. Wertenbaker joins with other playwrights in this volume in viewing the century's end as a moment, as she describes it, of 'sadness', of 'uncertainty' in which 'human beings are in trouble in some way'.[25] As *The Break of Day* illustrates, in terms of women's lives specifically, at the century's end women find themselves 'in trouble' through the loss of 'certainty' experienced in the 1970s, when the possibility of radical change and empowerment was in view. Looking back to the 1970s as a more positive, 'certain' time for women, is themed in two further, albeit quite different, plays that I introduce here as a point of comparison with *The Break of Day*: Catherine Johnson's *Shang-a-Lang* (Bush Theatre, 1998) and April de Angelis's *The Positive Hour* (Hampstead Theatre, 1997).

Johnson's *Shang-a-Lang* focuses on a friendship between three women – marking a gender shift from her early, debut play at the Bush, *Boys Mean Business* (1989).[26] Like *The Break of Day*, Pauline, Jackie and Lauren are three long-standing friends who get together to celebrate Pauline's fortieth birthday party at a Bay City Rollers weekend at Butlins in Minehead. As the names, setting and event suggest, unlike Tess, Nina and April, these are working-class, not middle-class women. They do not talk of a feminist past as a moment of empowerment in their lives, but their teenage lives figure retrospectively as the best time of their lives. After some delightful 'bad' behaviour and several quarrels, the play ends with the friendship between the women dismissed by Pauline as not a friendship but a 'habit',[27] and with them all going their separate ways: Jackie goes home to a husband to confess to having had a one-night stand; Lauren takes off with members of the Roller's tribute band, and Pauline stays on at the Rollers weekend, with her dreams of Woody.[28] The idea that women from the 1970s have grown up with only their teenage pop idols to sustain their emotionally and financially impoverished lives, overall makes for a depressing drama, despite some very funny observational moments (which I, and several of the other fortysomething women in the matinee audience of the touring production of *Shang-a-Lang* clearly enjoyed).[29] Johnson since has found commercial success with the 1970s, going on to create the Abba musical *Mamma Mia*.

What haunts *Shang-a-Lang* is feminism's failure in the 1970s to bring 'adventure' to the working-class lives of young girls like Pauline and her 'mates'. The failings of a 1970s feminism is the subject of April de Angelis's ironically titled, *The Positive Hour*. There are points of continuity between the production of *The Break of Day* and *The Positive Hour*: both were directed by Stafford-Clark, and performed by Out of Joint (*Positive Hour* was in a co-production with Hampstead Theatre). As the titles to both plays suggest, each interrogates a moment of (feminist) hope, but missing from *The Positive Hour* is the glimmer of optimism that heralds the possibility of change. 'Because I do not hope to know again/ The infirm glory of the positive hour' is the quote from T.S. Eliot which prefaces the play,[30] for which read the 'infirm glory' of feminism's 'positive hour'.[31]

There are connections between Wertenbaker and de Angelis as writers – not in respect of style (de Angelis is far more eclectic), but in terms of interests. Like Wertenbaker (although towards the end rather than near the beginning of the 1980s) de Angelis had support for her early work from women's and new writing companies (*Ironmistress* was staged by the women's company Resisters in 1988; other plays were staged by the new writing companies Paines Plough and Red Shift). *Playhouse Creatures*, premiered by The Sphinx Theatre Company in 1993, like *Our Country's Good* and *After Darwin*, works through a theatre setting (looking at Restoration actresses and historicising past and present inequalities for women working in the theatre.)

Where both women playwrights share materialist-feminist concerns in their earlier work, their attitudes to feminism in the 1990s, as reflected in their respective plays, are quite different. All of the characters in *The Positive Hour* are in crisis and the forum used to stage this is a women's group counselling session – an echo of earlier consciousness-raising sessions in the WLM. As in *The Break of Day*, women come together to talk, but it is a much darker conversation and much harder for the women to make connections. Participants in *The Positive Hour* group include Paula (working-class, single mother with violent boyfriend whose daughter, Victoria, has been placed with foster parents), Nicola (young single woman whose alcoholic bereaved father refuses to let her have a life of her own) and Emma (middle-class, divorced and dealing with the break-up of her marriage). These are women having troubles, not adventures. Even Miranda, the group leader and social worker is dysfunctional (she has recently had a nervous breakdown and her own marriage breaks up during the course of the play). Systems of self-help, deemed so important in the climate of 1970s feminism, are now seen not only as insufficient, but possibly even dangerous to lives in the 1990s, as attempts of the group, under Miranda's direction, to form a women's only space to make 'positive' changes in their lives, fail to cope with dangerous realities. The most poignant evocation of this comes in the closing moments of the play as Miranda reveals that the real reason behind her breakdown was finding a dead child: a child left to starve to death and whose body was covered in 'hundreds of tiny cuts', that someone, Miranda explains, made not out of anger, but satisfaction (*The Positive Hour*, p.84).

Feminism is represented in the play as having failed women in its promise of a better life.[32] Having lived by the feminist creed, for example, Emma finds herself getting increasingly angry with feminism for the way in which her life has turned out: 'Just do this and this and all the good talented things inside you will come out. Abandon the life of your mothers. Well, I did and now I've got nothing. No career, no husband, no child. Nothing's turned out the way it was supposed to' (*The Positive Hour*, p. 48). Disillusioned and angry with feminism she begins to explore other (previously repressed) ways of living: experimenting with S&M, or earning money through commercial art work, rather than living as a failed artist. Faced with Emma's anger Miranda is forced to admit that 'perhaps things haven't turned out the way we wanted', though she also recognises that that '[feminist] moment of absolute certainty' is what makes 'you choose to go on acting on that faith because you know it's the best thing you've got' (*The Positive Hour*, p.48). De Angelis's dark, bitter, though also funny, play involves all of the women moving out of Miranda's feminist orbit: the group breaks up, as does Miranda's marriage. The play ends on a note of uncertainty, as suggested in De Angelis's final stage directions: '*There is a bright flash of light, noise. Whether it is frightening, as in a thunderstorm, or hopeful, as in a bright future, is ambiguous. Nicky stands unsure.*' (*The Positive Hour*, p.86.)

That the two playwrights, whose theatre had earlier shared points of materialist-feminist contact, should come to such very different conclusions about feminism in the 1990s makes for an interesting point of divergence. Both writers variously articulate, as do all of the women playwrights in this study, the desire not to be constrained or limited by the label of 'woman writer'. Similarly, for those women, like Wertenbaker and De Angelis, whose playwriting spans across decades (rather than, for example, Kane's exclusively 1990s canon), the role of feminism necessarily changes in their work. De Angelis describes feminism, for example, as an 'umbrella' that she needed to get out from under, in order, as she explains it to 'address the world without those ideas, whilst somehow taking them with me'.[33] This point brings me back to what I earlier described as Wertenbaker's critically misunderstood project in *The Break of Day*: of taking feminism forward as a part of a bigger, epic political struggle.

Nevertheless, where I detect the root of the divergence is in the writers' attitudes towards the 'energy' that feminism may still have to offer the world. Clearly, Wertenbaker views this more 'positively' than De Angelis. The world may be a darker, more violent place, as so much of women's (and men's) dramatic work from the 1990s suggests, and feminism has not (could not) have delivered all the demands made of it and by it as *The Positive Hour* dramatises. However, to understand, rather than to blame a feminist past and to resist a 'post-feminist' present (and future) through an agency dependent upon cross-border collaborations offers a way forward. Without this kind of feminist collaboration, then the likelihood is, Wertenbaker's theatre suggests, that a future history will be an 'adventure' determined by gender, class and race in which less able 'sisters' are unlikely to survive.

Adventures for the boys
After Darwin

In this part of this chapter, I return to where I began this study: with representations of masculinity and the culture of the masculine in the 1990s. If feminism is to pursue a more enabling, less disabling, politics as argued for in this and previous chapters, it must also counter accusations that it is to 'blame' for the 'crisis in masculinity'; must invite a response to this 'crisis' that involves an understanding of how men's roles are changing in work and family, and must actively discourage a colonialist legacy of white, masculinist 'supremacy'. To pursue this discussion, I turn to Wertenbaker's *After Darwin*, staged the year following *The Positive Hour* at the Hampstead Theatre (1998).

Briefly, and in stark contrast to Wertenbaker's feminist belief in the need for women to have adventures, *After Darwin* dramatises the 'boys-only' 1831 adventure of Captain Robert FitzRoy, and the clergyman–naturalist, Charles Darwin, on their voyage aboard *The Beagle* to the Galapagos Islands. Unable to tolerate Darwin's emergent theory of evolution that unsettles spiritual belief in God the Creator, but also unable to persuade Darwin to desist from his views,

friendship turns to enmity, and, ultimately, results in FitzRoy's suicide (staged as the opening scene to the play). Compositionally, *After
Darwin* emerges as a play about a play about the voyage, a device that
enables Wertenbaker to introduce a second set of contemporary theatre characters: the play's director, Millie (a Turkish–Bulgarian dissident); the writer, Lawrence (a black-American tutor of the 'Meta-
physics of Cultural Genealogy'), and two actors: Tom (who is gay and
plays Darwin), and Ian (who is straight and divorced and plays Fitzroy).

After Darwin dramaturgically works to pursue the idea of theatre as a space in which ideas and self-knowledge might evolve. The
play's two-act structure works through two different historical settings: Act One is set on board *The Beagle* (at sea, where ideas are fluid
and subject to change); Act Two is set in Darwin's study (on land,
where new ideas are explored and shaped). These settings also work
metatheatrically as the fictional spaces for Lawrence's play. As a spectator, I found that the metatheatricality of this jolted you backwards
and forwards between past and present, in a way that mirrored the
shifts in perception that the characters are forced to make about their
own lives and the lives of others.

In working through a dual timeframe, Wertenbaker establishes
a parallel between the breakdown of certainty in the nineteenth century after the dawn of Darwin's theory of evolution and the uncertainty that colours the close of the twentieth century. Moreover, the
misappropriation of Darwin's theory in the interests of supporting a
late twentieth-century view of competitive survival (ironically embodied in the character of Darwin's interpreter, Tom), come under
the dramatic microscope. The complex present/past relations between
Tom/Darwin and Ian/Fitzroy affords a dialectical staging of the selfish
and selfless; of travelling light or being willing to take responsibility
for the luggage of the past,[34] all of which echoes Mihail's plea in *The
Break of Day* for a way of re-visioning a contemporary world that has
'no ideal but selfishness'.

Given the feminist debate that is dramatised in *The Break of
Day* and the foregrounding of the 'three sisters', I was initially sur-
prised in *After Darwin* by Wertenbaker's male-dominated stage picture. On (post-production) reflection, however, I began to see certain

kinds of connections between the two plays, though obviously from very differently gendered perspectives. The historical framing of *After Darwin* takes us back to a nineteenth-century (pre-First Women's Liberation Movement) moment of change when the 'order of things' shifts from a God-made to a man-made world. At no point, however, does the 'birth' of man as self-creator/self-created involve 'woman'.

As the only woman in the play, and as the director of Lawrence's play, Millie is temporally located in the fictional present. The 'past' has no roles for women, except as middle-class domestic creatures in English homes,[35] or as a colonised other in territories charted by FitzRoy – 'foreign' countries, such as 'Tierra del Fuego, where, so we are told, women, once they have outlived their usefulness, get eaten by their tribes in times of famine' (*After Darwin*, p.134). In sum, as the voyage of intellectual and geographical discovery was gendered, raced, classed and nationed, Millie could have no part in it. As she states, 'a woman's territory is already so insecure' (*After Darwin*, p.132).

A question that the play poses, however, is whether Millie can have a role in the future? As theatre director she has the task of shaping the drama, events and ideas, but her role is constantly beset by the difficulties of holding the production together, especially in the light of Tom's selfish behaviour. In the final scene Millie and Lawrence are represented as tourists visiting Darwin's house. Millie's attention is drawn to the 'imaginary line of bookshelves' (*After Darwin*, p.175), and she browses the titles of man-made history, thought and creation, that have brought her, as a displaced Eastern European woman, to the point of extinction. Can that change? Fitzroy appeals to Lawrence as the writer to bring him back and to make him a part of things: a different cultural vision in the interests of progressive social change. They all need to be included if there is to be a chance of a less selfish, more democratic future, one that allows Millie not just to survive but also to flourish.[36]

Negotiating masculinities

Reviews of *After Darwin*, although mixed, were significantly better than those Wertenbaker received for *The Break of Day*.[37] It would be oversimplistic and polemical of me to argue that this is an issue of straightforward prejudice: that a play about women is far less attractive than a play that (appears to be) predominantly about men. Moreover, to pursue this line of argument would be to elide an important issue in both plays: the way in which re-figuring masculinity is represented as a part of Wertenbaker's epic, feminist picture.

While Wertenbaker looked to feminism in the mid-1980s to bring some energy into the world, it is clear, looking briefly at the representation of masculinity in *Abel's Sister*, that men were not contributing to this energisation. Neither Chris nor Howard are represented as particularly useful or inspiring to the idea of a better world. Howard designs posters for alternative causes, but does not appear to be active in or committed to any himself. Chris, the American, ex-Vietnam fighter and protestor, is physically and emotionally damaged. Where there is energy in the play it comes, ultimately, from Sandra, the least 'abled' 'sister', but the most capable of 'seeing' a more inclusive way of imagining the world.

The dysfunctionality of Chris and Howard is one kind of representation of the masculine in the 1980s. *Three Birds Alighting*, at the beginning of the 1990s, showed another: the masculine ethos of a materially driven culture. For masculinity to adopt a less selfish, less materialistic, creed in the 1990s then men have to be more reflective than they have been about the lives they live. Traditionally, it has been women who have found the space to reflect on their lives – most specifically in the consciousness-raising, women-only groups in the 1970s, as satirised in *The Positive Hour*.[38] When the women come together in *The Break of Day* they are meeting to talk; the men are going to play sport (tennis). Yet, as Act One illustrates, the men also have a need to talk about and to reflect on their personal and professional lives.[39] (In the end the game of tennis is never played.) Moreover, in *After Darwin*, the complex paralleling of Ian and Tom, FitzRoy and Darwin centrally stages the inability to communicate and to share the anxieties, feelings and emotions that arise as history (in both centuries) shifts and redefines systems of belief and social orders. Metatheatrically, as the performers play actors preparing, through Stanislavski's system of rehearsal, to play Darwin and FitzRoy, space is created for Tom and Ian to reflect on the emotional states of their respective characters.

Given the doubling of roles, this involves them talking about their own lives, as well as the lives of their characters. As a device, the dual role play also suggests the idea of a more fluid concept of subjectivity: one which might allow for the possibility of change.

In *The Break of Day*, Tess's gardener, Paul, is someone who has made a significant change of lifestyle. Paul recollects the 1980s as a materialistically driven decade, and, in consequence, in the 1990s explains that he has turned his back on money, family, luxury home. He earns a wage as a gardener, and while he knows he could make lots of money as a landscape gardener, chooses not to go down that route in order not to get caught up again in the ethos of greed. Paul's recantation of his 1980s lifestyle is not, however, expressed as a consequence of feminism: he did not lose his job and status because of women, his change in lifestyle is a choice he makes. This is in contradistinction to the widely held belief in the 1990s of the feminist empowerment of women necessitating the dispossession of men.

Wertenbaker, by contrast, shows that the issue is not one of men falling victim to women's success, but of the difficulty men experience in negotiating their roles and lives in relation to shifting social structures. In *The Break of Day* it is not that the women are represented as simply doing 'better' than the men and at their expense, but that political, social and economic change conditions lives, employment prospects or job satisfaction, for which feminism alone cannot be held responsible, but for which it is frequently used as a scapegoat. As Imelda Whelehan in *Overloaded* argues:

> The logic of the backlash [against feminism] is maintained by identifying social ills and foisting them onto the shoulders of bad old feminists. But if we attempt to see past this, what we assuredly find is a highly technologised world and a shifting economy with which people in their ordinary lives, expectations and attitudes have trouble keeping up.[40]

None of the men in *The Break of Day* are represented as victims of women's success. Rather, each has to give consideration to work in what is represented as a volatile economy: where theatre is poorly funded (Robert), hospitals are closing (Jamie) and contracts are lost

(Hugh). Each, to borrow the argument from *After Darwin*, has to adapt to survive. Moreover, just as the capitalist idea of man as 'breadwin-ner', the main wage earner, is no longer as stable as it once was, then neither, given the new reproductive technology, is patriarchy. A low sperm count also has implications for paternity: a 'father' may no longer be the biological father of 'his' child.[41]

Both *The Break of Day* and *After Darwin* attempt to shift us out of the familiar patterns of biological thinking and parenting, towards the possibility of new, cross-border collaborations: to help the child from Eastern Europe in *The Break of Day*, and the young woman, Millie, in *After Darwin*. For this to happen, the impulse to stay inside our own colonialist histories, to reproduce the 'selfsame', has to be resisted.[42]

Theatre: a space to imagine

While the shift towards Europe and questions of citizenship in Werten-baker's theatre in the 1990s may be due in part to what Billington and others identify as her 'outsider' status, it is also a response, I would argue, to social and political changes in Europe. In a roundtable discus-sion broadcast on radio in December 1989, Timberlake Wertenbaker and other theatre guests looked back on the 1980s and forward to the 1990s.[43] Looking back, the changes in Europe, particularly the coming down of the Berlin Wall, were discussed as radically altering our per-ception of the world. Looking to the future, Wertenbaker forecast the writers in the West as the new dissidents of a theatre that while cul-turally vital, struggles to survive. As testimony to that view, we can contrast the energy, hope and sense of community that the convicts, exiled from Britain to Australia, experience through the opportunity offered to them of putting on a play in Wertenbaker's *Our Country's Good* (1988), with the way in which the theatre is represented in *The Break of Day* and *After Darwin* as still hopeful, but barely surviving.

As a feminist 'dissident' of the 1990s in a theatre struggling to survive, Wertenbaker's advocacy of theatre as one of the few arenas left to us for shared discussion and public debate is undaunted. At the close of *The Break of Day* as the characters group together in the dressing-room of the theatre, Tess says 'We only want to try and understand what's happened', and, in response, Robert delivers the last line of the play: 'you could even say that's hopeful' (*The Break of Day*, p.98). Trying to 'understand what's happened' is, therefore, metatheatrically situated: theatre, Wertenbaker suggests, is a space that allows us to understand, and (hopefully) to know more about ourselves (not just personally, but socially, culturally, politically). In *After Darwin*, the rehearsal room is represented not as a space for the fixing and plotting of dramatic events, but for different ways of creating characters, playing scenes and exploring different emotional states.[44] Ideas need to be embodied in feelings and emotions so as to be shared and understood by others. In brief, while vulnerable (to cinema and to new technologies) theatre, Wertenbaker argues, is necessary and vital to culture. 'It is quite possible – that human beings have come to the end of their evolution . . . but . . . we will never come to the end of our imagination' claims the writer, Lawrence, in *After Darwin* (p.160). Imagining is also a form of evolving. 'The idea of cultural evolution, separated from biological evolution, is an interesting one', argues Wertenbaker:

> Ideas compete just as genes do. Ideas need to propagate to survive. If they do not find a suitable host and a friendly environment they perish. But they also need to adapt to the environment. Quite a good metaphor for feminism?[45]

9 Tales for the twenty-first century: final reflections

Churchill's *The Skriker* established a recurrent concern of the 1990s: the child at risk. Where second-wave feminism in the 1970s took account of a 'lost' past, women's absence from history, culture and society, in the hope of securing a radical transformation of women's lives in a contemporary present, feminism at century's end is more concerned with the future, or more specifically, the 'uncertain' dark future in which children, girl children especially, are increasingly at risk. When the Skriker transports Lily forward in time, she meets her women descendants. The girl child from the future *'bellows wordless rage'* at Lily. She hates her as one of 'the distant past master class' responsible for her inheriting a black 'cemetery' of a world.[1] Fairy tales traditionally encompass the idea of transformation: of a better world, but the tales that women write for the English stage in the 1990s tell of the inequalities and injustices that militate against the idea of a better future. To conclude and to reflect on past chapters, I offer a brief look at some final, additional tales that sound a cautionary note for the twenty-first century, though not without a glimmer of hope, a glimpse at the possibility of change.

The future at risk in *The Skriker* is bound up in a society that fails to care enough about its vulnerable young mothers. Josie kills her baby and Lily does not manage to save the 'future' for her child. *Jordan*, by Anna Reynolds (with Moira Buffini, Lilian Baylis Theatre, 1992) works a fairy tale frame of Rumpelstiltskin into the 'f'real' story of Shirley Jones: a mother who took the life of her baby, was tried, acquitted of murder, but committed suicide on her release. Reynolds writes from her own experience of psychiatric prison, of the kind Daniels portrays in *Head-Rot Holiday*, and also has close links with Clean

169

Break.[2] In *Jordan*, Shirley is a mother that society fails to protect from a violent partner and who is hounded rather than helped by welfare systems. In the fairy tale woven into the play's dramatic one-woman monologue (played by Buffini), the queen saves herself and her child by fleeing to another, magical land. In Shirley's story, there is no other 'land', no means of escape and mother and baby do not survive.

Keeping children safe is a difficult task for mothers, as Chapter 3 illustrated, and especially when the burden of care and provision falls increasingly on women. *The Maiden Stone* by Scottish writer and feminist, Rona Munro,[3] that played London's Hampstead Theatre in 1995, is steeped in the folk culture of East Scotland. The play tells the story of Harriet, a travelling actress from the nineteenth century, who struggles to find theatre engagements that will keep herself and her children alive. When the father of her children dies of cold and hunger, Harriet survives with the help of Bidie: a travelling woman surrounded by a brood of children. Munro's tale images the father either as a figure who tries, but can no longer manage to provide, or the father who fails to provide altogether. Consequently, the children seek out, gather round the maternal body, travelling with Bidie, or haunting Harriet as she transforms into the rock, 'the maiden stone' (a monument to unmarried mothers).[4] In contrast to the hostility towards lone mothers in the 1990s, Bidie's brood turn against, violently against, the idea of the father who conceived them, but absented himself from their care.

As theatre by Daniels and others illustrates, if women fail each other, or their children, the consequences can be fatal. In finding ways to help each other, Harriet and Bidie construct a different kind of 'family'; make connections across class and national difference (Harriet is originally from a wealthy family in the north of England; Bidie is a poor woman from the North of Scotland).[5] Harriet and Bidie attempt to help each other, and together they help a young woman Mary on her way to adventure and fortune. Setting her up to join a travelling company and to start a life as an actress, depends, however, on Harriet and Bidie taking 'care' of her new born baby: seeing that it dies. Together, neither mother nor baby will survive. Alone, performing the role of 'innocent', Mary may yet have adventures.

If young working-class women, like those in theatre by Prichard and Upton, are going to have adventures and better lives, then mutuality not materiality (as in 'girl power' style of 'feminism') is needed. Wertenbaker's *The Ash Girl* (Birmingham Repertory Theatre, 2000) is based on the Cinderella story and retells the tale with an emphasis on the dangers of keeping 'inside' familial and cultural traditions. Mother and daughters are mutilated, toes are cut off and legs made lame, in attempts to 'fit' the 'ideal' feminine: to win riches and a prince for a husband. Others, with difficulty, learn to change their lives. The prince, Indian, nomadic and in exile from his own country learns to find beauty in a country he finds ugly and unwelcoming. Like Cordelia in *King Lear*, Ashgirl decides to 'love and be silent' and unlike her sisters does not express greed through words. She learns that she cannot rely on external (magical) agency alone, but that she must also gain knowledge to choose for herself. In the interests of knowing and choosing she must learn, as Cixous argues, not to be afraid to go into the forest and to conquer her fear of the dark.[6] Family, culture and tradition may all conspire to map our lives for us, as Nagy and others show. It takes courage to break with 'cruel convention' in order for lives to be lived differently; for stories, like Lavery's lesbian romances, to find different endings.

One tradition that must be broken is the cult of the 'feminine'. Tanika Gupta's *Skeleton* (Soho Theatre, 1997), inspired by a story by Rabindranath Tagore, tells a cautionary tale about the idolatry of women. A medical student, Gopal, falls in love with the image of a woman, rather than her person. His nemesis is a female skeleton, given to him as a present from his father for his medical training. Through Gopal's worship of the feminine form, the skeleton, Nayani, is brought back to life at the time of Durga Puja (the time of the mighty ten armed Goddess Durga, equipped with a 'weapon in each hand').[7] Nayani's story, told through nightly encounters with Gopal, is one of living as a prized possession of men, whom consequently she murders. In a reversal of the Scheherazade tale, it is Gopal, the object of Nayani's 'fatal attraction' who struggles to stay alive. Both Gopal and Nayani are damaged by the gaze that desires to own/be owned, to possess/be possessed: the gaze that encourages a violent 'othering' and, as Kane illustrated, 'engenders' war.

While an experienced writer for radio and television, *Skeleton* was Gupta's debut stage play, enabled by a writer's residency at the theatre. *Skeleton* had a lukewarm critical reception,[8] but Gupta has since held a further residency at the Royal National Theatre, where a new writers' programme, 'Springboards', launched her play *The Waiting Room* (2000). I take Gupta as my final point of reflection and as a hopeful sign: 'breaking down the door' of the Royal National Theatre at the beginning of a new century.

The Waiting Room blends magic and realism, white suburbia with Indian tradition exceptionally to 'naturalise' Asian family drama on the 'national', English stage. Like *East is East, The Waiting Room* explores familial relations and tensions, but primarily in relation to the mother, rather than the father. Western traditions of dramatic realism, governed by mimetic rules that separate the living and the dead, are refigured through the haunting, 'dead' presence of an Asian mother, Priya. Like Churchill's various bodies that refuse to stay dead, or Lavery's car crash victims, Mary and Gary, who are reluctant to die, Priya is unwilling to accept that she is dead. While the family struggle to cope with Hindu funeral rituals in English suburbia, Priya endeavours to come to terms with her life so that she can leave for the heavenly 'waiting room'. In contrast to a life-after-death determined by her own Hindu faith, Priya hovers in a pan-spiritual world, secularised through an 'Immortal Soul' (spirit guide) in the image of her favourite Bombay film star.

The exposition of family 'secrets' that include a daughter's coming out as a lesbian and revelations surrounding the paternity and death of a third child, is both deeply moving and darkly comic. From 'outside' the family, in a non-mimetic space and in a state of 'unbeing', Priya is able to look back at her past and forward to the future of her surviving two children, a son and a daughter. While she expresses regret at her own lost opportunities, she also discovers self-knowledge and acquires the agency to help change her children's future: she acts as a catalyst for them to reassess their own lives and also reassesses her own view of each child. In particular, negotiating the difficult relationship Priya has had with her son ensures that his future will be less damaged by their past: more certain of happiness. 'Frozen' feelings about the child she could not save thaw, and, as Priya finally walks into the waiting room, she is overwhelmed by beauty and the presence of children. Kane believed it possible to experience hell imaginatively through art, through theatre, in order to avoid it in reality. Conversely, Gupta's play suggests, it may also be possible to stage an idea, a 'feeling' of a better world, a 'heaven', in the interests of making it a reality.

At the threshold of the twenty-first century the stories women tell may be dark and uncertain, but the possibility, albeit a fragile possibility, of a more hopeful future, one that is less oppressive and combative, more progressive and democratic, remains in the ability to move 'outside' past histories, 'fixed' categories of gender, race or sexuality. At which point 'woman' as playwright may, finally, be 'subject' to erasure.

Notes

I A FEMINIST VIEW ON THE 1990S

1 David Edgar, ed., *State of Play: Playwrights on Playwriting* (London: Faber and Faber, 1999), p.19, states that between 1985 and 1990 the percentage of new work in regional and London repertory theatres dropped to 7 per cent of the total number of plays performed (from 12 per cent between 1970 and 1985), and that new work also 'performed' less well at the box office.

2 Christopher Innes, *Modern British Drama 1890–1990* (Cambridge: Cambridge University Press, 1992), p.448.

3 Innes uses three main types of theatre – Realism, Comedy and Poetic Drama – to organise his study, rather than working to a strict chronology. The final section of the book, however, is set apart as a 'new departure'. Innes explains how: 'troupes have sprung up performing for special interest groups, based on ethnic or sexual identity. Out of these some of the more challenging new writing has emerged, the most highly developed being feminist drama. The feminist playwrights consciously reject conventional forms as inherently masculinist, and as a consequence their criteria demand separate treatment' (*Modern British Drama*, p.7).

4 Edgar, *State of Play*, p.8; Benedict Nightingale, *Predictions: The Future of Theatre* (London: Phoenix, 1998), p.17.

5 Not everyone has agreed with the importance of this 1990s new writing. For dissenting views see Peter Ansorge, *From Liverpool to Los Angeles: On Writing for Theatre, Film and Television* (London: Faber and Faber, 1997), and Vera Gottlieb, 'Lukewarm Britannia', in Vera Gottlieb and Colin Chambers, eds., *Theatre in a Cool Climate* (Oxford: Amber Lane Press, 1999), pp.201–12.

6 Alex Sierz, *In-Yer-Face Theatre: British Drama Today* (London: Faber and Faber, 2001).

7 Sierz acknowledged this possibility in his keynote presentation at the 'In-Yer-Face? British Drama in the 1990s' Conference, University of the West of England, Bristol, 6–7 September 2002, specifically citing the problems of 'laddish sensibility' that risks 'push[ing] more gentle sensibilities to the sidelines'.

8 Susan Faludi, *Backlash: The Undeclared War Against Women* (London: Vintage, 1992).

9 Faludi, *Backlash*, p.498.

10 Ibid.

11 See also Marilyn French, *The War Against Women* (London: Hamish Hamilton, 1992).

12 For a feminist response to Lyndon's *No More Sex War*, see Yvonne Roberts, *Mad About Women: Can There Ever Be Fair Play Between the Sexes?* (London: Virago, 1992).

13 Audience responses to *Oleanna* have frequently been extreme and highly gendered. Alex Sierz, for example, describes how, at the opening of the play's production at the Royal Court in June 1993, under Harold Pinter's direction, some men in the audience cheered as the professor attacked the student. Or, how, in the New York production, 'there had been shouts of "Hit the bitch!"' (*In-Yer-Face Theatre*, pp.31–2). My own observations on seeing a later, regional production at Leicester Haymarket were not dissimilar. Some men actually walked out as the student pursued her allegations.

14 Susan Faludi, *Stiffed: The Betrayal of Modern Man* (London: Vintage, 2000), p.14.

15 For overview information about British film in the 1990s, I am indebted to Robert Murphy, ed., *British Cinema of the 90s* (London: BFI, 2000).

16 Robert Murphy, ibid., explains that *The Full Monty* made £46.2 million at the box office (p.4), compared to *Trainspotting's* £12.3 million (p.3).

17 Edgar, *State of Play*, p.270.

18 See Lynda Hart, *Fatal Women: Lesbian Sexuality and the Mark of Aggression* (London: Routledge, 1994), p.67.

19 See Imelda Whelehan, *Overloaded: Popular Culture and the Future of Feminism* (London: The Women's Press, 2000), p.54.

20 Mark Ravenhill, 'Dramatic Moments', *Guardian*, 9 April 1997, p.14.

21 Wolf dates her genderquake from the 1991 Anita Hill and Clarence Thomas hearings, that ultimately forced male officialdom to take account of Hill's alleged case of sexual harassment against Thomas, when he sought confirmation to the US Supreme Court. See Wolf, *Fire with Fire* (London: Vintage, 1994), pp.3–5.

22 The first televised date rape case in America was that of William Kennedy Smith in 1991. See Katie Roiphe, *The Morning After* (London: Hamish Hamilton, 1993), p.51. For a report on the growing incidence of date rape in Britain see 'Schools Alert over "Date-rape" Drug', *The Times*, 15 December 1997, p.8.

23 Natasha Walter, *The New Feminism* (London: Virago, 1999), p.4.

24 Ibid., p.4.

25 Imelda Whelehan, *Modern Feminist Thought: From the Second-Wave to 'Post-Feminism'* (Edinburgh: Edinburgh University Press, 1995), p.140.

26 Editorial, *Feminist Review: The Past Before Us, Twenty Years of Feminism*, Spring 1989, 31, p.3.

27 Peggy Phelan, *Unmarked: The Politics of Performance* (London: Routledge, 1993), p.6.

28 Sue-Ellen Case, *The Domain-Matrix: Performing Lesbian at the End of Print Culture* (Bloomington and Indianapolis: Indiana University Press, 1996), p.12. See also Janelle Reinelt, 'Staging the Invisible: The Crisis of Visibility in Theatrical Representation', *Text and Performance Quarterly*, 14, 1994, pp.1–11.

29 Sarah Kane, interview, in Heidi Stephenson and Natasha Langridge, eds., *Rage and Reason: Women Playwrights on Playwriting* (London: Methuen, 1997), p.134.

30 Raymond Williams, *The Long Revolution* (Harmondsworth: Pelican/Penguin, 1961), p.69.

31 Principally there were three feminisms: bourgeois feminism, linked to staging realism with more roles for women; radical feminism, looking to ways of undermining patriarchy and representing women's

culture; and socialist feminism, harnessed to a Brechtian/feminist dramaturgy.

32 Williams, *The Long Revolution*, pp.64, 69.

33 One area where such acknowledgement is urgently needed is in the matter of critical reception. Feminist theatre has always been beset by the difficulty created by the ideological gap between the feminist makers on the one hand and the rather more conservative (mostly male) 'body' of critical reviewers on the other. But an additional problem for the reception of women's playwriting in the 1990s was that critics were often still looking and assessing theatre through an outdated feminist lens.

34 Williams, *The Long Revolution*, p.65; my emphasis.

35 Graham Saunders, '"Just a Word on a Page and There is the Drama": Sarah Kane's Theatrical Legacy' *Contemporary Theatre Review*, Vol. 13, issue 1, 2003, pp.97–110, p.99.

36 Stephenson and Langridge, eds., *Rage and Reason*, p.135.

37 For a more inclusive, general list of contemporary writers see Dominic Dromgoole's *The Full Room: An A–Z of Contemporary Playwriting* (London: Methuen, 2002). For women playwrights specifically see Heidi Stephenson and Natasha Langridge, eds., *Rage and Reason: Women Playwrights on Playwriting*, London: Methuen, 1997.

38 For overviews of past and contemporary work by women playwrights in Scotland, Wales and Northern Ireland, see relevant essays in Elaine Aston and Janelle Reinelt, eds., *Cambridge Companion to Modern British Women Playwrights* (Cambridge: Cambridge University Press, 2000), 'Part 2: National, Tensions and Intersections'. On contemporary Scottish women dramatists, see also Adrienne Scullion, 'Self and Nation: Issues of Identity in Modern Scottish Drama by Women', *New Theatre Quarterly*, 68, November 2001, pp.373–90.

39 For detailed discussion of the changeover between Stafford-Clark and Daldry see Philip Roberts, *The Royal Court Theatre and the Modern Stage* (Cambridge: Cambridge University Press, 1999), Chapters 8 and 9.

40 Soho Theatre Company now operates a Theatre and Writer's Centre out of a converted synagogue in Dean Street in the fashionable part

of London's Soho. The Hampstead Theatre has also secured itself a new building through lottery funding, and the Royal Court bid for and carried out a programme of major refurbishment under Stephen Daldry's direction.

41 For details of the difficult financial pressures facing the company, see David Benedict's article, 'Making Drama Out of a Crisis', *Independent*, 8 September, 1997.

42 'What Share of the Cake?: The Employment of Women in the English Theatre', commissioned and published by the Women's Playhouse Trust in 1987 was the first report to study women's employment in companies funded by the Arts Council. While the 1986 Cork Report suggested an improving picture for women, 'What Share of the Cake?' proved otherwise. A subsequent survey in the 1990s, 'What Share of the Cake Now?', by Jenny Long, indicated no further improvement for women's employment in the theatre. For further details see Stephenson and Langridge, eds., *Rage and Reason*, pp.ix–x.

43 *Full Room*, p.154.

44 For further details of feminist companies see Elaine Aston, ed., *Feminist Theatre Voices* (Loughborough: Loughborough Theatre Texts, 1997).

45 For documentation of productions by all three companies – Scarlet Theatre, Foursight and The Sphinx Theatre Company – see Geraldine Cousin, ed., *Recording Women: A Documentation of Six Theatre Productions* (Amsterdam: Harwood Academic Publishers, 2000).

46 Sarah Kane had been commissioned by The Sphinx Theatre Company for an adaptation of *Medea*, a commission she did not fulfil because of her suicide. See Graham Saunders, *'Love Me or Kill Me': Sarah Kane and the Theatre of Extremes* (Manchester: Manchester University Press, 2002), conversation with Mel Kenyon, p.151.

47 Sue Parrish, quoted in Geraldine Cousin, *Recording Women*, p.105.

48 Judith Butler, *Bodies that Matter* (London: Routledge, 1993), p.222.

49 Eileen Atkins, *Vita & Virginia* (London: Samuel French, 1995), p.24. This fusion and confusion of identities is also to be found in the experimental British film, *Orlando* (1992) directed by Sally Potter.

50 *Vita & Virginia*, p.32.

51 Innes, *Modern British Drama*, p.449.

52 Subsequently, Andrzej Wajda based his film *Danton* on her 600-page manuscript, and Gems also re-shaped it into a play for the RSC, *The Danton Affair* (1986), before turning to her fascination with the writer herself in *The Snow Palace*. For further details see Pam Gems, introduction, *The Snow Palace* (London: Oberon Books, 1998), pp.7–9.

53 Stated in interview, *Writers Revealed*, radio broadcast, BBC Radio 4, 20 June 1991.

54 Edgar, ed., *State of Play*, p.60. Prichard gives Kane's *Blasted* and Nagy's *The Sphinx* as examples.

55 Michael Billington, *Guardian*, 27 December 1995, p.6. Billington goes on, however, to use this observation to refute the idea that women are being marginalised by the 'boys' plays', a point of view that, given my own observations and comments in this chapter, I have to disagree with.

56 Cixous, 'Excerpts from the Oxford Amnesty Lecture', reproduced in *Black Sail/White Sail*, programme, 1994.

57 Hélène Cixous, 'Black Sail/White Sail', trans. Donald Watson, unpublished manuscript from The Sphinx Theatre, p.78.

58 Faludi, *Backlash*, p.498.

2 TELLING FEMINIST TALES: CARYL CHURCHILL

1 Caryl Churchill, interview in Kathleen Betsko and Rachel Koenig, eds., *Interviews with Contemporary Women Playwrights* (New York: Beech Tree Books, 1987), pp.75–84, p.78.

2 Martin Crimp, quoted in Caroline Egan, 'The Playwright's Playwright', *Guardian*, 21 September 1998, p.13.

3 Sarah Daniels, interview, in Heidi Stephenson and Natasha Langridge, eds., *Rage and Reason: Women Playwrights on Playwriting* (London: Methuen, 1997), pp.1–8, p.6.

4 Churchill, quoted in Judith Thurman, 'The Playwright Who Makes You Laugh about Orgasm, Racism, Class Struggle, Homophobia, Woman-Hating, the British Empire, and the Irrepressible Strangeness of the Human Heart', *Ms.*, May 1982, pp.51–7, p.54.

5 Mark Ravenhill, *Guardian*, 9 April 1997, p.14.

6 Michael Billington, *Guardian*, 3 September 1997, p.14.

7 Quoted in Egan, 'The Playwright's Playwright', p.13.

8 See, for example, Churchill's *Light Shining in Buckinghamshire*.

9 See her interview in Kathleen Betsko and Rachel Koeing, eds., *Interviews with Contemporary Women Playwrights*, p.78.

10 Clare Bayley, *What's On*, reproduced in *Theatre Record*, 9–22 April 1991, p.460. See also my commentary on Sarah Daniels's opening scene to *Beside Herself*, Chapter 3, p.41.

11 Robert Cushman, *Observer*, reproduced in *Theatre Record*, 26 August–8 September 1982, p.469.

12 Mark Ravenhill, in David Edgar, ed., *State of Play: Playwrights on Playwriting* (London: Faber and Faber, 1999), p.50.

13 Caryl Churchill, *Top Girls*, in *Plays Two* (London: Methuen, 1990), p.92.

14 The time of the play's original production was also the time of the Greenham Common peace protest by women, which opposed the militarism of the base at which they camped out with a vigil by women for peace. For a reading of Kit and Angie's shelter scene as evocative of the Greenham Camp, see Harry Lane, 'Secrets as Strategies for Protection and Oppression in *Top Girls*', in Sheila Rabillard, ed., *Essays on Caryl Churchill: Contemporary Representations* (Blizzard: Winnipeg, 1998), pp.60–8.

15 For further details see Aston, *Caryl Churchill* (Plymouth: Northcote, 2nd edition 2001), pp.75–9.

16 James Christopher, *Time Out*, reproduced in *Theatre Record*, 9–22 April 1991, p.460.

17 Ros Asquith, *City Limits*, reproduced in *Theatre Record*, ibid.

18 Ravenhill, *Guardian*, 9 April 1997, p.14.

19 Joni Lovenduski and Vicky Randall, *Contemporary Feminist Politics: Women and Power in Britain* (Oxford: Oxford University Press, 1993), p.41.

20 Natasha Walter, *The New Feminism* (London: Virago, 1999), p.174.

21 See Lesley Manville's comments, quoted in Lizbeth Goodman in 'Overlapping Dialogue in Overlapping Media: Behind the Scenes of *Top Girls*', in Rabillard, ed., *Essays on Caryl Churchill*, pp.77–8.

22 Ian Dodd, *Tribune*, reproduced in *Theatre Record*, 9–22 April 1991, p.462.

23 Like so many of Churchill's plays, *Top Girls* has been performed and published in slightly different arrangements: originally written as three acts but performed as two. Churchill has stated her preference for the three-act version: 'Act One, the dinner; Act Two, Angie's story; Act Three, the year before', *Top Girls*, production note, in Churchill, *Plays Two*, p.54. This arrangement highlights Angie's story; brings her disadvantaged position more clearly into view.

24 Churchill signals the possibility of Angie as a disturbing, disruptive presence through the belief that Angie has in her possession supernatural powers, in her dabbling in black magic, and her licking of Kit's menstrual blood. In other Churchill plays, belief in supernatural powers also accompanies oppressed, damaged and violent figures. The *Gestus* for this in *Top Girls* is the moment in which Angie puts on the dress that Marlene gave her, a dress that is now too small for her, as she threatens to kill her mother. The misfit, adult–child body erupts into violence.

25 Marina Warner, *From the Beast to the Blonde: On Fairy Tales and their Tellers* (London: Vintage, 1995), p.210.

26 I am thinking of the current Harry Potter vogue (an orphaned boy with special magic powers), and the cinematic interpretation of Tolkien's *The Lord of the Rings* that has a very boyish-looking hobbit on a quest to save the world from total destruction. That said, the 1990s also produced heroines on a mission to save the world, as exemplified in American television series such as *Buffy the Vampire Slayer* and *Charmed*, series that portray young women in constant battle with the forces of evil (though significantly, never managing completely to defeat them).

27 This concern also surfaces in other plays, most notably in her dramatisation of the Fenland community of women in *Fen*, 1983.

28 Caryl Churchill, *The Skriker* in *Plays Three* (London: Nick Hern Books, 1998), p.243.

29 Elin Diamond, *Unmaking Mimesis* (London: Routledge, 1997), p.93.

30 The temptation is always there, however, to 'read' from or to see 'out' from the 'real': to follow Churchill's narrative of the two

working-class girls. I know that I have done this myself. Print culture, the publication of Churchill's words, as opposed to the movement text of the spirit world for which we only have stage directions, tends to pull us in that direction. The response of the critics shows that it is easier to pick out the dramatic rather than the physical for analysis and commentary.

31 Benedict Nightingale, *The Times*, reproduced in *Theatre Record*, 15–28 January 1994, p.93.

32 That said, it has typically been the case that Churchill's more stylistically experimental work – *A Mouthful of Birds* or *Lives of the Great Poisoners*, for example – has been critically less well received. Without wishing to make a one-sided case for Churchill's theatre, what this does point to is the unease that reviewers experience (and sometimes confess to) when faced with reviewing cross-disciplinary forms that tax their more conventional, dramatic backgrounds and training.

33 Jann Parry, *Observer*, reproduced in *Theatre Record*, 15–28 January 1994, p.94.

34 Charles Spencer, *Daily Telegraph*, reproduced in *Theatre Record*, 15–28 January 1994, p.96.

35 See Irving Wardle, *Independent on Sunday*, reproduced in *Theatre Record*, 15–28 January 1994, p.95.

36 Janelle Reinelt, 'Caryl Churchill and the Politics of Style', in Elaine Aston and Janelle Reinelt, eds., *The Cambridge Companion to Modern British Women Playwrights* (Cambridge: Cambridge University Press, 2000), pp.174–93, p.188.

37 Alice Rayner, 'All Her Children: Caryl Churchill's Furious Ghosts' in Rabillard, ed., *Essays on Caryl Churchill*, pp.206–24, p.216.

38 See Caryl Churchill, *Cloud Nine*, in *Plays One* (London: Methuen, 1985), p.308.

39 Rayner's analysis of *Cloud Nine* brought back my own memory of trying to play this scene in a late 1980s college production and in a social climate quite different to that of the play's first staging in 1979. The performers, like the characters in the scene, found it hard to take the ritual seriously, and, after several attempts to find a way of making the scene do serious work in the production, we actually

agreed to cut it. The difficulty then was twofold: the danger of the essentialist risks arising from the idea of Isis and a 'maternal line', and the disjunction between the desire for a different, less oppressive organisation of sexuality and the repressive climate of the 1980s. If it was impossible to conjure a goddess that might offer an alternative to the Christian and patriarchal idea of the Mother at the close of the 1970s, the 1980s certainly was not, we felt, a moment in which she had a greater chance of putting in an appearance.

40 Churchill also talked about the Skriker's damaged language in terms of a schizophrenic breakdown of language; a language that s/he is not entirely in control of (Interview, *Late Theatre*, BBC 2, January 1994).

41 E. Ann Kaplan, *Motherhood and Representation: The Mother in Popular Culture and Melodrama* (London: Routledge, 1992), p.51.

42 Programme notes to the production of *The Skriker* offered explanations of the spirit figures, including for example, Jenny Greenteeth 'A water fairy who drowns children'; Nellie Longarms, 'A water spirit who drags children into ponds', or Black Annis 'A hag with a blue face and only one eye, she devours lambs and young children'.

43 Mother–child separation is a recurrent feature in Churchill's work. A woman, starving and unable to feed her baby, leaves her child in a church in *Light Shining*. Marion in *Owners* tries to 'own' Lisa's baby for her husband, Clegg. Val separates (temporarily) from her children in *Fen*. See also later discussion on *Blue Heart*.

44 Marina Warner. *From the Beast to the Blonde*, p.xv.

45 'The Mother of Invention', title of a review of *Blue Heart* by Benedict Nightingale, *The Times*, 25 September 1997, p.36.

46 Betty Friedan, *The Feminine Mystique* (London: Victor Gollancz, 1963), p.32.

47 This was due to having a break from playwriting. For details see Churchill's interview with David Benedict, Arts section, *Independent*, 19 April 1997, p.4.

48 Caryl Churchill, *Blue Heart* (London: Nick Hern Books, 1997), p.5.

49 *The Times*, 25 September 1997, p.36.

50 Paul Taylor, Features section, *Independent*, 25 September 1997, p.4.

51 John Peter, Culture section, *The Sunday Times*, 31 August 1997, p.14.

52 Having become accustomed over the years to Churchill's technique of adult-child playing, in the production of *Far Away* I was incredibly struck by Churchill's introduction of a young girl to play Joan and by her use of children in the parade-of-the-prisoners scene.

53 Churchill, *Far Away* (London: Nick Hern Books, 2000), p.38.

3 SAYING NO TO DADDY

1 Caryl Churchill, *Far Away* (London: Nick Hern Books, 2000), p.14.

2 Sarah Daniels, *Head-Rot Holiday*, in *Plays: Two* (London: Methuen, 1994), p.244.

3 Subsequent to a 1981 conference organised by the Women Against Violence Against Women network, women in Britain set up the organisation Incest Survivors, to arrange self-help groups around the country. See Joni Lovenduski and Vicky Randall, eds., *Contemporary Feminist Politics: Women and Power in Britain* (Oxford: Oxford University Press, 1993) p.260.

4 Louise Armstrong, *Rocking the Cradle of Sexual Politics: What Happened when Women Said Incest* [1994], first British edition (London: Women's Press, 1996), p.65.

5 See *Rocking the Cradle*, Chapter 7: 'The Great Incest Massacre II'.

6 For an overview, see Gerrilyn Smith's 'Foreword' to the British edition (1996) of *Rocking the Cradle*.

7 Presenter Esther Rantzen, working with the results of a survey into abuse conducted by her consumer watchdog team from the popular *That's Life* series, instigated the programme. The survey revealed that 'the majority of those who responded were women and girls who had been victims of sexual abuse' (Jean La Fontaine, *Child Sexual Abuse*, Oxford: Polity Press and Basil Blackwell, 1990, p.3).

8 Jean La Fontaine, *Child Sexual Abuse*, pp.10–11.

9 Beatrix Campbell, *Unofficial Secrets: Child Sexual Abuse: The Cleveland Case* (London: Virago, 1988, fully revised, 1997), p.63.

10 See Campbell's poignant commentary on 'the ghosts of dead children' tortured and killed by fathers in the 1980s, *Unofficial Secrets*, p.121.

11 Sarah Daniels, interview, in Heidi Stephenson and Natasha Langridge, eds., *Rage and Reason: Women Playwrights on Playwriting* (London: Methuen, 1997), p.2.

12 Sarah Daniels, *Ripen Our Darkness* and *The Devil's Gateway* (London: Methuen, 1986), p.33.

13 Daniels also has pursued a career in radio and television drama, including the children's series, *Grange Hill*. Her commitment to young audiences is one that she shares with many of the women dramatists featured in this volume. *Taking Breath*, a play for young people about environmental protest, is published in the Faber collection, *New Connections 99: New Plays for Young People* (1999).

14 Stephenson and Langridge, *Rage*, p.3.

15 All three plays are published in Daniels, *Plays: Two* (London: Methuen, 1994).

16 Judith Herman, *Trauma and Recovery: From Domestic Abuse to Political Terror* (London: Pandora, 1992), p.7.

17 Ibid., p.110.

18 In *My Father's House: A Memoir of Incest and of Healing* (London: Virago, 1989), Sylvia Fraser explains how she 'created a secret accomplice', another self to cope with the sexual relationship with her father (p.15). By splitting herself into two she was able to repress the trauma of abuse.

19 Daniels also stages the idea of a reconciliation between Evelyn and Eve, as first Eve then Evelyn enfolds her other 'self' in a large bath towel, wiping clean her hands, face and neck. See *Beside Herself*, *Plays: Two*, p.186.

20 Herman, *Trauma and Recovery*, p.112. Herman further explains: 'It is not uncommon to find adult survivors who continue to minister to the wishes and needs of those who once abused them and who continue to permit major intrusions without boundaries or limits. Adult survivors may nurse their abusers in illness, defend them in adversity, and even, in extreme cases, continue to submit to their sexual demands.' (p.112.)

21 Reading Daniels's play and accounts of the Cleveland case, I was struck by the way in which the fun that Daniels pokes at the Reverend Teddy Kegwin in *Beside Herself*, works as a kind of antidote

to the antifeminist campaigning of the Reverend Michael Wright in the Cleveland case. See Campbell, *Unofficial Secrets*, p.49.

22 Louise Armstrong explains how in some cases, memories of abuse can remain buried and dormant, and then can be triggered by 'something apparently neutral' (*Kiss Daddy Goodnight: Ten Years Later*, New York: Hawthorn Books, 1987, p.27).

23 Campbell, *Unofficial Secrets*, p.70.

24 How to 'stage' abuse is clearly an issue that playwrights have to consider. In *Paper Walls* (1994), Scarlet Theatre's physical theatre piece about women and domestic violence, for example, abuse was recreated through dolls, thereby imitating the way in which children are invited to narrate what has happened to them through puppetry. A less convincing technique is to be found in Claire Macintyre's abstract personification of an abused figure in *My Heart's a Suitcase* (1990), where the figure 'luggage' carries the burden of abuse, and advises resignation, rather than protest.

25 Controversially in the Cleveland case, anal dilation in children was taken to be a sign of sexual abuse.

26 Lynda Hart, *Fatal Women* (London: Routledge, 1994), p.95.

27 *Unofficial Secrets*, p.65.

28 Sheridan Morley, *Herald Tribune*, reproduced in *Theatre Record*, 26 March–8 April 1990, p.468.

29 That said, the women's physical theatre company, Spin/Stir, whose first show about abuse survivors, *Naming*, played the Oval House in 1994, did look to a target audience of survivors' support groups. For details see Barbara Egervary, 'Profile of a Company: Spin/Stir', *Glint Journal*, Vol. 2, no.2, 1994, pp.16–17.

30 The WPT production costs were estimated by Jules Wright as £86,000, with £28,000 from the Court. Jules Wright, 'In Her Wright Mind', *Plays and Players*, April 1990, pp.14–16, p.16.

31 In the 1980s, Daniels went so far as to state that she would never allow men to direct her work. See Sarah Daniels, 'There are 52% of Us', *Drama*, 152, 1984, pp.23–4, p.24. She since has modified this view: 'I've since learnt to use the "would never" more sparingly. It is rather a luxury now. There often isn't the choice and although it

would perhaps serve the feminist argument to leave it there, it would be untruthful' (Interview, *Rage and Reason*, p.8).

32 See also Daniels's radio play, *Purple Side Coasters* (1995) that examines two mothers who, suffering from puerperal psychosis, are separated from their children. Published in Lizbeth Goodman, ed., *MythicWomen/Real Women* (London: Faber, 2000), pp.197–239.

33 See reviews reproduced in *Theatre Record*, 12–25 February 1994, pp.186–8.

34 Benedict Nightingale, *The Times*, reproduced in *Theatre Record*, 12–25 February 1994, p.187.

35 Neil Smith, *What's On*, reproduced in *Theatre Record*, 12–25 February 1994, p.188.

36 See Michelene Wandor, *Post-War British Drama: Looking Back in Gender* (London: Routledge, 2001), p.216.

37 This is especially true in the context of child abuse. Consider, for example, the consequences of Lil's failure to believe Nicola (*Beside Herself*), or, worse still, the cycle of violence and selfharm that follows in the wake of Helen's refusal to believe her stepdaughter Ruth (*Head-Rot Holiday*).

38 Daniels, interview, *Rage and Reason*, p.4.

39 My anger prompted me to write 'Daniels in the Lion's Den: Sarah Daniels and the British Backlash', *Theatre Journal*, October 1995, pp.393–403.

40 Claire Armistead, 'Nostalgia for the Future', *Guardian*, 22 February 1994, p.6.

41 Sylvia Fraser, *My Father's House*, p.252.

42 In Armstrong's *Kiss Daddy Goodnight: Ten Years Later*, women who have suffered abuse show different ways of dealing, or not dealing with abuse; of getting over, or not getting over the trauma. That said the life stories of these women are generally characterised by a difficulty of forming relations as adults. In one case this leads to a mother giving away her children (see Maggie's story, 'Forgive and Forget', pp.95–11). Another woman describes her violent thoughts towards children and babies, and her actual cruelty towards a girl-child whose female body she wanted to destroy because her own body

had been abused by her step-father (see June's story, 'The Psychic Center Violated', pp.117–31).

43 Elaine Showalter, *Hystories: Hysterical Epidemics and Modern Culture* (London: Picador, 1997), p.40.

44 *Unofficial Secrets*, p.9.

45 Dora was a patient of Freud's who resisted and walked out of analysis, which explains the feminist interest in her case. Cixous, for example, has written extensively about Dora. Dora's case is also relevant to the discussion of this chapter in so far as she was another victim of Freud's insistence that her experience of unwanted sexual attentions (from the husband of her father's lover) was fantasy rather than reality. For further details of Dora's case and of feminist dramatic treatments of Dora see Elaine Showalter's *Hystories*, pp.42–3 and p.107.

46 Furse was appointed director in 1990 and remained in post until 1994.

47 For further details see Anna Furse, 'Written on My Body', *The Open Page*, no.2, March 1997, pp.38–43, pp.42–3.

48 Anna Furse, *Augustine (Big Hysteria)* (Amsterdam: Harwood Academic Publishers, 1997), p.36.

49 Ibid., p.41.

50 Hysterical fitting is often characteristic of the abused child. See Sylvia Fraser's account, *My Father's House*, p.222.

51 Drugs, most notably sodium amytal, are still, somewhat controversially, used by therapists to help patients release their traumatic memories.

52 Furse's line is an echo of Cixous: 'You only have to look at the Medusa straight on to see her. And she's not deadly. She's beautiful and she's laughing', in 'The Laugh of the Medusa', Elaine Marks and Isabelle de Courtivron, eds., *New French Feminisms* (Brighton: The Harvester Press, 1981), pp.245–64, p.255. Augustine's final speech is written in the style of Cixous's manifesto and other points in the play also index French feminist writing, most notably the reference to the 'theatre for forgotten scenes' (p.31), which is Clément's description of the hysteric's body in *The Newly Born Woman* (Manchester: Manchester University Press, 1987), p.5.

53 Furse also introduced surrealism into her stage picture. At one point both the violinist and Augustine reveal the F stops of the Man Ray photograph tattooed on their backs (*Augustine*, p.21). For Furse this reflects her concern for taking issue with 'the Surrealists' appropriation of hysteria in their peculiar use of female psychic disorder in their aesthetic' (introduction to *Augustine*, p.10).

54 David Thomas, *Not Guilty: In Defence of Modern Man* (London: Weidenfeld & Nicolson, 1993), Chapter 5 'The Myth of the Bad Man', pp.123–46.

55 One of the most widely publicised was that of Gary Romana in the USA who sued his daughter's therapists after she accused him of abuse in 1990. For an account of this case see Katy Butler 'You Must Remember This', *Guardian*, 23 July 1994, p.6.

56 For a more detailed overview see Elaine Showalter, *Hystories*, pp.156–8.

57 Claire Dowie, *Easy Access (for the boys) & All Over Lovely* (London: Methuen, 1998), p.30.

58 See Michael's video diary monologue, *Easy Access*, p.8.

59 *Frozen* was revived for the Cottesloe Studio at the Royal National Theatre in 2002. For more on Lavery, see pp. 100–10.

60 David Benedict, *Independent*, reproduced in *Theatre Record*, 23 April–6 May 1998, p.587.

61 Nancy's other daughter, Ingrid, who discovers Eastern ways of thinking, is instrumental in helping her mother to reach a state of forgiveness.

62 Bryony Lavery, *Frozen* (London: Faber and Faber, 2002), p.34.

63 Lavery in 'Read. Imagine. Write. Check.', in programme notes, *Frozen*, National Theatre, 2002.

64 Eve Ensler, *The Vagina Monologues* (London, Virago, 2001), p.xxiv.

65 Melba Wilson, *Crossing the Boundary: Black Women Survive Incest* (London: Virago, 1993), p.8.

66 Madeline North, *Time Out*, reproduced in *Theatre Record*, 1–28 January 1999, p.85.

67 For details see Julie Holledge, *Innocent Flowers: Women in the Edwardian Theatre* (London: Virago, 1981), Chapter 3: 'Kisses or Votes: The AFL 1908–10', pp.49–101.

4 GIRL POWER, THE NEW FEMINISM?

1 Angela McRobbie and Trisha McCabe, eds., *Feminism for Girls: An Adventure Story* (London: Routledge & Kegan Paul, 1981), p.1.

2 *Feminism for Girls*, p.5.

3 Women's Theatre Group, *My Mother Says I Never Should*, in Michelene Wandor, ed., *Strike While the Iron is Hot* (London: Journeyman Press, 1980).

4 Angela McRobbie, *Feminism and Youth Culture* [1991], second edition (Basingstoke: Macmillan, 2000), p.212.

5 Imelda Whelehan, *Overloaded: Popular Culture and the Future of Feminism* (London: The Women's Press, 2000), p.45.

6 Katie Roiphe, *The Morning After: Sex, Fear, and Feminism* (London: Hamish Hamilton, London, 1993).

7 Roiphe writes from a position of privilege, as she was a scholar at Harvard in 1986 and then went on to graduate school to study English literature at Princeton. While her style of writing oozes college-brat-confidence, it fails (among many things) to take account of how advocacy of personal and sexual empowerment is relevant to the lives of young women less privileged than herself who live outside the protective confines of a highly privileged campus life – an image that Sarah Kane challenges or reverses in *Cleansed* where the 'marginal' or the 'undesirable' are confined to a campus styled institution, see p.89.

8 *Coming on Strong: New Writing from the Royal Court Theatre*, preface by Stephen Daldry, introduction by Dominic Tickell (London: Faber and Faber, 1995).

9 *Peaches* was actually written as part of the Writers' Group at the Royal Court Young People's Theatre, rather than the festival.

10 Lyn Gardner, reviewing for the *Guardian*, 24 October 1996, p.6, offered this observation: 'Future anthropologists studying this double bill of winning plays from the Royal Court Young Writers Festival could be forgiven for thinking that late 20th century Britain was peopled just by two curious tribes . . . these two tribes are called Teenage Boys and Teenage Girls respectively.'

11 Rebecca Prichard, 'Plays by Women' in David Edgar, ed., *State of Play: Playwrights on Playwriting* (London: Faber and Faber, 1999), p.61.

12 *State of Play*, p.60.

13 *Evening Standard Hot Tickets Magazine*, 7 May 1998.

14 Prichard, *Essex Girls* in *Coming on Strong*, p.225.

15 'One to Watch: Rebecca Prichard', *Guardian*, 16 May 1998, p.5.

16 See Andrew Smith, 'Play for Today', *Observer Magazine*, 31 October 1999, pp.34–9, p.35. As dramatists of 'disenchantment' Smith also lists Mark Ravenhill, Sarah Kane, Conor McPherson, Martin McDonagh, Sebastian Barry, Martin Crimp, Nick Grosso and Simon Bennett.

17 Rebecca Prichard, *Fair Game: A Free Adaptation of Games in the Backyard by Edna Mazya* (London: Faber and Faber, 1997).

18 For further details and discussion see Jeremy Kinston's review of *Fair Game, The Times*, 4 November 1997, p.38.

19 Prichard, correspondence with the author, January 2003.

20 See Dalaya Alberge, 'Charities Alarmed at Casting of Children in "Gang Rape" Play', *The Times*, 26 August 1997, p.4. The article also details Mazya's concern over the age of the performers (her own actors had been in their early twenties) and the proposal for a more realistic style of production (the original Israeli production opted for greater stylisation).

21 See, for example, Eve Lewis, *Ficky Stingers* in Mary Remnant, ed., *Plays By Women: Volume Six* (London: Methuen, 1987) and Franca Rame, *The Rape*, in Stuart Hood, ed., *A Woman Alone and Other Plays: Franca Rame and Dario Fo* (London: Methuen [1975], 1991).

22 Prichard, quoted in correspondence with the author, January 2003.

23 That said, one should note that while Prichard aims at social condemnation of rape, Kane's dramatic world attempts to find tenderness or love where such love is morally forbidden – as, for example, in the love and sex between (a dead) brother and a sister in *Cleansed*, see pp.91–2.

24 Explained in David Benedict, '"Essex Girl writes Play" Shock Horror', Features, *Independent*, 22 October 1997, p.18.

25 See Graham Saunders, *'Love Me, Or Kill Me'* (Manchester: Manchester University Press, 2002), p.4.

26 Quoted in 'About the Red Room' in Kay Adshead, *The Bogus Woman* (London: Oberon Books, 2001), p.9.

27 'One to Watch: Lisa Goldman', Features, *Guardian*, 2 May 1998, p.5.

28 Benedict Nightingale, 'Ten with the Playwright Stuff', *The Times*, 1 May 1996, p.33.

29 Ibid.

30 See Nightingale's interview with Ian Rickson, 'Court in the Delicate Bubble Act', *The Times*, 14 January 1998, p.31.

31 Nightingale, review of Conor McPherson's *This Time Tree Bower*, *The Times*, 9 July 1996, p.36.

32 See Rickson interview, note 30.

33 See also Clare McIntyre's Brighton seafront setting in *My Heart's a Suitcase* (London: Nick Hern Books, 1994), which functions in a similar way.

34 Judy Upton, *Confidence* (London: Methuen, 1998), p.62.

35 See Ella's attempt to beat the slot machine in *Confidence*, Scene Three, pp.12–23.

36 Ella's get-rich-quick schemes are always 'cheap' and tacky – like her initial idea of going to Hollywood, not to be in the movies, but to root around in the dustbins for 'celebrity rubbish' to sell (see *Confidence*, p.3).

37 See Ian Burrell and Lisa Brinkworth, 'Sugar 'n' Spice but . . . Not at all Nice', *The Sunday Times*, 27 November 1994. The article reports on a number of cases in which wealthy women, out alone, get attacked by girl gangs.

38 See Upton's 'Afterword' to *Ashes and Sand*, in Pamela Edwardes, *Frontline Intelligence 3: New Plays for the Nineties* (London: Methuen, 1995), p.261.

39 Statistic quoted in Ian Burrell and Lisa Brinkworth, 'Sugar 'n' Spice but . . . Not at all Nice', *The Sunday Times*, 27 November 1994. Burrell and Brinkworth also note that in 1993 the government recorded 101,000 serious crimes by women, a 12 pre cent increase over five years, and an increase of four times the rate of increase in crimes by men.

40 Upton, 'Afterword' to *Ashes and Sand*, in Pamela Edwardes, *Frontline Intelligence 3*, p.261.

41 Nightingale, *The Times*, 1 May 1996, p.33.

42 *Ashes*, in *Plays One* (London: Methuen, 2002), p.15.

43 Directed by Rachel Talalay, the film stars Lori Petty as Tank Girl. The figure was also created on the catwalk by model Sarah Stockbridge for punk designer Vivienne Westwood, and photographed in a number of magazines such as *Vogue* and *Elle*.

44 Upton also addresses the issue of selfharm in her treatment of eating disorders in *Sunspots*.

45 Upton represents this tension or contradiction through imaging Daniel in scenes that both show him fetishising women's shoes and taking a hammer to them.

46 Ian Rickson, quoted in Sarah Hemmings, 'Look Forward with Anger', *Weekend Financial Times, 18 November 1990, p.17.*

47 Rebecca Prichard, *Yard Gal* (London: Faber and Faber, 1998).

48 Benedict Nightingale, *The Times*, 13 May 1998, p.34.

49 Judith Johnson's *Somewhere* is published in Pamela Edwardes, ed., *Frontline Intelligence 1: New Plays for the Nineties* (London: Methuen, 1993).

50 See Mica Nava, 'Youth Service Provision, Social Order and the Question of Girls', in Angela McRobbie and Mica Nava, eds., *Gender and Generation* (Basingstoke: Macmillan, 1984), pp.1–30, pp.4–5.

51 American girl gang researchers Meda Chesney-Lind and John M. Hagedorn observe that 'on the whole, girls come from more troubled families than boys' and 'the female gang acts as a kind of refuge for many girls, while for most boys the male gang is an extension of a mainstream, aggressive, male role' (*Female Gangs in America*, Chicago: Lake View Press, 1999, p.5).

52 Not even the Spice Girls managed to sustain the myth of girlbonding they helped to foster in the 1990s given the fragmenting of the group after Geri Halliwell's departure in 1998.

53 Girl gang dramas at the Court continue. In 2000 the Court staged Kia Corthron's *Breath, Boom*, an American drama set among black Bronx teenagers.

54 Sarah Hemming, 'Look Forward with Anger', p.17.

5 THE 'BAD GIRL OF OUR STAGE'?

1 Jack Tinker, *Daily Mail*, reproduced in *Theatre Record*, 1–28 January 1995, p.42.

2 In the *Daily Telegraph* Charles Spencer wrote that *Blasted* was 'a grave error of judgement by the theatre's artistic director Stephen Daldry' (20 January 1995, reproduced in *Theatre Record*, 1–28 January, p.40). Michael Billington wrote in the *Guardian* 'I was simply left wondering how such naïve tosh managed to scrape past the Court's normally judicious play-selection committee' (20 January 1995, reproduced in *Theatre Record*, 1–28 January, p.40). See also Tom Morris's 'Damned and Blasted?', *The Sunday Times*, 29 January 1995, pp.6–7.

3 Kane in interview with Clare Bayley, Arts section, *Independent*, 23 January 1995, p.20.

4 Kane in interview with David Benedict, *Independent on Sunday*, 22 January 1995, p.3.

5 Obituary for Sarah Kane, Mark Ravenhill, *Independent*, 23 February 1999, p.6.

6 Ibid., p.6.

7 Due to renovation work on the Royal Court's Sloane Square venue, the Court at that time was occupying theatres in St Martin's Lane (Downstairs) and West Street (Upstairs). *Cleansed* opened on 30 April 1998; *Yard Gal* on 7 May 1998.

8 See 'Conversation with Mel Kenyon' in Graham Saunders *'Love Me or Kill Me': Sarah Kane and the Theatre of Extremes* (Manchester: Manchester University Press, 2002), p.153.

9 James Macdonald, interview with James Christopher, Features section, *Independent*, 4 May 1998, pp.6–7, p.6.

10 Caryl Churchill, 'A Bold Imagination for Action', *Guardian*, 25 January 1995, p.19. Mel Kenyon, in discussion with me over this chapter, confirmed that Kane had been thinking in terms of a trilogy, and at one stage had drafted a page-length description for a play about nuclear devastation as a possible commission for the RSC. Introducing Kane's *Complete Plays* (London: Methuen, 1991), David Greig notes, however, that 'Kane abandoned the idea of a trilogy after *Cleansed* and instead she pushed her writing in a new and surprising direction'

(p.xiii). While stylistically different, *Crave*, in my view, connects to the earlier two plays in its concern for love in a loveless, dark and violent world, making it possible to think of these plays as a cycle.

11 'Fabulous Five', Michael Billington with Lyn Gardner, *Guardian*, 13 March 1996, p.10.

12 Veronica Lee, 'Young Guns', Culture section, *The Sunday Times*, 22 March 1998, p.8.

13 See Andrew Smith's 'Play for Today', *Observer Magazine*, 31 October 1999, pp.34–9, and Benedict Nightingale 'Ten with the Playwright Stuff', *The Times*, 1 May 1996, p.33. Sarah Hemming's review of the Bush's 1995 'Walk on the Wild Side' season, 'The Best of Time, the Worst of Time – The Present Bush', Arts section, *Independent*, 22 February 1995, p.24, also refers to the Court's Theatre Upstairs playing host to 'the bad girls Judy Upton and Sarah Kane'.

14 In a review of *Cleansed* in the *Daily Mail*, 7 May 1998.

15 In a review of *Cleansed* by Robert Gore-Langton, *Express*, 16 May 1998, p.56.

16 Jane Edwardes, *Time Out*, reproduced *Theatre Record*, 1–28 January 1995, p.38.

17 On a related point, see also Alex Sierz's analysis of Naomi Wallace's *The War Boys* (Finborough theatre, 1993), a production that Sierz states 'caused controversy not because of its subject matter [male vigilantes controlling the Kentucky–Mexico border in the USA] but because of its author's gender' (*In-Yer-Face Theatre*, London: Faber and Faber, 2001, p.156).

18 See interview with David Benedict, *Independent on Sunday*, 22 January 1995, p.3; Kane on 'The Only Thing I Remember is', *Guardian*, 13 August 1998, p.12, and 'Drama with Balls', *Guardian*, 20 August 1998, p.12.

19 Kane in Heidi Stephenson and Natasha Langridge, eds., *Rage and Reason* (London: Methuen, 1997), pp.129–35, pp.134–5.

20 Michelene Wandor, *Post-War British Drama: Looking Back In Gender* (London: Routledge, 2001), pp.232–4 (revised and updated edition of *Look Back in Gender*, London: Methuen, 1987).

21 Elaine Aston and Janelle Reinelt, eds., *Companion to Modern British Women Playwrights*, (Cambridge: Cambridge University

Press, 2000), p.1, pp.214–15. When this volume was conceived in 1995, *Blasted* was the only play of Kane's to have been performed. If the commission had been later, Kane would certainly have warranted a substantial entry.

22 See Chapter 1, p.10.

23 *Love Me Or Kill Me*, p.30.

24 'Fabulous Five', Michael Billington with Lyn Gardner, p.10.

25 Arts section, *Independent*, 20 January 1995, p.27.

26 Paul Taylor, *Independent*, 2 October 1996, pp.8–9.

27 Bert O. States 'The Phenomenological Attitude' in Janelle G. Reinelt and Joseph R. Roach, eds., *Critical Theory and Performance* (Ann Arbor: University of Michigan Press, 1992), pp.369–79, p.370.

28 States quoting Shelley, 'Phenomenological Attitude', p.370.

29 Ibid., p.370.

30 Quoted in Saunders, *Love Me Or Kill Me*, p.28.

31 'Sorties: Out and Out: Attacks/ Ways Out/Forays' in Hélène Cixous and Catherine Clément, *The Newly Born Woman*, translation Betsy Wing (Manchester: Manchester University Press, 1987), pp.63–132.

32 *The Newly Born Woman*, p.83.

33 Actress Kate Ashfield who played the part of Cate in the original production explains that Cate has a mental age of 12. See interview, Dominic Cavendish, Features, *Independent*, 9 September 1998, p.11.

34 In one particular moment, for example, Ian places one of her hands on his penis to help him to masturbate, while she sucks her thumb with the other. There is also a suggestion in the text that she is abused by her father, given that Cate explains that her fits have started since her dad came back home. See *Complete Plays* (London: Methuen, 2001) p.10. References to play texts of *Blasted, Cleansed* and *Crave* are all from this edition.

35 See *The Newly Born Woman*, p.5.

36 'Phenomenological Attitude', p.377, his emphasis. States elucidates the 'bridge of recognition' through his analysis of Barthes's comparison between the face of Greta Garbo and that of Charlie Chaplin. Looking at the 'intertextual makeup' is the point at which the possibility of another feeling or sensation arises, before 'the image begins giving in to these [known] significations'.

37 Interview with Bayley, see note 3.

38 Kane also explained in her interview in *Rage and Reason* that 'the play collapses into one of Cate's fits' (p.130).

39 Kane frequently uses images around food and the body to mark social disorder. In her first unpublished writing for theatre she produced a monologue on bulimia. In *Phaedra's Love* she replaces the ancient, athletic figure of Hippolytus as beautiful and chaste, disciplined and purposeful, with an Hippolytus that is overweight, oversexed and purposeless, as an observation on contemporary masculinities, that given Hippolytus' royal status, extends to a comment on the 'health' of the nation.

40 Reviewing the dark second half to Caryl Churchill's *Hotel* in 1997, Benedict Nightingale wrote 'after a couple of days in some modern hotels, I can share graveyard feelings like those', *The Times*, 24 April 1997, p.37.

41 Claire Monk, 'Men in the 90s', in Robert Murphy, ed., *British Cinema of the 90s* (London: BFI, 2000), pp.156–66, p.157.

42 See note 13 in her article, p.166.

43 As an extension to this discussion, see Kane on violence and Tarantino's films in Saunders, *Love Me Or Kill Me*, pp.25–6.

44 In the context of talking about a student performance by Kane as Bradshaw in Barker's *Victory*, Dan Rebellato also writes of her 'sympathy for the oppressed but grim understanding of the oppressor'. In 'Sarah Kane: An Appreciation', *New Theatre Quarterly*, 59, August 1999, pp.280–1, p.281.

45 See Andrew Smith, 'Play for Today', *Observer Magazine*, 31 October 1999, pp.34–9, p.34. See also my comments on Upton's dramaturgy in the last chapter.

46 Director James Macdonald explains how 'holocaust literature . . . shadows the play'. See Saunders, *Love Me or Kill Me*, p.126.

47 Michael Billington, *Guardian*, 7 May 1998, p.2.

48 Judith Butler, *Bodies that Matter* (London: Routledge, 1993), p.96.

49 See Michel Foucault, *Discipline and Punish*, translation Alan Sheridan (Harmondsworth: Penguin, 1977), p.9.

50 When Carl first declares his love to Rod it is a love that leads first to betrayal, and Kane models the betrayal on the biblical betrayal of Jesus by Judas. Grace is strung up and beaten for loving Graham in a way that suggests a crucifixion.

51 Elaine Scarry, *The Body in Pain: The Making and the Unmaking of the World* (Oxford: Oxford University Press, 1985), p.20.

52 Scarry, *The Body in Pain*, p.27.

53 Butler, *Bodies that Matter*, p.96.

54 Kane in Claire Armistead interview, 'No Pain. No Kane', *Guardian*, 29 April 1998, p.12.

55 Mark Ravenhill, 'Obituary: Sarah Kane', *Independent*, 23 February 1999, p.6.

56 Kane's own philosophy was that to face the very worst that life has to offer, requires not only love, but also humour. In the Bayley interview cited in note 3, she said 'Once you have perceived that life is very cruel, the only response is to live with as much humanity, humour and freedom as you can.' Characteristic of *Phaedra's Love* is the way in which even the darkest, most violent moments, are faced with grim humour and touches of irony. Hippolytus, castrated, bowels torn out, motionless, and surrounded by the bodies of his stepsister, Strophe, and his father, Theseus, opens his eyes and '*manages a smile*'. 'If there could have been more moments like this', he says as he dies and a vulture descends to eat his body (*Phaedra's Love*, in *Complete Plays*, p.103).

57 Kane, *Guardian*, 20 August 1998.

58 See 'Conversation with Vicky Featherstone', in Saunders, *Love Me or Kill Me*, pp.128–33 for details of how Featherstone and Kane worked together on *Crave*.

59 Paul Taylor, Features, *Independent*, 23 February 1999, p.1.

60 Upton made a similar point in *People on the River*, although dramaturgically Upton's play is much more conventional than the experimental *Crave*.

61 There are two significant patriarchal framings of the child in stories that are told: M's story about seeing her grandparents kiss that her mother told her could not be true: 'My father died before you were

born' (*Crave*, p.159), and B's 'impossible' inheritance of a broken nose from his father (*Crave*, p.162).

62 There is a reference on p.187 to ES3, which I understand in the light of the dedication of *Cleansed* – 'For the patients and staff of ES3' – to refer to a clinic or ward of a clinic where Kane was treated for depression.

63 'Drama with Balls', Sarah Kane, *Guardian*, 20 August 1998, p.12.

6 PERFORMING IDENTITIES

1 See Caryl Churchill, *Cloud Nine*, in *Plays One* (London: Methuen, 1985), p.283. Anna Marie Smith, *New Right Discourse on Race and Sexuality: Britain, 1968–1990* (Cambridge University Press: Cambridge, 1994) states that 'opinion polls found that homophobic attitudes both became more common and increased in severity in the late 1980s' (p.16).

2 Anna Marie Smith, ibid., p.198.

3 A similar homophobic response occurred on the performance scene in America at roughly the same time. In 1990 the NEA (National Endowment for the Arts) decided to defund four artists, three of whom were gay, while the other, Karen Finley, conjures the abject, defiling, contaminating body through her work.

4 It was repealed in Scotland in 2000.

5 Sue-Ellen Case, *The Domain-Matrix: Performing Lesbian at the End of Print Culture* (Bloomington and Indianapolis: Indiana University Press, 1996), p.11.

6 For further discussion of this point see Janelle Reinelt, 'Staging the Invisible: The Crisis of Visibility in Theatrical Representation', *Text and Performance Quarterly*, 14 (1994), pp.1–11.

7 'The essentialist risk' is taken from lesbian critic Teresa De Lauretis, quoted and explained in Case, *The Domain-Matrix*, p.12.

8 Sandra Freeman, *Putting Your Daughters on the Stage: Lesbian Theatre from the 1970s to the 1990s* (London: Cassell, 1997), pp.136–65.

9 Ibid., p.136.

10 Judith Butler, 'Imitation and Gender Insubordination', in Diana Fuss, ed., *Inside/Out: Lesbian Theories, Gay Theories* (London: Routledge, 1991), pp.13–31, pp.13–14.

11 The radical lesbian label has been used reductively against Sarah Daniels since *Masterpieces*. While readers might reasonably expect to find her work discussed in this chapter, I chose to present her theatre in the themed chapter on abuse (Chapter 3), in part to upset the expectation that her work only gets taken up in a lesbian context or is 'abused' by it.

12 Mary McCusker, Monstrous Regiment interview in Elaine Aston, ed., *Feminist Theatre Voices* (Loughborough: Loughborough Theatre Texts, 1997), p.71. For Lavery's comments on her lack of 'mainstream recognition' see her interview in Heidi Stephenson and Natasha Langridge, eds., *Rage and Reason: Women Playwrights on Playwriting* (London: Methuen, 1997), pp.105–14, p.107.

13 Lavery's first production at the Birmingham Repertory Theatre was actually in the 1980s when Monstrous Regiment produced *Origin of the Species* on the Studio stage in 1984. In 2002 *Frozen* was revived for the National Theatre, albeit like Churchill's *The Skriker* for the Cottesloe, the studio stage, and *A Wedding Story* transferred in 2001 to the Soho Theatre, London.

14 Bryony Lavery, *Her Aching Heart*, in *Plays 1* (London: Methuen, 1998), p.99.

15 Claire Grove in 'The Women's Theatre Group', interview, in Elaine Aston, ed., *Feminist Theatre Voices*, p.43.

16 Diana Fuss, ed., *Inside/Out: Lesbian Theories, Gay Theories* (London: Routledge, 1991), p.1.

17 Lynda Hart, *Fatal Women: Lesbian Sexuality and the Mark of Aggression* (London: Routledge, 1994), p.42.

18 Jill Posener's *Any Woman Can* is published in Jill Davis, ed., *Lesbian Plays* (London: Methuen, 1987).

19 *Fatal Women*, p.16.

20 Du Maurier's novel opens, 'Last night I dreamt I went to Manderley again'. Lavery's attraction to Du Maurier (bi-sexual 'mistress' of historical romance), is demonstrated in her adaptation for radio of *A High Wind in Jamaica* (2000) and *My Cousin Rachel* (1994).

21 For a discussion of venues and lesbian theatre, see Sandra Freeman, *Putting Your Daughters on the Stage*, Chapter 8, 'A Look at Venues', pp.124–35.

22 See also *Two Marias* in *Plays 1*, and *Frozen*, discussed later.

23 *Goliath*, Lavery's adaptation of the Beatrix Campbell study (discussed in Chapter 7) also opens with a monologue by a dead driver.

24 The first series of *Friends* was shown in 1994–5. Other comedy series towards the close of the decade, however, such as the American show *Will and Grace* (1998) or the British series *Gimme, Gimme, Gimme* (1999) have examined friendships between roommates who are straight and gay.

25 Kevin Elyot's 1995 gay play for the Royal Court, *My Night with Reg* works in a similar way. Drawing on conventions of the 'drawing room' play, Elyot overturns expectations of a bourgeois family drama by populating his domestic interior with a circle of gay friends to create his black comedy about Aids.

26 See also Lavery's *Origin of the Species* in *Plays 1*, which is set on New Year's Eve, and offers a feminist slant to the subject of evolution as Molly 'births' and educates an ancestral 'daughter', Victoria, to go out into the world.

27 Explained in author's correspondence with Lavery, 2003.

28 *A Wedding Story* (London: Faber, 2000), Scene Ten, pp.48–51.

29 Mary Douglas, *Purity and Danger: An Analysis of the Concepts of Pollution and Taboo* (London: Routledge, 1966), pp.36–7.

30 See for example Scene Five in *A Wedding Story* that recounts Peter and Evelyn's wedding and includes a description of Peter's suit that meant, as Sally says, that 'you couldn't see how *packed* his lunchbox was . . . you could only speculate as the size and *magnificence* of his fishing tackle' (p.34).

31 Peggy Phelan, *Unmarked: The Politics of Performance* (London: Routledge, 1993), p.4.

32 When Robin fails to cope with the facts of his mother's illness, Lavery instructs that he '*alchemises*' them into film (*A Wedding Story*, p.57). This is Robin's key strategy for coping with his mother's illness and other situations that he finds difficult – for example his estrangement from his children: if he cannot be with them, he can fantasise the film script in which they come to seek him out (see Scene Seventeen).

33 For a detailed analysis of this point, see Lynda Hart, 'Identity and Seduction: Lesbians in the Mainstream' in Lynda Hart and Peggy Phelan, *Acting Out: Feminist Performances* (Ann Arbor: The University of Michigan Press, 1993), pp.119–37. Hart's analysis in this essay focuses on the Split Britches show, *Anniversary Waltz*, which visually and controversially presented the lesbian relationship of performers Lois Weaver and Peggy Shaw in a wedding context.

34 In 1994 Nagy also had the following plays produced in America: *Trip's Cinch* (Actors' Theatre of Louisville); *Girl Bar* (written in 1988, Celebration Theatre Los Angeles), and an adaptation of Nathaniel Hawthorne's *The Scarlet Letter* (Denver Centre Theatre, 1994).

35 In Phyllis Nagy, *Plays One* (London: Methuen, 1998), p.vi.

36 My views expressed in this paragraph are consequent upon detailed study of Nagy's theatre and extended discussion with the playwright.

37 *Guardian*, 4 December 1995, p.7.

38 Phyllis Nagy, interview, in Heidi Stephenson and Natasha Langridge, eds., *Rage and Reason: Women Playwrights on Playwriting* (London: Methuen, 1997), p.27.

39 *Guardian*, 21 September 1998, p.13.

40 See Phyllis Nagy, afterword to *Weldon Rising*, in Annie Castledine, ed., *Plays By Women: Ten* (London: Methuen, 1994), p.144.

41 Ibid.

42 *Weldon Rising* originally was published in *Plays International* in 1992.

43 Stephenson and Langridge, eds., *Rage and Reason*, p.24.

44 This makes the matricide of *Butterfly Kiss* rather different, for example, to that staged in Martin McDonagh's *The Beauty Queen of Leenane* (1996) where the domestic, social constraints of a harsh and isolated rural Irish setting ultimately give way to a portrait of filial madness.

45 One other character also has a direct address moment: Teddy Roosevelt Hayes, Lily's first lover (see *Butterfly Kiss*, p.66). The lawyer's name 'Trouver' is an interesting play on words – trouver, meaning to 'find' in French. Similarly, Nagy playfully assigns presidential overtones to Teddy's surname.

46 *Tallulah Bankhead*, Bryony Lavery (Bath, Somerset: Absolute Press, 1999).

47 Sloan keeps a photograph of Christine in his wallet which Jenny steals, leaving a photograph of herself, age 5, that her father also keeps in the wallet, in full view: 'young Lily, hidden, at last, by nothing' (*Butterfly Kiss*, p.87).

48 For commentary on this see Jeremy Kingston's review for *The Times*, reproduced in *Theatre Record*, 9–22 April 1994, pp.447–8.

49 For an analysis of the centrality of the father to Lily's life and the possibility that 'Lily attempts to save Jenny from Sloan through murder', see Claudia Barnett, 'Phyllis Nagy's Fatal Women', *Modern Drama*, 42, 1999, pp.28–44, p.31.

50 Reviews cited are collected in *Theatre Record*, 26 February–11 March 1995, pp.266–70.

51 Phyllis Nagy, 'Hold Your Nerve: Notes for a Young Playwright', in David Edgar, ed., *State of Play: Playwrights on Playwriting* (London: Faber and Faber, 1999), pp.123–32, p.125, observes that:

> critics report on them [plays] as if they can be reduced to their literal, factual components for the benefit of any potential audience. And when it is impossible to attain either an instant understanding of plays or an instant sense of how to describe them for others, the natural tendency of commentary is to reject such work as being incoherent or incomprehensible.

52 In *The Sunday Times* John Peter wrote that 'Nagy uses the elements of drama – characters (sort of), motivation (vaguely), and the dynamics of plotting (arbitrarily)', reproduced in *Theatre Record*, 26 February – 11 March 1995, pp.269–70, p.270.

53 Nightingale, *The Times*, reproduced in *Theatre Record*, 26 February – 11 March 1995, p.268.

54 Steven Pimlott, interview with David Benedict, Features, *Independent*, 7 January 1998, p.14. With Pimlott, Nagy had found the kind of successful director–writer partnership of, for example, Caryl Churchill and Max Stafford-Clark, a success perhaps in part due to Pimlott's background in opera and musicals finding affinity with Nagy's own music training.

55 Michael Billington also wrote that while *The Strip* is 'bewildering and hallucinatory' it also 'has a built-in structure' (*Guardian* review, reproduced in *Theatre Record*, 26 February – 11 March 1995, p.266).

56 In his review for the *Independent*, Paul Taylor suggested an affinity between Otto Mink and the Duke in Shakespeare's *Measure for Measure*, *Theatre Record*, 26 February – 11 March 1995, pp.268–9, p.269.

57 See Nagy's commentary on this in *Rage and Reason*, pp.26–7.

58 Nagy describes Ava as her 'commentary on modern womanhood gone berserk' (*Rage and Reason*, p.24).

59 For more on this point, see Nagy's commentary in *State of Play*, p.125.

60 Nagy with Mel Kenyon, *Guardian*, 4 December 1995, p.7.

61 *Never Land* played in the Court's studio venue, temporarily housed in The Ambassadors, West Street (during the period of the Royal Court refurbishment). *Never Land* was originally commissioned by Hampstead Theatre, but the production fell through when Nagy refused to make changes to her script. While the Court had also turned *Never Land* down, it finally got taken on as a co-production with Helen McCory's company, The Foundry.

62 See *Never Land* (London: Methuen, 1998), pp.52–6. Much of the comedy in *Fawlty Towers* centred on the way hotelier Basil Fawlty (played by John Cleese) mistreated his Spanish waiter Manuel. The episode acted out is the one in which the hotel has German guests and creates the occasion for anti-German humour, specifically about the Second World War.

63 *Guess Who's Coming to Dinner* (1967) starred Spencer Tracy and Katherine Hepburn as the father and mother who have to come to terms with the daughter's (Katharine Houghton) decision to marry a black doctor (Sidney Poitier).

7 FEMINIST CONNECTIONS TO A MULTICULTURAL 'SCENE'

1 Winsome Pinnock in David Edgar, ed., *State of Play: Playwrights on Playwriting* (London: Faber and Faber, 1999), p.58.

2 The Methuen *Plays by Women* series began under Michelene Wandor's editorship in 1982. The first volume of *Black Plays* was

published in 1987, followed by two further volumes in 1989 and 1995. Jacqueline Rudet, for example, had *Money to Live* published in Volume Five of the *Plays by Women* series and *Basin* was published in the first volume of *Black Plays.*

3 Patricia Hilaire, Paulette Randall and Bernardine Evaristo founded Theatre of Black Women in 1982. Playwright Jacqueline Rudet set up Iamni-Faith in 1982. Later in 1990, Denise Wong also founded Women's Troop as a 'sister' company to Black Mime Theatre.

4 The Birmingham-based group, Women and Theatre, also sought to move toward a multi-racial composition in the late 1980s. For further details of both groups and their multi-racial aims, see Elaine Aston *Introduction to Feminism and Theatre* (London: Routledge, 1995), Chapter 6, 'Black Women, Shaping Feminist Theatre', pp.78–91.

5 Beatrix Campbell, *Goliath: Britain's Dangerous Places* (London: Methuen, 1993).

6 Ibid., p.107.

7 Ibid., p.109.

8 Caryl Churchill, *Cloud Nine*, in *Plays One* (London: Methuen, 1985), p.251.

9 Spivak, 'Criticism, Feminism and the Institution', 1984 interview with Elizabeth Grosz, published in Sarah Harasym, ed., *The Post-Colonial Critic: Interviews, Strategies, Dialogues* (London: Routledge, 1990), pp.1–16, p.9.

10 Heidi Safia Mirza, ed., *Black British Feminism: A Reader* (London: Routledge, 1997), p.9.

11 Pratibha Parmar, 'Other Kinds of Dreams', *Feminist Review*, 31, Spring 1989, pp.55–65, p.57.

12 M. Jacqui Alexander and Chandra Talpade Mohanty, eds., *Feminist Genealogies, Colonial Legacies, Democratic Futures* (London: Routledge, 1997), p.xix.

13 Although Spivak notes that 'essentialising' and 'universalising' have their strategic uses. See 'Criticism, Feminism and the Institution', p.11.

14 Alexander and Mohanty, eds., *Feminist Genealogies*, p.xxxi.

15 'Breaking Down the Door' is the title of Winsome Pinnock's essay in Vera Gottlieb and Colin Chambers, eds., *Theatre in a Cool Climate* (Oxford: Amber Lane Press, 1999), pp.27–38.

16 Winsome Pinnock, 'Breaking Down the Door', p.33 and p.29. For more views on this subject see comments from Michael Billington's interviewees (who include Nicolas Kent, Tricycle Theatre), in 'White Out', *Guardian*, 18 October 2000.

17 Explained in Heidi Stephenson and Natasha Langridge, eds., *Rage and Reason: Women Playwrights on Playwriting* (London: Methuen, 1997), McLeod interview, pp.98–104; Gupta interview, pp.115–21.

18 Stephenson and Langridge, eds., *Rage and Reason*, p.116.

19 Ibid., pp.103–4.

20 Pinnock's *Leave Taking* is published in Kate Harwood, ed., *First Run: New Plays by New Writers* (London : Nick Hern Books, 1989), pp.139–89.

21 Jenny McLeod, *Raising Fires* (London: Bush Theatre, 1994). *Raising Fires* is reminiscent of Miller's *The Crucible*, but, like Churchill's *Vinegar Tom*, removes martyred masculinity as the dramatic focus to concentrate more fully on witchcraft as a site of social, gender, and in McLeod's case, racial, prejudice.

22 Bonnie Greer, *Munda Negra*, in Yvonne Brewster, ed., *Black Plays 3* (London: Methuen, 1995), pp.41–99.

23 Edgar, ed., *State of Play*, p.58.

24 Kadija George, ed., *Six Plays by Black and Asian Women Writers* (London: Aurora Metro Press, 1993). The volume also contains a series of essays treating aspects of theatre and playwriting by black and Asian women.

25 Jenny McLeod, *Island Life*, in *Monstrous Regiment*, compiled by Gillian Hanna (London: Nick Hern Books, 1991), pp.147–212, p.155.

26 See Judith Johnson, 'Afterword: *Uganda*', in Pamela Edwardes, ed., *Frontline Intelligence 3: New Plays for the Nineties* (London: Methuen, 1995), p.133.

27 Winsome Pinnock, *Talking in Tongues* is published in Yvonne Brewster, ed., *Black Plays 3* (London: Methuen, 1995), pp.171–227.

28 Edgar, ed., *State of Play*, p.58.

29 Winsome Pinnock, interview, in Heidi Stephenson and Natasha Langridge, eds., *Rage and Reason: Women Playwrights on Playwriting* (London: Methuen, 1997), p.49.

30 Meenakshi Ponnuswami, 'Small Island People: Black British Women Playwrights', in Elaine Aston and Janelle Reinelt, eds., *The Cambridge Companion to Modern British Women Playwrights* (Cambridge: Cambridge University Press, 2000), pp.217–34, p.224.

31 Ibid., p.224.

32 See also Bonnie Greer's *Munda Negra* for engagement with this trauma in the representation of Greer's art critic Anna Eastman.

33 Judith Butler, *Gender Trouble* (London: Routledge, 1990).

34 In her later study, *Bodies that Matter* (London: Routledge, 1993), Butler brings race more fully into the frame, arguing the need for white feminism to 'contest' the idea 'that sexual difference is more primary or more fundamental than other kinds of difference, including racial difference' (p.181).

35 Stephenson and Langridge, eds., *Rage and Reason*, p.52.

36 Edgar, ed., *State of Play*, p.59.

37 See Winsome Pinnock, *Mules* (London: Faber and Faber, 1996), p.52.

38 Stephenson and Langridge, eds., *Rage and Reason*, p.52.

39 Alexander and Mohanty, eds., *Feminist Genealogies*, p.xii.

40 'Breaking Down the Door', p.36.

41 Reviews collected in *Theatre Record*, 22 April–5 May 1996, p.323.

42 Temba, formed in 1972, lasted twenty years, but lost its funding in 1992.

43 Both of these plays have also been broadcast on Radio 4 and both won CRE Race in the Media Awards for Drama. *Women of the Dust* had an Indian tour in 1993. Also for radio, Bhuchar, along with Shaheen Khan has written a series for BBC Radio 4, *Girlies* (following the lives of four Asian women).

44 Ruth Carter, *Women of the Dust* (London: Nick Hern Books, 1999), p.17.

45 For further discussion of the complexity of racial identities that belies an idea of 'the British character' as homogenous, see Mary Karen Dahl, 'Postcolonial British Theatre', in J. Ellen Gainor, ed.,

Imperialism and Theatre: Essays on World Theatre, Drama and Performance (London: Routledge, 1995), pp.38–55, p.46.

46 Jatinder Verma, 'Cultural Transformations' in Theodore Shank, ed., *Contemporary British Theatre* (Basingstoke: Macmillan), pp.55–61, p.58.

47 *Black British Feminism*, pp.262–3.

48 Kiranjit Ahluwalia, quoted in Pragna Patel, 'Third Wave Feminism and Black Women's Activism', in Heidi Safia Mirza, ed., *Black British Feminism*, pp.255–68, p.262. In support of Ahluwalia's claim for the hidden suffering of Asian women in Britain, Patel gives statistics for suicide rates of Asian women in Britain between the ages of 16 and 35 as being three times the national average (*Black British Feminism*, p.263).

49 Tanika Gupta, interview, in *Rage and Reason*, p.117. Gupta has since had residences at and work staged by the Soho Theatre Company and the Royal National Theatre. See chapter 9 for details.

50 The Khans have one more child: their eldest, Nazir, not seen in the play, but frequently spoken about on account of how he has already left home after violently quarrelling with George over the possibility of an arranged marriage.

51 Ayub Khan-Din, *East is East* (London: Nick Hern Books, 1997), p.45.

52 The first British Asian soap, *Family Pride*, was broadcast on Channel 4 in 1991. In 1996, BBC Radio 4 launched an Asian sketch show, *Goodness Gracious Me*, that transferred to television where it has proved highly popular and successful.

53 Ella's working-class identity is foregrounded in the production through the interpretation of the role by Linda Bassett. Bassett is closely identified with socially orientated roles on account of her several performances in plays by, among others, Churchill and Wertenbaker.

54 *The Story of M* is published with images and text in SuAndi, ed., *4 For More* (Manchester: ArtBlacklive Publication, 2002).

55 Influenced by Ntozake Shange, Kay's work, notably *Chiaroscuro* (1986) always has tended towards the experimental, more recently evidenced in her creation of a poetry text for a music-theatre production *Twice Through the Heart* (1997). For a description of

Chowdhry's slide and video piece, *The Sacred House* (1993), see Catherine Ugwu, *Let's Get it On* (London: Institute of Contemporary Arts, 1995), p.71. Her poetically styled *Monsoon* can be found in the Kadija George anthology of *Black and Asian Women Writers.*

56 *Lets Get it On*, p.68.

57 Ibid., p.68.

58 Kum-Kum Bhavani and Margaret Coulson, 'Transforming Socialist Feminism: The Challenge of Racism', in Heidi Safia Mirza, ed., *Black British Feminism*, pp.59–62, pp.60–1.

59 For a dramatic treatment of police harassment and a black mother, see black American playwright Adrienne Kennedy's *Motherhood 2000* in Bonnie Mauranca, ed., *Plays for the End of the Century* (Baltimore: PAJ/ John Hopkins, 1997). The opening line to *Motherhood 2000* reads: 'I finally found the policeman who beat my son that January night in 1991', p.3.

60 Carolyn Steedman, *Landscape for a Good Woman: A Story of Two Lives* (London: Virago, 1986), p.5.

61 *The Colour of Justice* was performed in a series of plays, edited by Richard Norton-Taylor and Nicolas Kent, that are based on courtroom and inquiry transcripts. They have become known as the 'Tricycle Tribunal Plays'. *The Colour of Justice* also toured nationally and was broadcast on BBC television.

62 For a full description of the production see Geraldine Cousin, ed., *Recording Women: A Documentation of Six Theatre Productions* (Amsterdam: Harwood Academic Publishers, 2000), pp.134–55.

63 Castledine, Production note, theatre programme, *Goliath*, 1997.

64 Lavery explains that ultimately she was not so 'certain about Anna Deavere Smith's working method' and opted for creating her own scenes inspired by Campbell's book. Lavery in Geraldine Cousin, ed. *Recording Women*, p.150.

65 This was not without difficulty, however. On occasion, McAuliffe's naturalist performance style was problematic in relation to particular roles, most especially in her interpretation of an Asian shopkeeper that was in danger of becoming a westernised, mimicking of 'Asian-ness'.

66 *Goliath*, p. 90.

67 In Cousin, ed., *Recording Women*, p.150.

68 My final point of reference is to the collection of monologues: Stuart Hood, ed., *A Woman Alone and Other Plays: Franca Rame and Dario Fo* (London: Methuen, 1991). My desire is to signal the context of the female monologue as a form that occupies the latter section of this chapter and, at the same time, invoke it as a point of reference to suggest the move towards diversity and difference.

8 FEMINISM PAST, AND FUTURE?

1 WTG commissioned *New Anatomies* (1982) at a time when Wertenbaker was in financial difficulty and in need of a supportive women's environment for her work. Wertenbaker discussed this time in an interview broadcast on BBC Radio 4, June 1991.

2 Wertenbaker in interview with Michael Billington, *Guardian*, 25 November 1999, p.10.

3 See Billington interview, ibid., for further commentary on this point.

4 Ibid., p.10.

5 Ibid., p.10.

6 With regard to *The Love of the Nightingale*, Wertenbaker states that she 'was actually thinking of the violence that erupts in societies when they have been silenced for too long', but notes that 'it has been interpreted as being about women' (*Plays 1*, London: Faber and Faber, 1996, viii).

7 Interview, *Writers Revealed*, BBC Radio 4, 20 June 1991. See also Chapter 4, p.59 for related discussion of the idea of women having adventures.

8 An audio recording of *Abel's Sister* is, however, held in the National Sound Archive, British Library, London.

9 The director was Les Waters and the production also involved collaboration between the Royal Court's Studio Theatre Upstairs and the Royal Court Young People's Theatre.

10 Martin Hoyle, *Financial Times*, 8 August 1984, reproduced in *London Theatre Record*, 30 July–12 August, 1984, p.662.

11 Radio interview, June 1991.

12 *The Sisters* is a physically orientated re-working of *Three Sisters* that Scarlet Theatre Company has regularly revived since their first tour

of this show in 1995. Latterly they have also devised a companion piece, *Sisters* and *Others* – where *Others* brings together the male characters from the play. For details of *The Sisters* see Geraldine Cousin (ed.), *Recording Women: A Documentation of Six Theatre Productions* (Amsterdam: Harwood, 2000), Section One.

13 Around the time that *The Break of Day* was staged, the issue of overseas adoption was headlining the news as couples in the UK and USA adopted baby girls from China. The issue of unwanted girl children in China received widespread publicity in the UK following the television documentary *The Dying Rooms* (June 1995) which alleged that in a country which restricts families to one child, making boys the priority, the girls are abandoned and left to die in orphanages.

14 M. Jacqui Alexander and Chandra Talpade Mohanty (eds.) *Feminist Genealogies, Colonial Legacies, Democratic Futures* (New York and London: Routledge, 1997), p.xli.

15 Timberlake Wertenbaker, *The Break of Day*, in *Plays 2* (London: Faber and Faber, 2002), p.86.

16 It is important that the adoption in the play is not an economic transaction. Mihail's anti-capitalist attitude signals that his motive for helping the childless British couple is selfless rather than selfish; that he is not one of the businessmen profiting from the (very real) trading in East to West babies.

17 Coveney, *Observer*, reproduced in *Theatre Record*, 19 November– 2 December 1995, p.1,624.

18 Nathan, *Jewish Chronicle*, reproduced in *Theatre Record*, 19 November–2 December 1995, p.1,620.

19 De Jongh, *Evening Standard*, reproduced in *Theatre Record*, 19 November–2 December 1995, pp.1,620–1, p.1,621.

20 Susan Bordo, *Unbearable Weight: Feminism, Western Culture and the Body* (Berkeley and Los Angeles: University of California Press, 1993), p.95.

21 *Unbearable Weight*, p.95.

22 De Jongh, *Theatre Record*, p.1620.

23 Spencer, *Daily Telegraph*, reproduced in *Theatre Record*, p.1,624.

24 Charlotte Canning, 'Feminists Perform their Past: Constructing History in *The Heidi Chronicles* and *The Break of Day*', in

Maggie B. Gale and Viv Gardner (eds.) *Women, Theatre and Performance* (Manchester: Manchester University Press, 2000), pp.163–77, p.175.

25 Preface, *Plays 2*, p.viii.

26 *Boys Mean Business* takes the relationship between two brothers, Gary and Will, and their friend Elvis as its focus. The brothers had a moment of teenage 'fame' in their band 'The Heroes', but are now struggling to make something of their lives, friendships and relationships. Published in *Bush Theatre Plays*, introduced by Dominic Dromgoole (London: Faber and Faber, 1996).

27 Catherine Johnson, *Shang-a-Lang* (London: Faber and Faber, 1998), p.89.

28 For those readers too young to remember the Bay City Rollers, tartan band – Woody was one of the five band members (along with Les, Eric, Derek and Alan).

29 Curiously, *Shang-a-Lang*, scheduled to have an extract broadcast on Radio 4's Woman's Hour, with discussion, was withdrawn on the grounds that women were behaving too badly, though in terms of the fortysomething women in the theatre audience, this did not appear to be a problem: rather the opposite, the pleasure lay precisely in identification with the female comedy of bad behaviour.

30 Quoted as preface to *The Positive Hour*, April de Angelis (London: Faber and Faber, 1997).

31 More recently both playwrights have taken a dramatic interest in asylum-seeking: see De Angelis's libretto for Jonathan Dove's opera *Flight* (1998) that was inspired by the true story of a refugee found living in Charles de Gaulle Airport, and Wertenbaker's *Credible Witness*.

32 It is perhaps not, therefore, insignificant that *The Positive Hour* had a much more 'positive' critical reception than did *The Break of Day*.

33 Quoted in *Rage and Reason*, Stephenson and Langridge (eds.), p.59.

34 See Timberlake Wertenbaker, *After Darwin*, in *Plays 2*, p.122.

35 One woman who exceptionally does get mentioned on account of her writing is Jane Austen, see *After Darwin*, p.109. The reference to Austen, however, has a particular resonance in the 1990s given

the ubiquitous filmed and televised versions of her work – the kind of mainstream costume drama that promotes and endorses a universalising, conservative view of history restricted to white, middle- to upper-class, heterosexual, familial organisation.

36 Wertenbaker explained that, 'the last scene should be a fusion, musical, where the different strands of the arguments harmonise for a moment: the scientific view (Darwin), the imaginative view (Lawrence), the tragic view (Fitzroy), brought together and realised by Millie' (correspondence with the author, February 2003).

37 For a collection of these see *Theatre Record*, 2–15 July 1998, pp.896–900.

38 *The Positive Hour* also parodies the idea of a men's group: Miranda's husband, Roger, joins a men's group not concerned with men as sensitive partners to 'feminism', but as functioning as a group that allows men to be men again.

39 Robert comments that in Chekhov's stories 'the men never play sports, they talk', adding 'I envy civilizations where talking itself is a sport' (*The Break of Day*, p.17).

40 Imelda Whelehan, *Overloaded* (London: The Women's Press, 2000), p.117. The anxieties provoked by a 'highly technologised world' are more obviously dramatised in *After Darwin* than *The Break of Day*.

41 Dr Glad in *The Break of Day* argues that 'the twentieth century isn't kind to men with their sperm count' (p.53). In Tess's inability to conceive, Robert's low sperm count is problematic. Glad, however, prefers to exclude the biological mother before the father, giving up on Tess's eggs and using eggs from another, younger woman, with Robert's sperm. 'We like to include the chaps in all of this' he claims (p.69).

42 Wertenbaker continues to press this point. See also her radio play *Dianeira* (BBC Radio 3, 1999) and *Credible Witness* (2001), both in *Plays 2*. *Credible Witness* takes a critical look at Britain's role in relation to the asylum-seeker at the close of the twentieth century.

43 *Kaleidoscope*, BBC Radio 4, 26 December 1989. The other speakers we Ian McDermott, Sheila Hancock and Bob Carlton.

44 Millie frequently instructs her actors to find the emotion of their character in a particular scene, and Wertenbaker takes emotional states for framing her scenes: Scene One 'Despair'; Scene Two 'Hope', Scene Three, 'Emotion', and so on.

45 From correspondence with the author, February 2003.

9 TALES FOR THE TWENTY-FIRST CENTURY: FINAL REFLECTIONS

1 Churchill, *The Skriker* in *Plays Three* (London: Nick Hern Books, 1998), p.290.

2 In the mid-1990s Reynolds was writer-in-residence for Clean Break. *Red* (1994), like Prichard's *Yard Gal* a two-character play cast with one black and one white performer, was a company commission. A third play, *Wild Things* (1994) also draws heavily on Reynold's own experience of psychiatric prison.

3 Munro also has worked with the MsFits feminist cabaret act.

4 As maiden traditionally means a young unmarried woman, the implication is that Harriet never actually married, only 'performed' the role of wife, and therefore, figuratively, comes to stand for the lone, unmarried mother struggling to provide for her children.

5 Cross-cultural connections may also be argued for the play's production: a Scottish playwright produced the play on the English stage. Under Jenny Topper's direction in the 1990s the Hampstead Theatre forged strong connections with Scottish women writers: Rona Munro's *Snake* was also staged there in 1999 and Liz Lochhead's *Perfect Days* transferred to the Hampstead after its sell-out run at The Traverse in 1998.

6 Cixous, 'The Laugh of the Medusa', in Elaine Marks and Isabelle de Courtivron, eds., *New French Feminisms* (Brighton: The Harvester Press, 1981), pp.245–64, p.248.

7 For further details, see Tanika Gupta, *Skeleton* (London: Faber and Faber, 1997), pp.91–2.

8 For reviews see *Theatre Record*, 21 May to 3 June 1997.

Bibliography

Full details about play reviews are given in the Notes. Where possible, these are referenced in Theatre Record, *otherwise full newspaper sources are given.*

Adshead, Kay. *The Bogus Woman.* London: Oberon Books, 2001.

Alberge, Dalya. 'Charities Alarmed at Casting of Children in "Gang Rape" Play', *The Times,* 4 November 1997: 38.

Alexander, Jacqui M., and Mohanty, Chandra Talpade, eds. *Feminist Genealogies, Colonial Legacies, Democratic Futures.* London: Routledge, 1997.

Ansorge, Peter. *From Liverpool to Los Angeles: On Writing for Theatre, Film and Television.* London: Faber and Faber, 1997.

Armistead, Claire. 'Arts Theatre: It Started with a Kiss . . .' *Guardian,* 7 January 1998: 12.

Armstrong, Louise. *Kiss Daddy Goodnight: Ten Years Later,* New York: Hawthorn Books, 1987.

——. *Rocking the Cradle of Sexual Politics: What Happened when Women Said Incest* [1994]. First British edition. London: Women's Press, 1996.

Ashfield, Kate. Interview, with Dominic Cavendish. Features, *Independent.* 9 September 1998: 11.

Aston, Elaine. 'Daniels in the Lion's Den: Sarah Daniels and the British Backlash'. *Theatre Journal,* October 1995: 393–403.

——. *An Introduction to Feminism and Theatre.* London: Routledge, 1995.

——. *Caryl Churchill.* [1997] Second edition. Plymouth: Northcote, 2001.

Aston, Elaine, ed. *Feminist Theatre Voices*. Loughborough: Loughborough Theatre Texts, 1997.

Aston, Elaine, and Janelle Reinelt, eds. *The Cambridge Companion to Modern British Women Playwrights*. Cambridge: Cambridge University Press, 2000.

Atkins, Eileen. *Vita and Virginia*. London: Samuel French, 1995.

Barnett, Claudia. 'Phyllis Nagy's Fatal Women'. *Modern Drama*, 42, 1999: 28–44.

Bhavani, Kum-Kum, and Coulson, Margaret. 'Transforming Socialist Feminism: The Challenge of Racism'. In Heidi Safia Mirza, ed., *Black British Feminism*: 59–62.

Billington, Michael. 'White Out', *Guardian*, 18 October 2000.

Billington, Michael, with Lyn Gardner. 'Fabulous Five'. *Guardian*, 13 March, 1996: 10.

Bordo, Susan. *Unbearable Weight: Feminism, Western Culture and the Body*. Berkeley and Los Angeles: University of California Press, 1993.

Bradwell, Mike, ed. *The Bush Theatre Book*. London: Methuen, 1997.

Brewster, Yvonne, ed. *Black Plays*. London: Methuen, 1987.

——. *Black Plays 2*. London: Methuen, 1989.

——. *Black Plays 3*. London: Methuen, 1995.

Brown, Georgina. 'Arts: Where Angels Fear to Tread'. *Independent*, 30 March 1996: 7.

Burrell, Ian, and Lisa Brinkworth. 'Sugar 'n' Spice but . . . Not all that Nice'. *The Sunday Times*, 27 November 1994: 16.

Butler, Judith. *Gender Trouble*. London: Routledge, 1990.

——. 'Imitation and Gender Insubordination'. In Diana Fuss, ed. *Inside/Out: Lesbian Theories, Gay Theories*. London: Routledge, 1991: 13–31.

——. *Bodies that Matter*. London: Routledge, 1993.

Butler, Katy. 'You Must Remember This'. *Guardian*, 23 July 1994: 6.

Campbell, Beatrix. *Unofficial Secrets: Child Sexual Abuse: The Cleveland Case*. London: Virago, 1988; fully revised, 1997.

Canning, Charlotte. 'Feminists Perform their Past: Constructing History in *The Heidi Chronicles* and *The Break of Day*'. In Maggie

B. Gale and Viv Gardner, eds. *Women, Theatre and Performance.* Manchester: Manchester University Press, 2000: 163–77.

Carter, Ruth. *Women of the Dust.* London: Nick Hern Books, 1999.

——. *A Yearning.* London: Nick Hern Books, 1999.

Case, Sue-Ellen. 'Toward a Butch-Femme Aesthetic'. In Lynda Hart, ed., *Making a Spectacle: Feminist Essays on Contemporary Women's Theatre.* Ann Arbor: University of Michigan Press, 1989: 282–99.

——. *The Domain-Matrix: Performing Lesbian at the End of Print Culture.* Bloomington and Indianapolis: Indiana University Press, 1996.

Castledine, Annie. Production note, theatre programme, *Goliath.* The Sphinx Theatre Company, 1997.

Chambers, Colin. 'That's Entertainment'. In Vera Gottlieb and Colin Chambers, eds. *Theatre in a Cool Climate.* Oxford: Amber Lane Press, 1999: 169–78.

Chesney-Lind, Meda, and John M. Hagedorn, eds. *Female Gangs in America.* Chicago: Lake View Press, 1999.

Churchill, Caryl. *Plays One: Owners, Traps, Vinegar Tom, Light Shining in Buckinghamshire, Cloud Nine.* London: Methuen, 1985.

——. Interview. In Kathleen Betsko and Rachel Koenig, eds. *Interviews with Contemporary Women Playwrights.* New York: Beech Tree Books, 1987: 75–84.

——. *Plays Two: Softcops, Top Girls, Fen, Serious Money.* London: Methuen, 1990.

——. 'A Bold Imagination for Action'. *Guardian,* 25 January 1995:19.

——. *Blue Heart.* London: Nick Hern Books, 1997.

——. Interview with David Benedict. Arts section, *Independent,* 19 April 1997: 4.

——. *Plays Three: Icecream, Mad Forest, Thyestes, The Skriker, Lives of the Great Poisoners, Mouthful of Birds* (with David Lan). London: Nick Hern Books, 1998.

——. *Far Away.* London: Nick Hern Books, 2000.

Cixous, Hélène. 'The Laugh of the Medusa'. In Elaine Marks and Isabelle de Courtivron, eds. *New French Feminisms.* Brighton: The Harvester Press, 1981: 245–64.

——. *Black Sail/White Sail* Trans. Donald Watson. Manuscript from The Sphinx Theatre; touring show, 1994.

——. 'Excerpts from the Oxford Amnesty Lecture'. *Black Sail/White Sail.* Theatre programme, 1994.

Cixous, Hélène and Catherine Clément. *The Newly Born Woman.* Translated by Betsy Wing. Manchester: Manchester University Press, 1987.

Cousin, Geraldine, ed. *Recording Women: A Documentation of Six Theatre Productions.* Amsterdam: Harwood Academic Publishers, 2000.

Cullen, Mike. *Anna Weiss.* London: Nick Hern Books, 1997.

Dahl, Mary Karen. 'Postcolonial British Theatre'. In J. Ellen Gainor, ed. *Imperialism and Theatre: Essays on World Theatre, Drama and Performance.* London: Routledge, 1995: 38–55.

Daldry, Stephen. Preface. *Coming On Strong: New Writing from the Royal Court Theatre.* London: Faber and Faber, 1995: vii–viii.

Daniels, Sarah. 'There are 52% of Us', *Drama*, 152, 1984: 23–4.

——. *Ripen Our Darkness and The Devil's Gateway.* London: Methuen, 1986.

——. *Plays: Two: The Gut Girls, Beside Herself, Head-Rot Holiday, The Madness of Esme and Shaz.* London: Methuen, 1994.

——. Interview. In Heidi Stephenson and Natasha Langridge, eds. *Rage and Reason: Women Playwrights on Playwriting.* London: Methuen, 1997: 1–8.

——. *Purple Side Coasters* [1995]. In Lizbeth Goodman, ed. *Mythic Women/Real Women.* London: Faber and Faber, 2000: 197–239.

De Angelis, April. *The Positive Hour.* London: Faber and Faber, 1997.

Diamond, Elin. *Unmaking Mimesis.* London: Routledge, 1997.

Douglas, Mary. *Purity and Danger: An Analysis of the Concepts of Pollution and Taboo.* London: Routledge, 1966.

Dowie, Claire. *Easy Access (for the Boys) and All Over Lovely.* London: Methuen, 1998.

Dromgoole, Dominic. *The Full Room: An A–Z of Contemporary Playwriting.* London: Methuen, 2002.

Edgar, David, ed. *State of Play: Playwrights on Playwriting.* London: Faber and Faber, 1999.

Edwardes, Pamela, ed. *Frontline Intelligence 1: New Plays for the Nineties.* London: Methuen, 1993.

———. *Frontline Intelligence 2.* London: Methuen, 1994.

———. *Frontline Intelligence 3.* London: Methuen, 1995.

Egan, Caroline. 'The Playwright's Playwright'. *Guardian.* 21 September 1998: 13.

Egervary, Barbara. 'Profile of a Company: Spin/Stir', *Glint Journal,* Vol. 2, no. 2, 1994: 16–17.

Ensler, Eve. *The Vagina Monologues.* London, Virago, 2001.

Faludi, Susan. *Backlash: The Undeclared War Against Women.* London: Vintage, 1992.

———. *Stiffed: The Betrayal of Modern Man.* London: Vintage, 2000.

Foucault, Michel. *Discipline and Punish.* Translated by Alan Sheridan. Harmondsworth: Penguin, 1977.

Fraser, Sylvia. *In My Father's House: A Memoir of Incest and of Healing.* London, Virago, 1989.

Freeman, Sandra. *Putting Your Daughters on the Stage: Lesbian Theatre from the 1970s to the 1990s.* London: Cassell, 1997.

French, Marilyn. *The War Against Women.* London: Hamish Hamilton, 1992.

Friedan, Betty. *The Feminine Mystique.* London: Victor Gollancz, 1963.

Furse, Anna. *Augustine (Big Hysteria).* Amsterdam: Harwood Academic Publishers, 1997.

———. 'Written on My Body'. *The Open Page.* No. 2, March 1997: 38–43.

Fuss, Diana, ed. *Inside/Out: Lesbian Theories, Gay Theories.* London: Routledge, 1991.

Gardiner, Caroline. *What Share of the Cake? The Employment of Women in the English Theatre.* London: Women's Playhouse Trust, 1987.

Gems, Pam. *The Snow Palace.* London: Oberon Books, 1998.

George, Kadija, ed. *Six Plays by Black and Asian Women Writers.* London: Aurora Metro Press, 1993.

Goodman, Lizbeth. 'Overlapping Dialogue in Overlapping Media: Behind the Scenes of *Top Girls*'. In Sheila Rabillard, ed. *Essays on Caryl Churchill: Contemporary Representations.* Winnipeg: Blizzard Publishing, 1998: 69–101.

Gottlieb, Vera. 'Lukewarm Britannia'. In Vera Gottlieb and Colin Chambers, eds. *Theatre in a Cool Climate*. Oxford: Amber Lane Press, 1999: 201–12.

Gottlieb, Vera, and Colin Chambers, eds. *Theatre in a Cool Climate*. Oxford: Amber Lane Press, 1999.

Greer, Bonnie. *Munda Negra*. In Yvonne Brewster, ed. *Black Plays 3* London: Methuen, 1995: 41–99.

Greig, David. Introduction. *Sarah Kane, Complete Plays*. London: Methuen, 2001: ix–xviii.

Gupta, Tanika. Interview. In Heidi Stephenson and Natasha Langridge, eds. *Rage and Reason: Women Playwrights on Playwriting*. London: Methuen, 1997: 115–21.

——. *Skeleton*. London: Faber and Faber, 1997.

——. *The Waiting Room*. London: Faber and Faber, 2000.

Hart, Lynda. 'Identity and Seduction: Lesbians in the Mainstream'. In Lynda Hart and Peggy Phelan, *Acting Out: Feminist Performances* (Ann Arbor: The University Of Michigan Press, 1993): 119–37.

——. *Fatal Women: Lesbian Sexuality and the Mark of Aggression*. London: Routledge, 1994.

Hemming, Sarah. 'The Best of Time, the Worst of Time – The Present Bush'. Arts section, *Independent*, 22 February 1995: 24.

Herman, Judith. *Trauma and Recovery From Domestic Abuse to Political Terror*. London: Pandora, 1992.

Holledge, Julie. *Innocent Flowers: Women in the Edwardian Theatre*. London: Virago, 1981.

Hood, Stuart, ed. *A Woman Alone and Other Plays: Franca Rame and Dario Fo*. London: Methuen, 1991.

Innes, Christopher. *Modern British Drama 1890–1990*. Cambridge: Cambridge University Press, 1992.

Johnson, Catherine. *Boys Mean Business*. In *Bush Theatre Plays*. London: Faber and Faber, 1996: 77–172.

——. *Shang-a-Lang*. London: Faber and Faber, 1998.

Johnson, Judith. *Somewhere*. In Pamela Edwardes, ed. *Frontline Intelligence 1: New Plays for the Nineties*. London: Methuen, 1993: 131–204.

——. *Uganda*. In Pamela Edwardes, ed. *Frontline Intelligence 3: New Plays for the Nineties*: London: Methuen, 1995: 77–133.

Kane, Sarah. Interview with David Benedict. *Independent on Sunday*, 22 January 1995: 3.

——. Interview with Clare Bayley. Arts, *Independent*, 23 January 1995: 20.

——. Interview. In Heidi Stephenson and Natasha Langridge, eds. *Rage and Reason: Women Playwrights on Playwriting*. London: Methuen, 1997: 129–35.

——. 'No Pain. No Kane'. Interview with Claire Armistead. *Guardian*, 29 April 1998: 12.

——. 'The Only Thing I Remember is'. *Guardian*, 13 August 1998: 12.

——. 'Drama with Balls'. *Guardian*, 20 August 1998: 12.

——. *Crave*. London: Methuen, 1998.

——. *Complete Plays: Blasted, Phaedra's Love, Cleansed, Crave, 4.48 Psychosis. Skin*. London: Methuen, 2001.

Kaplan, Ann E. *Motherhood and Representation: The Mother in Popular Culture and Melodrama*. London: Routledge, 1992.

Kennedy, Adrienne. *Motherhood 2000*. In Bonnie Marranca, ed. *Plays for the End of the Century*. Baltimore: Johns Hopkins University Press, 1997.

Khan-Din, Ayub. *East is East*. London: Nick Hern Books, 1997.

La Fontaine, Jean. *Child Sexual Abuse*. Oxford: Polity Press and Basil Blackwell, 1990.

Lane, Harry. 'Secrets as Strategies for Protection and Oppression in *Top Girls*'. In Sheila Rabillard, ed. *Essays on Caryl Churchill: Contemporary Representations*. Winnipeg: Blizzard Publishing, 1998: 60–8.

Lavery, Bryony. 'But Will Men Like It? Or Living as a Feminist Writer Without Committing Murder'. In Susan Todd, ed. *Calling the Shots*. London: Faber and Faber, 1984: 24–32.

——. Interview. In Heidi Stephenson and Natasha Langridge, eds. *Rage and Reason: Women Playwrights on Playwriting*. London: Methuen, 1997: 105–14.

——. *Plays 1: Origin of the Species, Two Marias, Her Aching Heart, Nothing Compares to You*. London: Methuen, 1998.

——. *Tallulah Bankhead.* Bath, Somerset: Absolute Press, 1999.

——. *A Wedding Story.* London: Faber and Faber, 2000.

——. *Frozen.* London: Faber and Faber, 2002.

——. 'Read. Imagine. Write. Check.' Programme, *Frozen.* National Theatre, 2002.

Lee, Veronica. 'Young Guns'. Culture section, *The Sunday Times,* 22 March 1998: 8.

Lewis, Eve. *Ficky Stingers.* In Mary Remnant, ed. *Plays By Women: Volume Six.* London: Methuen, 1987: 116–27.

Lovenduski, Joni, and Randall, Vicky. *Contemporary Feminist Politics: Women and Power in Britain.* Oxford: Oxford University Press, 1993.

Lyndon, Neil. *No More Sex War: The Failures of Feminism.* London: Sinclair-Stevenson, 1992.

McDonagh, Martin. *The Beauty Queen of Leenane.* London: Methuen, 1996.

Macdonald, James. Interview with James Christopher. Features, *Independent,* 4 May 1998: 6–7.

McIntyre, Clare. *My Heart's a Suitcase & Low Level Panic.* London: Nick Hern Books, 1994.

McLeod, Jenny. *Island Life.* In *Monstrous Regiment.* Compiled by Gillian Hanna. London: Nick Hern Books, 1991: 147–212.

——. *Raising Fires.* London: Bush Theatre, 1994.

McRobbie, Angela. *Feminism and Youth Culture* [1991]. Second edition. Basingstoke: Macmillan, 2000.

McRobbie, Angela, and Trisha McCabe, eds. *Feminism for Girls: An Adventure Story.* London: Routledge & Kegan Paul, 1981.

Mamet, David. *Oleanna.* In *Mamet: Plays 4.* London: Methuen, 2002.

Mirza, Heidi Safia. *Black British Feminism: A Reader.* London: Routledge, 1997.

Monk, Claire. ' Men in the 90s'. In Robert Murphy, ed. *British Cinema of the 90s:* London: BFI, 2000: 156–66.

Murphy, Robert, ed. *British Cinema of the 90s.* London: BFI, 2000.

Nagy, Phyllis. Afterword to *Weldon Rising.* In Annie Castledine, ed. *Plays by Women: Ten.* London: Methuen, 1994: 144.

——. Adaptation of Nathaniel Hawthorne's *The Scarlet Letter.* London: Samuel French, 1995.

——. Interview with Michael Church. *The Times*, 20 February 1995: 15.

——. Interview. In Heidi Stephenson and Natasha Langridge, eds. *Rage and* Reason: *Women Playwrights on Playwriting*: London: Methuen, 1997: 19–28.

——. *Plays One: Weldon Rising, Butterfly Kiss, Disappeared, The Strip.* London: Methuen, 1998.

——. *Never Land.* London: Methuen, 1998.

——. *The Talented Mr Ripley.* Adaptation of the novel by Patricia Highsmith. London: Methuen, 1999.

——. 'Hold Your Nerve: Notes for a Young Playwright'. In David Edgar, ed. *State of Play: Playwrights on Playwriting.* London: Faber and Faber, 1999: 123–32

Nagy, Phyllis and Kenyon, Mel. 'Season of Lad Tidings'. *Guardian*, 4 December 1995: 7.

Nava, Mica. 'Youth Service Provision, Social Order and the Question of Girls'. In Angela McRobbie and Mica Nava, eds. *Gender and Generation.* Basingstoke: Macmillan, 1984: 1–30.

Nightingale, Benedict. 'Ten with the Playwright Stuff'. *The Times*, 1 May 1996: 33.

——. *Predictions: The Future of Theatre.* London: Phoenix, 1998.

Parmar, Pratibha. 'Other Kinds of Dreams'. *Feminist Review*, 31, Spring 1989: 55–65.

Patel, Pragna. 'Third Wave Feminism and Black Women's Activism'. In Heidi Safia Mirza, ed. *Black British Feminism: A Reader.* London: Routledge, 1997: 255–68.

Phelan, Peggy. *Unmarked: The Politics of Performance.* London: Routledge, 1993.

Pimlott, Stephen. Interview with David Benedict. Features. *Independent*, 7 January 1998: 14.

Pinnock, Winsome. *Leave Taking.* In Kate Harwood, ed. *First Run: New Plays by New Writers.* London: Nick Hern Books, 1989: 139–89.

——. *Talking in Tongues.* In Yvonne Brewster, ed. *Plays 3.* London: Methuen, 1995: 171–227.

——. *Mules.* London: Faber and Faber, 1996.

——. Interview. In Heidi Stephenson and Natasha Langridge, eds. *Rage and Reason: Women Playwrights on Playwriting*. London: Methuen, 1997: 45–53.

——. 'Plays by Women'. In David Edgar, ed. *State of Play: Playwrights on Playwriting*. London: Faber and Faber, 1999: 58–9.

——. 'Breaking Down the Door'. In Vera Gottlieb and Colin Chambers, eds. *Theatre in a Cool Climate*. Oxford: Amber Lane Press, 1999: 27–38.

Ponnuswami, Meenakshi. 'Small Island People: Black British Women Playwrights'. In Elaine Aston and Janelle Reinelt, eds. *The Cambridge Companion to Modern British Women Playwrights*. Cambridge: Cambridge University Press, 2000: 217–34.

Posener, Jill. *Any Woman Can*. In Jill Davis, ed. *Lesbian Plays*. London: Methuen, 1987: 14–27.

Prichard, Rebecca. *Essex Girls*. In *Coming on Strong: New Writing from the Royal Court Theatre*. London: Faber and Faber, 1995: 181–246.

——. *Fair Game: A Free Adaptation of Games in the Backyard by Edna Mazya*. London: Faber and Faber, 1997.

——. *Yard Gal*. London: Faber and Faber, 1998.

——. 'Plays by Women' in David Edgar, ed. *State of Play: Playwrights on Playwriting*. London: Faber and Faber, 1999: 61.

Rabillard, Sheila, ed. *Essays on Caryl Churchill: Contemporary Representations*. Winnipeg: Blizzard Publishing, 1998.

Rame, Franca. *The Rape*. In Stuart Hood, ed. *A Woman Alone and Other Plays: Franca Rame and Dario Fo*. London: Methuen, 1991.

Ravenhill, Mark. 'Dramatic Moments'. *Guardian*, 9 April 1997: 14.

——. 'Plays about Men'. In David Edgar, ed. *State of Play: Playwrights on Playwriting*. London: Faber and Faber, 1999: 48–51.

——. 'Obituary, Sarah Kane'. *Independent*, 23 February 1999: 6.

Rayner, Alice. 'All Her Children: Caryl Churchill's Furious Ghosts'. In Sheila Rabillard, ed. *Essays on Caryl Churchill: Contemporary Representations*. Winnipeg: Blizzard Publishing, 1998: 206–24.

Rebellato, Dan. 'Sarah Kane: An Appreciation'. *New Theatre Quarterly*, 59, August 1999: 280–1.

Reinelt, Janelle. 'Staging the Invisible: The Crisis of Visibility in Theatrical Representation'. *Text and Performance Quarterly*, 14, 1994: 1–11.

——. 'Caryl Churchill and the Politics of Style'. In Elaine Aston and Janelle Reinelt, eds. *The Cambridge Companion to Modern British Women Playwrights*. Cambridge: Cambridge University Press, 2000: 174–93.

Reynolds, Anna, and Moira Buffini. 'Jordan' 1992. Manuscript from the authors.

Rickson, Ian. 'Court in the Delicate Bubble Act'. Interview with Benedict Nightingale. *The Times*, 14 January 1998: 31.

Roberts, Philip. *The Royal Court Theatre and the Modern Stage*. Cambridge: Cambridge University Press, 1999.

Roberts, Yvonne. *Mad About Women: Can There Ever be Fair Play Between the Sexes?* London: Virago, 1992.

Roiphe, Katie. *The Morning After: Sex, Fear, and Feminism*. London: Hamish Hamilton, 1993.

Saunders, Graham. '"Just a Word on a Page and There is the Drama": Sarah Kane's Theatrical Legacy'. *Contemporary Theatre Review*, 2003, Vol. 13, issue 1: 97–110.

——. *'Love Me Or Kill Me': Sarah Kane and the Theatre of Extremes*. Manchester: Manchester University Press, 2002.

Scarry, Elaine. *The Body in Pain: The Making and the Unmaking of the World*. Oxford: Oxford University Press, 1985.

Scullion, Adrienne. 'Self and Nation: Issues of Identity in Modern Scottish Drama by Women'. *New Theatre Quarterly*, 68, November 2001: 373–90.

Shank, Theodore, ed. *Contemporary British Theatre*. Basingstoke: Macmillan, 1994.

Showalter, Elaine. *Hystories: Hysterical Epidemics and Modern Culture*. London: Picador, 1997.

Sierz, Alex. *In-Yer-Face Theatre: British Drama Today*. London: Faber and Faber, 2001.

——. 'Sarah Kane: NTQ Checklist'. *New Theatre Quarterly*, 67, August 2001: 285–90.

Smith, Andrew. 'Play for Today'. *Observer Magazine.* 31 October 1999: 34–9.

Smith, Anna Marie. *New Right Discourse on Race and Sexuality: Britain in 1968–1990.* Cambridge: Cambridge University Press, 1994.

Spivak, Gayatri Chakravorty. 'Criticism. Feminism and the Institution'. Interview with Elizabeth Grosz. In Sarah Harasym, ed. *The Post-Colonial Critic: Interviews, Strategies, Dialogues.* London: Routledge, 1990: 1–16.

States, Bert, O. 'The Phenomenological Attitude'. In Janelle G. Reinelt and Joseph R. Roach, eds. *Critical Theory and Performance.* Ann Arbor: University of Michigan Press, 1992: 369–79.

Steedman, Carolyn. *Landscape for a Good Woman: A Story of Two Lives.* London: Virago, 1986.

Stephenson, Heidi and Natasha Langridge, eds. *Rage and Reason: Women Playwrights on Playwriting.* London: Methuen, 1997.

Taylor, Paul. 'Theatre: The Agent, the Catcher, the Cradle-snatcher: The Fixers 3. Mel Kenyon'. *Independent,* 3 January 1996: 10–11.

——. 'Let's Do the New Plays Right Here'. *Independent,* 2 October 1996: 8–9.

Thomas, David. *Not Guilty: In Defence of Modern Man.* London: Weidenfeld & Nicolson, 1993.

Thurman, Judith. 'The Playwright Who Makes You Laugh about Orgasm, Racism, Class Struggle, Homophobia, Woman-Hating, the British Empire, and the Irrepressible Strangeness of the Human Heart'. *Ms.,* May 1982, 51–7.

Ugwu, Catherine, ed. *Let's Get it On.* London: Institute of Contemporary Arts, 1995.

Upton, Judy. 'Afterword'. *Ashes and Sand.* In Pamela Edwardes, *Frontline Intelligence 3: New Plays for the Nineties.* London: Methuen, 1995: 261.

——. *Confidence.* London: Methuen, 1998.

——. *Plays 1.* London: Methuen, 2002.

Verma, Jatinder. 'Cultural Transformations'. In Theodore Shank, ed. *Contemporary British Theatre.* Basingstoke: Macmillan, 1994: 55–61.

Walter, Natasha. *The New Feminism*. London: Virago, 1999.

Wandor, Michelene. *Post-War British Drama: Looking Back in Gender*. London: Routledge, 2001.

Warner, Marina. *From the Beast to the Blonde: On Fairy Tales and their Tellers*. London: Vintage, 1995.

Wertenbaker, Timberlake. *Plays 1: New Anatomies, The Grace of Mary Traverse, Our Country's Good, The Love of the Nightingale, Three Birds Alighting on a Field*. London: Faber and Faber, 1996.

——. Notes from 'About Now', Birmingham Theatre Conference, 1997. In *Studies in Theatre Production*, 15, June 1997: 88–92.

——. Interview. In Heidi Stephenson and Natasha Langridge, eds. *Rage and Reason: Women Playwrights on Playwriting*. London: Methuen, 1997: 136–45.

——. Interview. With Michael Billington. *Guardian*, 25 November 1999: 10.

——. *Plays 2. The Break of Day, After Darwin, Credible Witness, The Ash Girl, Dianeira*. London: Faber and Faber, 2002.

Whelehan, Imelda. *Modern Feminist Thought: From the Second Wave to 'Post-Feminism'*. Edinburgh: Edinburgh University Press, 1995.

——. *Overloaded: Popular Culture and the Future of Feminism*. London: The Women's Press, 2000.

Williams, Raymond. *The Long Revolution*. Harmondsworth: Pelican/ Penguin, 1961.

Wilson, Melba. *Crossing the Boundary: Black Women Survive Incest*. London: Virago, 1993.

Wolf, Naomi. *Fire with Fire*. London: Vintage, 1994.

Woolf, Virginia. *A Room of One's Own* [1929]. London: Granada, 1977.

Women's Theatre Group. *My Mother Says I Never Should*. In Michelene Wandor, ed. *Strike While the Iron is Hot*. London: Journeyman Press, 1980.

Wright, Jules. 'In Her Wright Mind'. Interview. *Plays and Players*, April 1990: 14–16.

SPECIAL JOURNAL EDITIONS

The Past Before Us, Twenty Years of Feminism. Feminist Review, Spring 1989, 31.

RADIO/AUDIO BROADCASTS

Wertenbaker, Timberlake. *Abel's Sister.* National Sound Archive, British Library, London.

Wertenbaker, Timberlake. Interview, *Writers Revealed.* BBC Radio 4, 20 June 1991.

Wertenbaker, Timberlake, with Ian McDermott, Sheila Hancock and Bob Carlton. *Kaleidoscope,* BBC Radio 4, 26 December 1989.

TELEVISION BROADCASTS

Goodbye to the '90s. BBC 2, December 1999.

Late Theatre. Caryl Churchill. Interview. BBC 2, January 1994.

Index